La Sorcière

*Satanism and Witchcraft - The Witch
of the Middle Ages*

By Jules Michelet

Translated by Lionel J. Trotter

PANTIANOS
CLASSICS

Published by Pantianos Classics

ISBN-13: 978-1-78987-089-3

First published in 1883

Contents

Preface

IN this translation of a work rich in the raciest beauties and defects of an author long since made known to the British public, the present writer has striven to recast the trenchant humour, the scornful eloquence, the epigrammatic dash of Mr. Michelet, in language not all unworthy of such a word-master. How far he has succeeded others may be left to judge. In one point only is he aware of having been less true to his original than in theory he was bound to be. He has slurred or slightly altered a few of those passages which French readers take as a thing of course, but English ones, because of their different training, are supposed to eschew. A Frenchman, in short, writes for men, an Englishman rather for drawing-room ladies, who tolerate grossness only in the theatres and the columns of the newspapers. Mr. Michelet's subject, and his late researches, lead him into details, moral and physical, which among ourselves are seldom mixed up with themes of general talk. The coarsest of these have been pruned away, but enough perhaps remain to startle readers of especial prudery. The translator, however, felt that he had no choice between shocking these and sinning against his original. Readers of a larger culture will make allowance for such a strait, will not be so very frightened at an amount of plain-speaking, neither in itself immoral, nor, on the whole, impertinent. Had he docked his work of everything condemned by prudish theories, he might have made it more conventionally decent; but Michelet would have been puzzled to recognize himself in the poor maimed cripple that would then have borne his name.

Nor will a reader of average shrewdness mistake the religious drift of a book suppressed by the Imperial underlings in the interests neither of religion nor of morals, but merely of Popery in its most outrageous form. If its attacks on Rome seem, now and then, to involve Christianity itself, we must allow something for excess of warmth, and something for the nature of inquiries which laid bare the rotten outgrowths of a religion in itself the purest known among men. In studying the so-called Ages of Faith, the author has only found them worthy of their truer and older title, the Ages of Darkness. It is against the tyranny, feudal and priestly, of those days, that he raises an outcry, warranted almost always by facts which a more mawkish philosophy refuses to see. If he is sometimes hasty and one-sided; if the Church and the Feudal System of those days had their uses for the time being; it is still a gain to have the other side of the subject kept before us by way of counterpoise to the doctrines now in vogue. We need not be intolerant; but Home is yet alive.

Taken as a whole, Mr. Michelet's book cannot be called unchristian. Like most thoughtful minds of the day, he yearns for some nobler and larger creed than that of the theologians; for a creed which, understanding Nature, shall reconcile it with Nature's God. Nor may he fairly be called irreverent for talking, Frenchman like, of things spiritual with the same freedom as he would of things temporal. Perhaps in his heart of hearts he has nearly as much religious earnestness as they who call Dr. Colenso an infidel, and shake their heads at the doubtful theology of Frederic Robertson. At any rate, no translator who should cut or file away so special a feature of French feeling would be doing justice to so marked an original.

For English readers who already know the concise and sober volumes of their countryman, Mr. Wright, the present work will offer mainly an interesting study of the author himself. It is a curious compound of rhapsody and sound reason, of history and romance, of coarse realism and touching poetry, such as, even in France, few save Mr. Michelet could have produced. Founded on truth and close inquiry, it still reads more like a poem than a sober history. As a beautiful speculation, which has nearly, but not quite, grasped the physical causes underlying the whole history of magic and illusion in all ages, it may be read with profit as well as pleasure in this age of vulgar spirit-rapping. But the true history of Witchcraft has yet to be written by some cooler hand.

L. T.
May 11th, 1863.

Introduction

IT was said by Sprenger, before the year 1500, "*Heresy of witches*, not of wizards, must we call it, for these latter are of very small account." And by another, in the time of Louis XIII.: "To one wizard, ten thousand witches."

"Witches they are by nature." It is a gift peculiar to woman and her temperament. By birth a fay, by the regular recurrence of her ecstasy she becomes a sibyl. By her love she grows into an enchantress. By her subtlety, by a roguishness often whimsical and beneficent, she becomes a Witch; she works her spells; does at any rate lull our pains to rest and beguile them.

All primitive races have the same beginning, as so many books of travel have shown. While the man is hunting and fighting, the woman works with her wits, with her imagination: she brings forth dreams and gods. On certain days she becomes a seeress, borne on boundless wings of reverie and desire. The better to reckon up the seasons, she watches the sky; but her heart belongs to earth none the less. Young and flower-like herself, she looks down toward the enamoured flowers, and forms with them a personal acquaintance. As a woman, she beseeches them to heal the objects of her love.

In a way so simple and touching do all religion and all science begin. Ere long everything will get parcelled out; we shall mark the beginning of the professional man as juggler, astrologer, or prophet, necromancer, priest, physician. But at first the woman is everything.

A religion so strong and hearty as that of Pagan Greece begins with the Sibyl to end in the Witch. The former, a lovely maiden in the broad daylight, rocked its cradle, endowed it with a charm and glory of its own. Presently it fell sick, lost itself in the darkness of the Middle Ages, and was hidden away by the Witch in woods and wilds: there, sustained by her compassionate daring, it was made to live anew. Thus, of every religion woman is the mother, the gentle guardian, the faithful nurse. With her the gods fare like men: they are born and die upon her bosom.

Alas! her loyalty costs her dear. Ye magian queens of Persia; bewitching Circe; sublime Sibyl! Into what have ye grown, and how cruel the change that has come upon you! She who from her throne in the East taught men the virtues of plants and the courses of the stars; who, on her Delphic tripod beamed over with the god of light, as she gave forth her oracles to a world upon its knees; she also it is whom, a thousand years later, people hunt down like a wild beast; following her into the public places, where she is dishonoured, worried, stoned, or set upon the burning coals!

For this poor wretch the priesthood can never have done with their faggots, nor the people with their insults, nor the children with their stones. The
poet, childlike, flings her one more stone, for a woman the cruellest of all. On
no grounds whatever, he imagines her to have been always old and ugly. The
word "witch" brings before us the frightful old women of *Macbeth*. But their
cruel processes teach us the reverse of that. Numbers perished precisely for
being young and beautiful.

The Sibyl foretold a fortune, the Witch accomplishes one. Here is the great,
the true difference between them. The latter calls forth a destiny, conjures it,
works it out. Unlike the Cassandra of old, who awaited mournfully the future
she foresaw so well, this woman herself creates the future. Even more than
Circe, than Medea, does she bear in her hand the rod of natural miracle, with
Nature herself aa sister and helpmate. Already she wears the features of a
modern Prometheus. With her industry begins, especially that queen-like
industry which heals and restores mankind. As the Sibyl seemed to gaze upon the morning, so she, contrariwise, looks towards the west; but it is just
that gloomy west, which long before dawn as happens among the tops of the
Alps gives forth a flush anticipant of day.

Well does the priest discern the danger, the bane, the alarming rivalry,
involved in this priestess of nature whom he makes a show of despising.
From the gods of yore she has conceived other gods. Close to the Satan of the
Past we see dawning within her a Satan of the Future.

The only physician of the people for a thousand years was the Witch. The
emperors, kings, popes, and richer barons had indeed their doctors of Saler-
no, their Moors and Jews; but the bulk of people in every state, the world as it
might well be called, consulted none but the Saga, or wise-woman. When she
could not cure them, she was insulted, was called a Witch But generally, from
a respect not unmixed with fear, she was called good lady or fair lady (belle
dame bella donna), [1] the very name we give to the fairies.

Soon there came upon her the lot which still befalls her favourite plant,
belladonna, and some other wholesome poisons which she employed as an-
tidotes to the great plagues of the Middle Ages. Children and ignorant passers-by would curse those dismal flowers before they knew them. Affrighted
by their questionable hues, they shrink back, keep far aloof from them. And
yet among them are the comforters (Solaneae) which, when discreetly employed, have cured so many, have lulled so many sufferings to sleep.

You find them in ill-looking spots, growing all lonely and ill-famed amidst
ruins and rubbish-heaps. Therein lies one other point of resemblance between these flowers and her who makes use of them. For where else than in
waste wildernesses could live the poor wretch whom all men thus evilly entreated; the woman accursed and proscribed as a poisoner, even while she
used L to heal and save; as the betrothed of the Devil and of evil incarnate,
for all the good which, according to the great physician of the Renaissance,
she herself had done? When Paracelsus, at Basle, in 1527, threw ail medicine

into the fire, [2] he avowed that he knew nothing but what he had learnt from witches.

This was worth a requital, and they got it. They were repaid with tortures, with the stake. For them new punishments, new pangs, were expressly devised. They were tried in a lump; they were condemned by a single word. Never had there been such wastefulness of human life. Not to speak of Spain, that classic land of the faggot, where Moor and Jew are always accompanied by the Witch, there were burnt at Treves seven thousand, and I know not how many at Toulouse; five hundred at Geneva in three months of 1513; at Wurtzburg eight hundred, almost in one batch, and fifteen hundred at Bamberg; these two latter being very small bishoprics! Even Ferdinand II., the savage Emperor of the Thirty Years' War, was driven, bigot as he was, to keep a watch on these worthy bishops, else they would have burned all their subjects. In the Wurtzburg list I find one Wizard a schoolboy, eleven years old; a Witch of fifteen: and at Bayonne two, infernally beautiful, of seventeen years.

Mark how, at certain seasons, hatred wields this one word *Witch,* as a means of murdering whom she will. Woman's jealousy, man's greed, take ready hold of so handy a weapon. Is such a one wealthy? *She is a Witch.* Is that girl pretty? *She is a Witch.* You will even see the little beggar-woman, La Murgui, leave a death-mark with that fearful stone on the forehead of a great lady, the too beautiful dame of Laneinena.

The accused, when they can, avert the torture by killing themselves. Remy, that excellent judge of Lorraine, who burned some eight hundred of them, crows over this very fear. "So well," said he, "does my way of justice answer, that of those who were arrested the other day, sixteen, without further waiting, strangled themselves forthwith."

Over the long track of my History, during the thirty years which I have devoted to it, this frightful literature of witchcraft passed to and fro repeatedly through my hands. First I exhausted the manuals of the Inquisition, the asinine foolings of the Dominicans.

(*Scourges, Hammers, Ant-hills, Floggings, Lanterns, &c.,* are the titles of their books.) Next, I read the Parliamentarists, the lay judges who despised the monks they succeeded, but were every whit as foolish themselves. One word further would I say of them here: namely, this single remark, that, from 1300 to 1600, and yet later, but one kind of justice may be seen. Barring a small interlude in the Parliament of Paris, the same stupid savagery prevails everywhere, at all hours. Even great parts are of no use here. As soon as witchcraft comes into question, the fine natured De Lancre, a Bordeaux magistrate and forward politician under Henry IV., sinks back to the level of a Nider, a Sprenger; of the monkish ninnies of the fifteenth century.

It fills one with amazement to see these different ages, these men of diverse culture, fail in taking the least step forward. Soon, however, you begin clearly to understand how all were checked alike, or let us rather say blinded, made hopelessly drunk and savage, by the poison of their guiding principle. That principle lies in the statement of a radical injustice: "On account of one man all are lost; are not only punished but worthy of punishment; *depraved and perverted beforehand,* dead to God even before their birth. The very babe at the breast is damned."

Who says so? Everyone, even Bossuet himself. A leading doctor in Rome, Spina, a Master of the Holy Palace, formulates the question neatly: "Why does God suffer the innocent to die? For very good reasons: even if they do not die on account of their own sins, they are always liable to death as guilty of the original sin." (*De Strigibus,* ch. 9.)

From this atrocity spring two results, the one pertaining to justice, the other to logic. The judge is never at fault in his work: the person brought before him is certainly guilty, the more so if he makes a defence. Justice need never beat her head, or work herself into a heat, in order to distinguish the truth from the falsehood. Everyhow she starts from a foregone conclusion. Again, the logician, the schoolman, has only to analyse the soul, to take count of the shades it passes through, of its manifold nature, its inward strifes and battles. He had no need, as we have, to explain how that soul may grow wicked step by step. At all such niceties and groping efforts, how, if even he could understand them, would he laugh and wag his head! And, oh! how gracefully then would quiver those splendid ears which deck his empty skull!

Especially in treating of the *compact with the Devil,* that awful covenant whereby, for the poor profit of one day, the spirit sells itself to everlasting torture, we of another school would seek to trace anew that road accursed, that frightful staircase of mishaps and crimes, which had brought it to a depth so low. Much, however, cares our fine fellow for all that! To him soul and Devil seem born for each other, insomuch that on the first temptation, for a whim, a desire, a passing fancy, the soul will throw itself at one stroke into so horrible an extremity.

Neither do I find that the moderns have made much inquiry into the moral chronology of witchcraft. They cling too much to the connection between antiquity and the Middle Ages; connection real indeed, but slight, of small importance. Neither from the magician of old, nor the seeress of Celts and Germans, comes forth the true Witch. The harmless "Sabasies" (from Bacchus Sabasius), and the petty rural "Sabbath" of the Middle Ages, have nothing to do with the Black Mass of the fourteenth century, with the grand defiance then solemnly given to Jesus. This fearful conception never grew out of a long chain of tradition. It leapt forth from the horrors of the day.

At what date, then, did the Witch first appear? I say unfalteringly, "In the age of despair:" of that deep despair which the gentry of the Church engendered. Unfalteringly do I say, "The Witch is a crime of their own achieving."

I am not to be taken up short by the excuses which their sugary explanations seem to furnish. "Weak was that creature, and giddy, and pliable under temptation. She was drawn towards evil by her lust." Alas! in the wretchedness, the hunger of those days, nothing of that kind could have ruined her even into a hellish rage. An amorous woman, jealous and forsaken, a child hunted out by her stepmother, a mother beaten by her son (old subjects these of story), if such as they were ever tempted to call upon the Evil Spirit, yet all this would make no Witch. These poor creatures may have called on Satan, but it does not follow that he accepted them. They are still far, ay, very far from being ripe for him. They have not yet learned to hate God.

For the better understanding of this point, you should read those hateful registers which remain to us of the Inquisition, not only in the extracts given by Llorente, by Lamothe-Langon, &c., but in what remains of the original registers of Toulouse. Head them in all their flatness, in all their dryness, so dismal, so terribly savage. At the end of a few pages you feel yourself stricken with a chill; a cruel shiver fastens upon you; death, death, death, is traceable in every line. Already you are in a bier, or else in a stone cell with mouldy walls. Happiest of all are the killed. The horror of horrors is the *In pace*. This phrase it is which comes back unceasingly, like an ill-omened bell sounding again and again the heart's ruin of the living dead: always we have the same word, "Immured."

Frightful machinery for crushing and flattening; most cruel press for shattering the soul! One turn of the screw follows another, until, all breathless, and with a loud crack, it has burst forth from the machine and fallen into the unknown world.

On her first appearance the Witch has neither father nor mother, nor son, nor husband, nor family. She is a marvel, an aerolith, alighted no one knows whence. Who, in Heaven's name, would dare to draw near her?

Her place of abode? It is in spots impracticable, in a forest of brambles, on a wild moor where thorn and thistle intertwining forbid approach. The night she passes under an old cromlech. If anyone finds her there, she is isolated by the common dread; she is surrounded, as it were, by a ring of fire.

And yet would you believe it? she is a woman still. This very life of hers, dreadful though it be, tightens and braces her woman's energy, her womanly electricity. Hence, you may see her endowed with two gifts. One is the *inspiration of lucid frenzy,* which in its several degrees, becomes poesy, secondsight, depth of insight, cunning simplicity of speech, the power especially of believing in yourself through all your delusions. Of such a gift the man, the wizard, knows nothing. On his side no beginning would have been made.

From this gift flows that other, the sublime power of *unaided conception,* that parthenogenesis which our physiologists have come to recognise, as touching fruitfulness of the body in the females of several species; and which is not less a truth with regard to the conceptions of the spirit.

By herself did she conceive and bring forth what?

A second self, who resembles her in his self-delusions. The son of her hatred, conceived upon her love; for without love can nothing be created. For

x

all the alarm this child gave her, she has become so well again, is so happily engrossed with this new idol, that she places it straightway upon her altar, to worship it, yield her life up to it, and offer herself up as a living and perfect sacrifice. Very often she will even say to her judge, "There is but one thing I fear; that I shall not suffer enough for him." - *(Lancre.)*

Shall I tell you what the child's first effort was? It was a fearful burst of laughter. Has he not cause for mirth on his broad prairie, far away from the Spanish dungeons and the "immured" of Toulouse? The whole world is his *In pace.* He comes, and goes, and walks to and fro. His is the boundless forest, his the desert with its far horizons, his the whole earth, in the fulness of its teeming girdle. The Witch in her tenderness calls him *"Robin mine,"* the name of that bold outlaw, the joyous Robin Hood, who lived under the green bowers. She delights too in calling him fondly by such names as *Little Green, Pretty-Wood, Greenwood;* after the little madcap's favourite haunts. He had hardly seen a thicket when he took to playing the truant. [3]

What astounds one most is, that at one stroke the Witch should have achieved an actual Being. He bears about him every token of reality. We have heard and seen him; anyone could draw his likeness.

The Saints, those darling sons of the house, with their dreams and meditations make but little stir; *they look forward waitingly,* as men assured of their part in Elysium. What little energy they have is all centred in the narrow round of *Imitation;* a word which condenses the whole of the Middle Ages. He on the other hand this accursed bastard whose only lot is the scourge has no idea of waiting. He is always seeking and will never rest. He busies himself with all things between earth and heaven. He is exceedingly curious; will dig, dive, ferret, and poke his nose everywhere. At the *consummatum est* he only laughs, the little scoffer! He is always saying "Further," or "Forward." Moreover, he is not hard to please. He takes every rebuff; picks up every windfall. For instance, when the Church throws out nature as impure and doubtworthy, Satan fastens on her for his own adornment. Nay, more; he employs her, and makes her useful to him as the fountain-head of the arts; thus accepting the awful name with which others would brand him; to wit, the *Prince of the World.*

Some one rashly said, "Woe to those who laugh." Thus from the first was Satan intrusted with too pretty a part; he had the sole right of laughing, and of declaring it an *amusement* - rather let us say a *necessity;* for laughing is essentially a natural function. Life would be unbearable if we could not laugh, at least in our afflictions.

Looking on life as nothing but a trial, the Church is careful not to prolong it. Her medicine is resignation, the looking for and the hope of death. A broad field this for Satan! He becomes the physician, the healer of the living. Better still, he acts as comforter: he is good enough to shew us our dead, to call up the shades of our beloved.

One more trifle the Church rejected, namely, logic or free reason. Here was a special dainty, to which *the other* greedily helped himself. The Church had carefully builded up a small *In pace*, narrow, lowroofed, lighted by one dim opening, a mere cranny. That was called *The School*. Into it were turned loose a few shavelings, with this commandment, "Be free." They all fell lame. In three or four centuries the paralysis was confirmed, and Ockham's standpoint is the very same as Abélard's. [4]

It is pleasant to track the Renaissance up to such a point. The Renaissance took place indeed, but how? Through the Satanic daring of those who pierced the vault, through, the efforts of the damned who were bent on seeing the sky. And it took place yet more largely away from the schools and the men of letters, in the *School of the Bush*, where Satan had set up a class for the Witch and the shepherd.

Perilous teaching it was, if so it happened; but the very dangers of it heightened the eager passion, the uncontrollable yearning to see and to know. Thus began those wicked sciences, physic debarred from poisoning, and that odious anatomy. There, along with his survey of the heavens, the shepherd who kept watch upon the stars applied also his shameful nostrums, made his essays upon the bodies of animals. The Witch would bring out a corpse stolen from the neighbouring cemetery; and, for the first time, at risk of being burned, you might gaze upon that heavenly wonder, "which men" as M. Serres has well said "are foolish enough to bury, instead of trying to understand."

Paracelsus, the only doctor whom Satan admitted there, saw yet a third worker, who, stealing at times into that dark assembly, displayed there his surgical art. This was the surgeon of those happy days, the headsman' stout of hand, who could play patly enough with the fire, could break bones and set them again; who if he killed, would sometimes save, by hanging one only for a certain time.

By the more sacrilegious of its essays this convict university of witches, shepherds, and headsmen, emboldened the other, obliged its rival to study. For everyone wanted to live. The Witch would have got hold of everything: people would for ever have turned their backs on the doctor. And so the Church was fain to suffer, to countenance these crimes. She avowed he belief in *good poisons* (Grillandus). She found herself driven and constrained to allow of public dissections. In 1306 one woman, in 1315 another, was opened and dissected by the Italian Mondino. Here was a holy revelation, the discovery of a greater world than that of Christopher Columbus! Fools shuddered or howled; but wise men fell upon their knees.

With such conquests the Devil was like enough to live on. Never could the Church alone have put an end to him. The stake itself was useless, save for some political objects.

Men had presently the wit to cleave Satan's realm in twain. Against the Witch, his daughter, his bride, they armed his son, the doctor. Heartily, utterly as the Church loathed the latter, yet to extinguish the Witch, she established his monopoly nevertheless. In the fourteenth century she proclaimed, that any woman who dared to heal others *without having duly studied,* was a witch and should therefore die.

But how was she to study in public? Fancy what a scene of mingled fun and horror would have occurred, if the poor savage had risked an entrance into the schools! What games and merry-makings there would have been! On Midsummer Day they used to chain cats together and burn them in the fire. But to tie up a Witch in that hell of caterwaulers, a Witch yelling and roasting, what fun it would have been for that precious crew of monklings and cowl-bearers!

In due time we shall see the decline of Satan. Sad to tell, we shall find him pacified, turned into *a good old fellow.* He will be robbed and plundered, until of the two masks he wore at the Sabbath, the dirtiest is taken by Tartuffe. His spirit is still everywhere, but of his bodily self, in losing the Witch he lost all. The wizards were only wearisome.

Now that we have hurled him so far downwards, are we fully aware of what has happened? Was he not an important actor, an essential item in the great religious machine just now slightly out of gear? All organisms that work properly are two-fold, two-sided. Life can otherwise not go on at all. It is a kind of balance between two forces, opposite, symmetrical, but unequal; the lower answering to the other as its counterpoise. The higher chafes at it, seeks to put it down. So doing, it is all wrong.

When Colbert, in 1672, got rid of Satan, with very little ceremony, by forbidding the judges to entertain pleas of witchcraft, the sturdy Parliament of Normandy with its sound Norman logic pointed out the dangerous drift of such a decision. The Devil is nothing less than a dogma holding on to all the rest. If you meddle with the Eternally Conquered, are you not meddling with the Conqueror likewise? To doubt the acts of the former, leads to doubting the acts of the second, the miracles he wrought for the very purpose of withstanding the Devil. The pillars of heaven are grounded in the Abyss. He who thoughtlessly removes that base infernal, may chance to split up Paradise itself.

Colbert could not listen, having other business to mind. But the Devil perhaps gave heed and was comforted. Amidst such minor means of earning -a livelihood as spirit-rapping or table-turning, he grows resigned, and believes at least that he will not die alone.

[1] Whence our old word Beldam, the more courteous meaning of which is all but lost in its ironical one. TRANS.
[2] Alluding to the bonfire which Paracelsus, as professor of medicine, made of the works of Galen and Avicenna. TRANS.
[3] Here, as in some other passages, the play of words in the original is necessarily lost. TRANS.
[4] Abélard flourished in the twelfth, William of Ockham (pupil of Duns Scotus) in the fourteenth century. TRANS

Book One

Chapter One - The Death of the Gods

CERTAIN authors have declared that, shortly before the triumph of Christianity, a voice mysterious ran along the shores of the Aegean Sea, crying, "Great Pan is dead!" The old universal god of nature was no more; and great was the joy thereat. Men fancied that with the death of nature temptation itself was dead. After the troublings of so long a storm, the soul of man was at length to find rest.

Was it merely a question touching the end of that old worship, its overthrow, and the eclipse of old religious rites? By no means. Consult the earliest Christian records, and in every line you may read the hope, that nature is about to vanish, life to be extinguished; that the end of the world, in short, is very near. It is all over with the gods of life, who have spun out its mockeries to such a length. Everything is falling, breaking up, rushing down headlong. The whole is becoming as nought: "Great Pan is dead!"

It was nothing new that the gods must perish. Many an ancient worship was grounded in that very idea. Osiris, Adonis die indeed in order to rise again. On the stage itself, in plays which were only acted for the feast days of the gods, Aeschylus expressly averred by the mouth of Prometheus, that some day they should suffer death: but how? As conquered and laid low by the Titans, the ancient powers of nature.

Here, however, things are quite otherwise. Alike in generals and particulars, in the past and the future, would the early Christians have cursed Nature herself. So utterly did they condemn her, as to find the Devil incarnate in a flower. Swiftly may the angels come again, who erst overwhelmed the cities of the Dead Sea! Oh, that they may sweep off, may crumple up as a veil the hollow frame of this world; may at length deliver the saints from their long trial!

The Evangelist said, "The day is coming:" the Fathers, "It is coming immediately." From the breaking-up of the Empire and the invasion of the Barbarians, St. Augustin draws the hope that very soon no city would remain but the city of God.

And yet, how hard of dying is the world; how stubbornly bent on living! Like Hezekiah, it begs a respite, one turn more of the dial. Well, then, be it so until the year one thousand. But thereafter, not one day.

Are we quite sure of what has been so often repeated, that the gods of old had come to an end, themselves wearied and sickened of living; that they were so disheartened as almost to send in their resignation; that Christianity had only to blow upon these empty shades?

They point to the gods in Rome; they point out those in the Capitol, admitted there only by a kind of preliminary death, on the surrender, I might say, of all their local pith; as having disowned their country, as having ceased to be the representative spirits of the nations. In order to receive them, indeed, Rome had performed on them a cruel operation: they were enervated, bleached. Those great centralized deities became in their official life the mournful functionaries of the Roman Empire. But the decline of that Olympian aristocracy had in no wise drawn down the host of home-born gods, the mob of deities still keeping hold of the boundless country-sides, of the woods, the hills, the fountains; still intimately blended with the life of the country. These gods abiding in the heart of oaks, in waters deep and rushing, could not be driven therefrom.

Who says so? The Church. She rudely gainsays her own words. Having proclaimed their death, she is indignant because they live. Time after time, by the threatening voice of her councils [1] she gives them notice of their death and lo! they are living still.

"They are devils." Then they must be alive. Failing to make an end of them, men suffer the simple folk to clothe, to disguise them. By the help of legends they come to be baptized, even to be foisted upon the Church. But at least they are converted? Not yet. We catch them stealthily subsisting in their own heathen character.

Where are they? In the desert, on the moor, in the forest? Ay; but, above all, in the house. They are kept up by the most intimate household usages. The wife guards and hides them in her household things, even in her bed. With her they have the best place in the world, better than the temple, the fireside.

Never was revolution so violent as that of Theodosius. Antiquity shows no trace of such proscription of any worship. The Persian fire-worshipper might, in the purity of his heroism, have insulted the visible deities, but he let them stand nevertheless. He greatly favoured the Jews, protecting and employing them. Greece, daughter of the light, made merry with the gods of darkness, the tunbellied Cabiri; but yet she bore with them, adopted them as workmen, even to shaping out of them her own Vulcan. Rome in her majesty welcomed not only Etruria, but even the rural gods of the old Italian labourer. She persecuted the Druids, but only as the centre of a dangerous national resistance.

Christianity conquering sought and thought to slay the foe. It demolished the schools, by proscribing logic and uprooting the philosophers, whom Valens slaughtered. It razed or emptied the temples, shivered to pieces the symbols. The new legend would have been propitious to the family, had the

15

father not been cancelled in Saint Joseph; had the mother been set up as an educatress, as having morally brought forth Jesus. A fruitful road there was, but abandoned at the very outset through the effort to attain a high but barren purity.

So Christianity turned into that lonely path where the world was going of itself; the path of a celibacy in vain opposed by the laws of the emperors. Down this slope it was hurled headlong by the establishment of monkery.

But in the desert was man alone? The Devil kept him company with all manner of temptations. He could not help himself, he was driven to create anew societies, nay whole cities of anchorites. We all know those dismal towns of monks which grew up in the Thebaid; how wild, unruly a spirit dwelt among them; how deadly were their descents on Alexandria. They talked of being troubled, beset by the Devil; and they told no lie.

A huge gap was made in the world; and who was to fill it? The Christians said, The Devil, everywhere the Devil: *ubique daemon.*[2]

Greece, like all other nations, had her energumens, who were sore tried, possessed by spirits. The relation there is quite external; the seeming likeness is really none at all. Here we have no spirits of any kind: they are but black children of the Abyss, the ideal of waywardness. Thenceforth we see them everywhere, those poor melancholies, loathing, shuddering at their own selves. Think what it must be to fancy yourself double, to believe in that other, that cruel host who goes and comes and wanders within you, making you roam at his pleasure among deserts, over precipices! You waste and weaken more and more; and the weaker grows your wretched body, the more is it worried by the devil. In woman especially these tyrants dwell, making her blown and swollen. They fill her with an infernal *wind*, they brew in her storms and tempests, play with her as the whim seizes them, drive her to wickedness, to despair.

And not ourselves only, but all nature, alas! becomes demoniac. If there is a devil in the flower, how much more in the gloomy forest! The light we think so pure teems with children of the night. The heavens themselves blasphemy! are full of hell. That divine morning star, whose glorious beams not seldom lightened a Socrates, an Archimedes, a Plato, what is it now become? A devil, the archfiend Lucifer. In the eventime again it is the devil Venus who draws me into temptation by her light so soft and mild.

That such a society should wax wroth and terrible is not surprising. Indignant at feeling itself so weak against devils, it persecutes them everywhere, in the temples, at the altars once of the ancient worship, then of the heathen martyrs. Let there be more feasts? they will likely be so many gatherings of idolaters. The Family itself becomes suspected: for custom might bring it together round the ancient Lares. And why should there be a family? the empire is an empire of monks.

But the individual man himself, thus dumb and isolated though he be, still watches the sky, still honours his ancient gods whom he finds anew in the stars. "This is he," said the Emperor Theodosius, "who causes famines and all the plagues of the empire." Those terrible words turned the blind rage of the people loose upon the harmless Pagan. Blindly the law unchained all its furies against the law.

Ye gods of Eld, depart into your tombs! Get ye extinguished, gods of Love, of Life, of Light! Put on the monk's cowl. Maidens, become nuns. Wives, forsake your husbands; or, if ye will look after the house, be unto them but cold sisters.

But is all this possible? What man's breath shall be strong enough to put out at one effort the burning lamp of God? These rash endeavours of an impious piety may evoke miracles strange and monstrous. Tremble, guilty that ye are!

Often in the Middle Ages 'will recur the mournful tale of the Bride of Corinth. Told at a happy moment by Phlegon, Adrian's freedman, it meets us again in the twelfth, and yet again in the sixteenth century, as the deep reproof, the invincible protest of nature herself.

"A young man of Athens went to Corinth, to the house of one who had promised him his daughter. Himself being still a heathen, he -knew not that the family which he thought to enter had just turned Christian. It is very late when he arrives. They are all gone to rest, except the mother, who serves up for him the hospitable repast and then leaves him to sleep. Dead fired, he drops down. Scarce was he fallen asleep, when a figure entered the room: 'tis a girl all clothed and veiled in white; on her forehead a fillet of black and gold. She sees him. In amazement she lifts her white hand: e Am I, then, such a stranger in the house already? Alas, poor recluse! ...But I am ashamed, and withdraw. Sleep on.'

"'Stay, fair maiden! Here are Bacchus, Ceres, and with thee comes Love. Fear not, look not so pale!'

"'Ah! Away from me, young man! I have nothing more to do with happiness. By a vow my mother made in her sickness my youth and my life are bound for ever. The gods have fled, and human victims now are our only sacrifices.'

"' Ha! can it be thou, thou, my darling betrothed, who wast given me from my childhood? The oath of our fathers bound us for evermore under the blessing of heaven. Maiden, be mine!'

"' No, my friend, not I. Thou shalt have my younger sister. If I moan in my chilly dungeon, do thou in her arms think of me, of me wasting away and thinking only of thee; of me whom the earth is about to cover again.'

"'Nay, I swear by this flame, the torch of Hymen, thou shalt come home with me to my father. Rest thee, my own beloved.'

"As a wedding-gift he offers her a cup of gold. She gives him her chain, but instead of the cup desires a curl of his hair.

"It is the hour of spirits; her pale lip drinks up the dark blood-red wine. He too drinks greedily after her. He calls on the god of Love. She still resisted,

17

though her poor heart was dying thereat. But he grows desperate, and falls weeping on the couch. Anon she throws herself by his side.

"'Oh! how ill thy sorrow makes me! Yet, if thou wast to touch me Oh, horror! white as the snow, and cold as ice, such, ah me! is thy bride.'

"'I will warm thee again: come to me, wert thou come from the very grave.'

"Sighs and kisses many do they exchange.

"'Dost thou feel how warm I am?'

"Love twines and holds them fast. Tears mingle with their joy. She changes with the fire she drinks from his mouth: her icy blood is aglow with passion; but the heart in her bosom will not beat.

"But the mother was there listening. Soft vows, cries of wailing and of pleasure.

"' Hush, the cock is crowing: to-morrow night!' Then with kiss on kiss they say farewell.

"In wrath the mother enters; sees what? Her daughter. He would have hidden her, covered her up. But freeing herself from him, she grew from the couch up to the roof.

"'O mother, mother, you grudge me a pleasant night; you would drive me from this cosy spot! Was it not enough to have wrapped me in my windingsheet and borne me to the grave? A greater power has lifted up the stone. In vain did your priests drone over the trench they dug for me. Of what use are salt and water, where burns the fire of youth? The earth cannot freeze up love. You made a promise; I have just reclaimed my own.

"'Alas, dear friend, thou must die: thou wouldst but pine and dry up here. I have thy hair; it will be white to-morrow...Mother, one last prayer! Open my dark dungeon, set up a stake, and let the loving one find rest in the flames. Let the sparks fly upward and the ashes redden. We will go to our olden gods.'" [3]

[1] See Mansi, Baluze; Council of Aries, 442; of Tours, 567; of Leptines, 743; the Capitularies, &c., and even Gerson, about 1400.

[2] See the Lives of the Desert Fathers, and 'the authors quoted by A. Maurie, *Magie,* 317. In the fourth century, the Messalians, thinking themselves full of devils, spat and blew their noses without ceasing; made incredible efforts to spit them forth.

[3] Here I have suppressed a shocking phrase. Goethe, so noble in the form, is not so in the spirit of his poem. He spoils the marvel of the legend by sullying the Greek conception with a horrible Slavish idea. As they are weeping, he turns the maiden into a vampire. She comes because she thirsts for blood, that she may suck the blood from his heart. And he makes her coldly say this impious and unclean thing: "When I have done with him, I will pass on to others: the young blood shall fall prey to my fury."

In the Middle Ages this story put on a grotesque garb, by way of frightening us with the *Devil Venus*. On the finger of her statue a young man imprudently places a ring, which she clasps tight, guarding it like a bride, and going in the night to his couch, to assert her rights. He cannot rid himself of his infernal spouse without an exorcism. The same tale, foolishly applied to the Virgin, is found in the *Fabliaux*. If my memory does not mislead me, Luther also, in his "Table Talk," takes up the old story in a very coarse way, till you quite smell the body. The Spanish. Del Rio shifts the scene of it to Brabant. The bride dies shortly before her marriage; the death-bells are rung. The bridegroom rushed wildly over the country. He hears a wail. It is she herself wandering about the heath. "Seest thou not" she says "who leads me?" But he catches her up and bears her home. At this point the story threatened to become too moving; but the hard inquisitor, Del Rio, cuts the thread. "On lifting her veil," says he, "they found only a log of wood covered with the skin of a corpse." The Judge le Loyer, silly though he be, has restored the older version.

Thenceforth these gloomy taletellers come to an end. The story is useless when our own age begins; for then the bride has triumphed. Nature conies back from the grave, not by 'stealth, but as mistress of the house.

Chapter Two - Why the Middle Ages Fell into Despair

"BE ye as newborn babes (*quasi modo geniti infants*); be thoroughly childlike in the innocence of your hearts; peaceful, forgetting all disputes, calmly resting under the hand of Christ." Such is the kindly counsel tendered by the Church to this stormy world on the morning after the great fall. In other words: "Volcanoes, ruins, ashes, and lava, become green. Ye parched plains, get covered with flowers."

One thing indeed gave promise of the peace that reneweth: the schools were all shut up, the way of logic forsaken. A method infinitely simple for the doing away with argument, offered all men a gentle slope, down which they had nothing to do but go. If the creed was doubtful, the life was all traced out in the pathway of the legend. From first to last but the one word *Imitation.*

"Imitate, and all will go well. Rehearse and copy." But is this the way to that true childhood which quickens the heart of man, which leads back to its fresh and fruitful springs? In this world that is to make us young and childlike, I see at first nothing but the tokens of age; only cunning, slavishness, want of power. What kind of literature is this, confronted with the glorious monuments of Greeks and Jews? We have just the same literary fall as happened in India from Brahminism to Buddhism; a twaddling flow of words after a noble inspiration. Books copy from books, churches from churches, until they cannot so much as copy. They pillage from each other: Aix-la-Chapelle is adorned with the marbles torn from Ravenna. It is the same with all the social life of those days. The bishop-king of a city, the savage king of a tribe, alike copy the Roman magistrates. Original as one might deem them, our monks in their monasteries simply restored their ancient Villa, as Chateaubriand well said. They had no notion either of forming a new society or of fertilizing the old. Copying from the monks of the East, they wanted their servants at first to be themselves a barren race of monkling workmen. It was in spite of them that the family in renewing itself renewed the world.

Seeing how fast these oldsters keep on oldening; how in one age we fall from the wise monk St. Benedict down to the pedantic Benedict of Aniane; [1] we feel that such gentry were wholly guiltless of that great popular creation which bloomed amidst ruins; namely, the Lives of the Saints. If the monks wrote, it was the people made them. This young growth might throw out some leaves and flowers from the crannies of an old Roman ruin turned into a convent: but most assuredly not thence did it first arise. Its roots go deep into the ground: sown by the people and cultivated by the family, it takes help from every hand, from men, from women, from children. The precarious, troubled life of those days of violence, made these poor folk imaginative, prone to believe in their own dreams, as being to them full of comfort: strange dreams withal, rich in marvels, in fooleries; absurd, but charming.

These families, isolated in forests and mountains, as we still see them in the Tyrol or the Higher Alps, and coming down thence but once a week, never wanted for illusions in the desert. One child had seen this, some woman had dreamed that. A new saint began to rise. The story went abroad in the shape of a ballad with doggrel rhymes. They sang and danced to it of an evening at the oak by the fountain. The priest, when he came on Sunday to perform service in the woodland chapel, found the legendary chant already in every mouth. He said to himself, "After all, history is good, is edifying. ... It does honour to the Church. *Vox populi, vox Dei!* But how did they light upon it?" He could be shown the true, the irrefragable proofs of it in some tree or stone which had witnessed the apparition, had marked the miracle. What can he say to that?

Brought back to the abbey, the tale will find a monk good for nothing, who can only write; who is curious, believes everything, no matter how marvellous. It is written out, broidered with his dull rhetoric, and spoilt a little. But now it has come forth, confirmed and consecrated, to be read in the refectory, ere long in the church. Copied, loaded and overloaded with ornaments chiefly grotesque, it will go on from age to age, until at last it comes to take high rank in the Golden. Legend.

When those fair stories are read again to us in these days, even as we listen to the simple, grave, artless airs into which those rural peoples threw all their young heart, we cannot help marking a great inspiration; and we are moved to pity as we reflect upon their fate.

They had taken literally the touching advice of the Church: "Be ye as newborn babes." But they gave to it a meaning, the very last that one would dream of finding in the original thought. As much, as Christianity feared and hated Nature, even so much did these others cherish her, deeming her all guileless, hallowing her even in the legends wherewith they mingled her up.

Those *hairy* animals, as the Bible sharply calls them, animals mistrusted by the monks who fear to find devils among them, enter in the most touching way into these beautiful stories; as the hind, for instance, who refreshes and comforts Geneviève of Brabant.

Even outside the life of legends, in the common everyday world," the humble friends of his hearth, the bold helpmates of his work, rise again in man's esteem. They have their own laws, [2] their own festivals. If in God's unbounded goodness there is room for the smallest creatures, if He seems to show them a pitying preference, "Wherefore," says the countryman, "should my ass not have entered the church? Doubtless, he has his faults, wherein he only resembles me the more. He is a rough worker, but has a hard head; is intractable, stubborn, headstrong; in short, just like myself." Thence come those wonderful feasts, the fairest of the Middle Ages; feasts of Innocents, of Fools, of the Ass. It is the people itself, moreover, which, in the shape of an ass, draws about its own image, presents itself before the altar, ugly, comical, abased. Verily, a touching sight! Led by Balaam, he enters solemnly between Virgil and the Sibyl; [3] enters that he may bear witness. If he kicked of yore against Balaam, it was that before him he beheld the sword of the ancient law. But here the law is ended, and the world of grace seems opening its two-leaved gate to the mean and to the simple. The people innocently believes it all. Thereon comes that lofty hymn, in which it says to the ass what it might have said to itself:

"Down on knee and say Amen!
Grass and hay enough hast eaten.
Leave the bad old ways, and go!

For the new expels the old:
Shadows fly before the noon:
Light hath hunted out the night."

How bold and coarse ye are! Was it this we asked of you, children rash and wayward, when we told you to be as children? We offered you milk; you are drinking wine. We led you softly, bridle in hand, along the narrow path. Mild and fearful, ye hesitated to go forward: and now, all at once, the bridle is broken; the course is cleared at a single bound. Ah! how foolish we were to let you make your own saints; to dress out the altar; to deck, to burden, to cover it up with flowers! Why, it is hardly distinguishable! And what we do see is the old heresy condemned of the Church, *the innocence of nature*: what am I saying? a new heresy, not like to end to-morrow, *the independence of man.*

Listen and obey! You are forbidden to invent, to create. No more legends, no more new saints: we have had enough of them. You are forbidden to in-troduce new chants in your worship: inspiration is not allowed. The martyrs you would bring to light should stay modestly within their tombs, waiting to be recognised by the Church. The clergy, the monks are forbidden to grant the tonsure of civil freedom to husbandmen and serfs. Such is the narrow fearful spirit that fills the Church of the Carlovingian days. [4] She unsays her words, she gives herself the lie, she says to the children, "Be old!"

21

A fall indeed! But is this earnest? They had bidden us all be young. Ah! but priest and people are no longer one. A divorce without end begins, a gulf unpassable divides them for ever. The priest himself, a lord and prince, will come out in his golden cope, and chant in the royal speech of that great empire which is no more. For ourselves, a mournful company, bereft of human speech, of the only speech that God would care to hear, what else can we do but low and bleat with the guileless friends who never scorn us, who, in winter-time will keep us warm in their stable, or cover us with their fleeces? We will live with dumb beasts, and be dumb ourselves.

In sooth there is less need than before for our going to church. But the church will not hold us free: she insists on our returning to hear what we no longer understand. Thenceforth a mighty fog, a fog heavy and dun as lead, enwraps the world. For how long? For a whole millennium of horror. Throughout ten centuries, a languor unknown to all former times seizes upon the Middle Ages, even in part on those latter clays that come midway betwixt sleep and waking, and holds them under the sway of a visitation most irksome, most unbearable; that convulsion, namely, of mental weariness, which men call a fit of yawning.

When the tireless bell rings at the wonted hours, they yawn; while the nasal chant is singing in the old Latin words, they yawn. It is all foreseen, there is nothing to hope for in the world, everything will come round just the same as before. The certainty of being bored to-morrow sets one yawning from to-day; and the long vista of wearisome days, of wearisome years to come, weighs men down, sickens them from the first with living. From brain to stomach, from stomach to mouth, the fatal fit spreads of its own accord, and keeps on distending the jaws without end or remedy. An actual disease the pious Bretons call it, ascribing it, however, to the malice of the Devil. He keeps crouching in the woods, the peasants say: if anyone passes by tending his cattle, he sings to him vespers and other rites, until he is dead with yawning. [5]

To be old is to be weak. When the Saracens, when the Norsemen threaten us, what will come to us if the people remain old? Charlemagne weeps, and the Church weeps too. She owns that her relics fail to guard her altars from these Barbarian devils. [6] Had she not better call upon the arm of that wayward child whom she was going to bind fast, the arm of that young giant whom she wanted to paralyse? This movement in two opposite ways fills the whole ninth century. The people are held back, anon they are hurled forward: we fear them and we call on them for aid. With them and by means of them we throw up hasty barriers, defences that may check the Barbarians, while sheltering the priests and their saints escaped thither from their churches.

In spite of the Bald Emperor's [7] command not to build, there grows up a tower on the mountain. Thither comes the fugitive, crying, "In God's name, take me in, at least my wife and children! Myself with my cattle will encamp

22

in your outer enclosure." The tower emboldens him and he feels himself a man. It gives him shade, and he in his turn defends, protects his protector.

Formerly in their hunger the small folk yielded themselves to the great as serfs; but here how great the difference! He offers himself as a *vassal*, one who would be called brave and valiant. [8] He gives himself up, and keeps himself, and reserves to himself the right of going elsewhere. "I will go further: the earth is large: I, too, like the rest, can rear my tower yonder. If I have defended the outworks, I can surely look after myself within."

Thus nobly, thus grandly arose the feudal world. The master of the tower received his vassals with some such words as these: "Thou shalt go when thou wiliest, and if need be with my help; at least, if thou shouldst sink in the mire, I myself will dismount to succour thee." These are the very words of the old formula. [9]

But, one day, what do I see? Can my sight be grown dim? The lord of the valley, as he rides about, sets up bounds that none may overleap; ay, and limits that you cannot see. "What is that? I don't understand." That means that the manor is shut in. "The lord keeps it all fast under gate and hinge, between heaven and earth."

Most horrible! By virtue of what law is this *vassus* (or *valiant* one) held to his power? People will thereon have it, that *vassus* may also mean *slave*. In like manner the word *servus,* meaning a *servant,* often indeed a proud one, even a Count or Prince of the Empire, comes in the case of the weak to signify a *serf,* a wretch whose life is hardly worth a halfpenny.

In this damnable net are they caught. But down yonder, on his ground, is a man who avers that his land is free, a *freehold,* a *fief of the sun.* Seated on his boundary-stone, with hat pressed firmly down, he looks at Count or Emperor passing near. "Pass on, Emperor; go thy ways! If thou art firm on thy horse, yet more am I on my pillar. Thou mayest pass, but so will not I: for I am Freedom."

But I lack courage to say what becomes of this man. The air grows thick around him: he breathes less and less freely. He seems to be *under a spell:* he cannot move: he is as one paralysed. His very beasts grow thin, as if a charm had been thrown over them. His servants die of hunger. His land bears nothing now; spirits sweep it clean by night.

Still he holds on: "The poor man is a king in his own house." But he is not to be let alone. He gets summoned, must answer for himself in the Imperial Court. So he goes, like an old-world spectre, whom no one knows any more. "What is he?" ask the young. "Ah, he is neither a lord, nor a serf! Yet even then is he nothing?"

"Who am I? I am he who built the first tower, he who succoured you, he who, leaving the tower, went boldly forth to meet the Norse heathens at the bridge. Yet more, I dammed the river, I tilled the meadow, creating the land itself by drawing it God-like out of the waters. From this land who shall drive me?"

23

"No, my friend," says a neighbour-- "you shall not be driven away. You shall till this land, but in a way you little think for. Remember, my good fellow, how in your youth, some fifty years ago, you were rash enough to wed my father's little serf, Jacqueline. Remember the proverb, 'He who courts my hen is my cock.' You belong to my fowl-yard. Ungird yourself; throw away your sword! From this day forth you are my serf."

There is no invention here. The dreadful tale recurs incessantly during the Middle Ages. Ah, it was a sharp sword that stabbed him. I have abridged and suppressed much, for as often as one returns to these times, the same steel, the same sharp point, pierces right through the heart.

There was one among them who, under this gross insult, fell into so deep a rage that he could not bring up a single word. It was like Roland betrayed. His blood all rushed upwards into his throat. His flaming eyes, his mouth so dumb, yet so fearfully eloquent, turned all the assembly pale. They started back. He was dead: his veins had burst. His arteries spurted the red blood over the faces of his murderers. [10]

The doubtful state of men's affairs, the frightfully slippery descent by which the freeman becomes a vassal, the vassal a servant, and the servant a serf, in these things lie the great terror of the Middle Ages, and the depth of their despair. There is no way of escape therefrom; for he who takes one step is lost. He is an *alien,* a *stray,* a *wild beast of the chase.* The ground grows slimy to catch his feet, roots him, as he passes, to the spot. The contagion in the air kills him; he becomes a thing in *mortmain*, a dead creature, a mere nothing, a beast, a soul worth twopence-halfpenny, whose murder can be atoned for by twopence-halfpenny.

These are outwardly the two great leading traits in the wretchedness of the Middle Ages, through which they came to give themselves up to the Devil. Meanwhile let us look within, and sound the innermost depths of their moral life.

[1] Benedict founded a convent at Aniane in Languedoc, in the reign of Charlemagne.
[2] See J. Grimm, Rechts *Alterthümer,* and my *Origines du Droit.*
[3] According to the ritual of Rouen. See Ducange on the words *Festum* and *Kalendae:* also Martène, iii. 110. The Sibyl was crowned and followed by Jews and Gentiles, by Moses, the Prophets, Nebuchadnezzar, &c. From a very early time, and continually from the seventh to the seventeenth century, the Church strove to proscribe the great people's feasts of the Ass, of Innocents, of Children, and of Fools. It never succeeded until the advent of the modern spirit.
[4] See the Capitularies, *passim.*
[5] An illustrious Breton, the last man of the Middle Ages, who had gone on a bootless errand to convert Rome, received there some brilliant offers. "What do you want?" said the Pope. "Only one thing: to have done with the Breviary."
[6] The famous avowal made by Hincmar.
[7] Charles the Bald. - TRANS
[8] A difference too little felt by those who have spoken of the *personal recommendation,* &c.

[9] Grimm, *Rechts Alterthümer,* and my *Origines du Droit.*
[10] This befell the Count of Avesnes when his freehold was declared a mere fief, himself a mere vassal, a serf of the Earl of Hainault. Read, too, the dreadful story of the Great Chancellor of Flanders, the first magistrate of Bruges, who also was claimed as a serf. - Gualterius, *Scriptores Rerum Francicarum,* viii. 334.

Chapter Three - The Little Devil of The Fireside

THERE is an air of dreaming about those earlier centuries of the Middle Ages, in which the legends were self-conceived. Among countryfolk so gently submissive, as these legends show them, to the Church, you would readily suppose that very great innocence might be found. This is surely the temple of God the Father. And yet the *penitentiaries,* wherein reference is made to ordinary sins, speak of strange defilements, of things afterwards rare enough under the rule of Satan.

These sprang from two causes, from the utter ignorance of the times, and from the close intermingling of near kindred under one roof. They seem to have had but a slight acquaintance with our modern ethics. Those of their day, all counterpleas notwithstanding, resemble the ethics of the patriarchs, of that far antiquity which regarded marriage with a stranger as immoral, and allowed only of marriage amongst kinsfolk. The families thus joined together became as one. Not daring to scatter over the surrounding deserts, tilling only the outskirts of a Merovingian palace or a monastery, they took shelter every evening under the roof of a large homestead (*villa*). Thence arose unpleasant points of analogy with the ancient *ergastulum,* where the slaves of an estate were all crammed together. Many of these communities lasted through and even beyond the Middle Ages. About the results of such a system the lord would feel very little concern. To his eyes but one family was visible in all this tribe, this multitude of people "who rose and lay down together, ...who ate together of the same bread, and drank out of the same mug."

Amidst such confusion the woman was not much regarded. Her place was by no means lofty. If the virgin, the ideal woman, rose higher from age to age, the real woman was held of little worth among these boorish masses, in this medley of men and herds. Wretched was the doom of a condition which could only change with the growth of separate dwellings, when men at length took courage to live apart in hamlets, or to build them huts in far-off forest-clearings, amidst the fruitful fields they had gone out to cultivate. From the lonely hearth comes the true family. It is the nest that forms the bird. Thenceforth they were no more things, but men; for then also was the woman born.

It was a very touching moment, the day she entered *her own home.* Then at last the poor wretch might become pure and holy. There, as she sits spinning

25

alone, while her goodman is in the forest, she may brood on some thought and dream away. Her damp, ill-fastened cabin, through which keeps whistling the winter wind, is still, by way of a recompense, calm and silent. In it are sundry dim corners where the housewife lodges her dreams.

And by this time she has some property, something of her own. The *distaff*, the *bed*, and the *trunk*, are all she has, according to the old song. [1] We may add a table, a seat, perhaps two stools. A poor dwelling and very bare; but then it is furnished with a living soul! The fire cheers her, the blessed box-twigs guard her bed, accompanied now and again by a pretty bunch of vervein. Seated by her door, the lady of this palace spins and watches some sheep. We are not yet rich enough to keep a cow; but to that we may come in time, if Heaven will bless our house. The wood, a bit of pasture, and some bees about our ground - such is our way of life! But little corn is cultivated as yet, there being no assurance of a harvest so long of coming. Such a life, however needy, is anyhow less hard for the woman: she is not broken down and withered, as she will be in the days of large farming. And she has more leisure withal. You must never judge of her by the coarse literature of the Fabliaux and the Christmas Carols, by the foolish laughter and license of the filthy tales we have to put up with by and by. She is alone; without a neighbour. The bad, unwholesome life of the dark, little, walled towns, the mutual spyings, the wretched dangerous gossipings, have not yet begun. No old woman comes of an evening, when the narrow street is growing dark, to tempt the young maiden by saying how for the love of her somebody is dying. She has no friend but her own reflections; she converses only with her beasts or the tree in the forest.

Such things speak to her, we know of what. They recall to her mind the saws once uttered by her mother and grandmother; ancient saws handed down for ages from woman to woman. They form a harmless reminder of the old country spirits, a touching family religion which doubtless had little power in the blustering hurly-burly of a great common dwelling house, but now comes back again to haunt the lonely cabin.

It is a singular, a delicate world of fays and hobgoblins, made for a woman's soul. When the great creation of the saintly Legend gets stopped and dried up, that other older, more poetic legend comes in for its share of welcome; reigns privily with gentle sway. It is the woman's treasure; she worships and caresses it. The fay, too, is a woman, a fantastic mirror wherein she sees herself in a fairer guise.

Who were these fays? Tradition says, that of yore some Gaulish queens, being proud and fanciful, did on the coming of Christ and His Apostles behave so insolently as to turn their backs upon them. In Brittany they were dancing at the moment, and never stopped dancing. Hence their hard doom; they are condemned to live until the Day of Judgment. [2] Many of them were turned into mice or rabbits; as the Kowriggwans for instance, or Elves, who meeting at night round the old Druidic stones entangle you in their dances.

26

The same fate befell the pretty Queen Mab, who made herself a royal chariot out of a walnut-shell. They are all rather whimsical, and sometimes ill-humoured. But can we be surprised at them, remembering their woeful lot? Tiny and odd as they are, they have a heart, a longing to be loved. They are good and they are bad and full of fancies. On the birth of a baby they come down the chimney, to endow it and order its future. They are fond of good spinning-women they even spin divinely themselves. Do we not talk of *spinning like a fairy?*

The fairy-tales, stripped of the absurd embellishments in which the latest compilers muffled them up, express the heart of the people itself. They mark a poetic interval between the gross communism of the primitive *villa*, and the looseness of the time when a growing burgess-class made our cynical Fabliaux. [3]

These tales have an historical side, reminding us, in the ogres, &c., of the great famines. But commonly they soar higher than any history, on the *Blue Bird's* wing, in a realm of eternal poesy; telling us our wishes which never vary, the unchangeable history of the heart.

The poor serf's longing to breathe, to rest, to find a treasure that may end his sufferings, continually returns. More often, through a lofty aspiration, this treasure becomes a soul as well, a treasure of love asleep, as in *The Sleeping Beauty:* but not seldom the charming person finds herself by some -fatal enchantment hidden under a mask. Hence that touching trilogy, that admirable *crescendo of Riquel with the Tuft, Ass's Skin,* and *Beauty and the Beast.* Love will not be discouraged. Through all that ugliness it follows after and gains the hidden beauty. In the last of these tales that feeling touches the sublime, and I think that no one has ever read it without weeping.

A passion most real, most sincere, lurks beneath it that unhappy, hopeless love, which unkind nature often sets between poor souls of very different ranks in life. On the one hand is the grief of the peasant maid at not being able to make herself fair enough to win the cavalier's fancy; on the other the smothered sighs of the serf, when along his furrow he sees passing, on a white horse, too exquisite a glory, the beautiful, the majestic Lady of the Castle. So in the East arises the mournful idyll of the impossible loves of the Rose and the Nightingale. Nevertheless, there is one great difference: the bird and the flower are both beautiful; nay, are alike in their beauty. But here the humbler being, doomed to a place so far below, avows to himself that he is ugly and monstrous. But amidst his wailing he feels in himself a power greater than the East can know. With the will of a hero, through the very greatness of his desire, he breaks out of his idle coverings. He loves so much, this monster, that he is loved, and, in return, through that love grows beautiful.

An infinite tenderness pervades it all. This soul enchanted thinks not of itself alone. It busies itself in saving all nature and all society as well. Victims of every kind, the child beaten by its step-mother, the youngest sister slighted, ill-used by her elders, are the surest objects of its liking. Even to the Lady of the Castle does its compassion extend j it mourns her fallen into the hands of so fierce a lord as Blue-Beard. It yearns with pity towards the beasts; it seeks to console them for being still in the shape of animals. Let them be patient, and their day will come. Some day their prisoned souls shall put on wings, shall be free, lovely, and beloved. This is the other side of *Ass's Skin* and such like stories. There especially we are sure of finding a woman's heart. The rude labourer in the fields may be hard enough to his beasts, but to the woman they are no beasts. She regards them with the feeling of a child. To her fancy all is human, all is soul: the whole world becomes ennobled. It is a beautiful enchantment. Humble as she is, and ugly as she thinks herself, she has given all her beauty, all her grace to the surrounding universe.

Is she, then, so ugly, this little peasant-wife, whose dreaming fancy feeds on things like these? I tell you she keeps house, she spins and minds the flock, she visits the forest to gather a little wood. As yet she has neither the hard work nor the ugly looks of the countrywoman as afterwards fashioned by the prevalent culture of grain crops. Nor is she like the fat townswife, heavy and slothful, about whom our fathers made such a number of fat stories. She has no sense of safety; she is meek and timid, and feels herself, as it were, in God's hand. On yonder hill she can see the dark frowning castle, whence a thousand harms may come upon her. Her husband she holds in equal fear and honour. A serf elsewhere, by her side he is a king. For him she saves of her best, living herself on nothing. She is small and slender like the women saints of the Church. The poor feeding of those days must needs make women fine-bred, but lacking also in vital strength. The children die off in vast numbers: those pale roses are all nerves. Hence, will presently burst forth the epileptic dances of the fourteenth century. Meanwhile, towards the twelfth century, there come to be two weaknesses attached to this state of half-grown youth: by night somnambulism; in the daytime seeing of visions, trance, and the gift of tears.

This woman, for all her innocence, still has a secret which the Church may never be told. Locked up in her heart she bears the pitying remembrance of those poor old gods who have fallen into the state of spirits; [4] and spirits, you must, know, are not exempt from suffering. Dwelling in rocks, and in hearts of oak, they are very unhappy in winter; being particularly fond of warmth. They ramble about houses; they are sometimes seen in stables warming themselves beside the beasts. Bereft of incense and burnt-offerings, they sometimes take of the milk. The housewife being thrifty, will not stint her husband, but. lessens her own share, and in the evening leaves a little cream.

Those spirits who only appear at night, regret their banishment from the day and are greedy of lamplight. By night the housewife starts on her perilous trip, bearing a small lantern, to the great oak where they dwell, or to the

28

secret fountain whose mirror, as it multiplies the flame, may cheer up those sorrowful outlaws.

But if anyone should know of it, good heavens! Her husband is canny and fears the Church: he would certainly give her a beating. The priest wages fierce war with the sprites, and hunts them out of every place. Yet he might leave them their dwelling in the oaks! What harm can they do in the forest? Alas! no-: from council to council they are hunted down. On set days the priest will go even to the oak, and with prayers and holy water drive away the spirits.

How would it be if no kind soul took pity on them? This woman, however, will take them under her care. She is an excellent Christian, but will keep for them one corner of her heart. To them alone can she entrust those little natural affairs, which, harmless as they are in a chaste wife's dwelling, the Church at any rate would count as blameworthy. They are the confidants, the confessors of these touching womanly secrets. Of them she thinks, when she puts the holy log on the fire. It is Christmastide; but also is it the ancient festival of the Northern spirits, the *Feast of the Longest Night.* So, too, the Eve of Mayday is the *Pervigilium of Maia*, when the tree is planted. So, too, with the Eve of St. John, the true feast-day of life, of flowers, and newly-awakened love. She who has no children makes it her especial duty to cherish these festivals, and to offer them a deep devotion. A vow to the Virgin would perhaps be of little avail, it being no concern of Mary's. In a low whisper, she prefers addressing some ancient genius, worshipped in other days as a rustic deity, and afterwards by the kindness of some local church transformed into a saint. [5] And thus it happens that the bed, the cradle, all the sweetest mysteries on which the chaste and loving soul can brood, belong to the olden gods.

Nor are the sprites ungrateful. One day she awakes, and without having stirred a finger, finds all her housekeeping done. In her amazement she makes the sign of the cross and says nothing. When the good man goes she questions herself, but in vain. It must have been a spirit. "What can it be? How came it here? How I should like to see it! But I am afraid: they say it is death to see a spirit." Yet the cradle moves and swings of itself. She is clasped by some one, and a voice so soft, so low that she took it for her own, is heard saying, "Dearest mistress, I love to rock your babe, because I am myself a babe." Her heart beats, and yet she takes courage a little. The innocence of the cradle gives this spirit also an innocent air, causing her to believe it good, gentle, suffered at least by God.

From that day forth she is no longer alone. She readily feels its presence, and it is never far from her. It rubs her gown, and she hears the grazing. It rambles momently about her, and plainly cannot leave her side. If she goes to the stable, it is there; and she believes that the other day it was in the churn. [6]

Pity she cannot take it up and look at it! Once, when she suddenly touched the brands, she fancied she saw the tricksy little thing tumbling about in the

29

sparks; another time she missed catching it in a rose. Small as it is, it works, sweeps, arranges, saves her a thousand cares.

It has its faults, however; is giddy, bold, and if she did not hold it fast, might perhaps shake itself free. It observes and listens too much. It repeats sometimes of a morning some little word she had whispered very, very softly on going to bed, when the light was put out. She knows it to be very indiscreet, exceedingly curious. She is irked with feeling herself always followed about, complains of it, and likes complaining. Sometimes, having threatened him and turned him off, she feels herself quite at ease. But just then she finds herself caressed by a light breathing, as it were a bird's wing. He was under a leaf. He laughs: his gentle voice, free from mocking, declares the joy he felt in taking his chaste young mistress by surprise. On her making a show of great wrath, "No, my darling, my little pet," says the monkey, "you are not a bit sorry to have me here."

She feels ashamed and dares say nothing more. But she guesses now that she loves him overmuch. She has scruples about it, and loves him yet more. All night she seems to feel him creeping up to her bed. In her fear she prays to God, and keeps close to her husband. What shall she do? She has not the strength to tell the Church. She tells her husband, who laughs at first incredulously. Then she owns to a little more, what a madcap the goblin is, sometimes even overbold. "What matters? He is so small." Thus he himself sets her mind at ease.

Should we too feel reassured, we who can see more clearly? She is quite innocent still. She would shrink from copying the great lady up there who, in the face of her husband, has her court of lovers and her page. Let us own, however, that to that point the goblin has already smoothed the way. One could not have a more perilous page than he who hides himself under a rose; and, moreover, he smacks of the lover. More intrusive than anyone else, he is so tiny that he can creep anywhere.

He glides even into the husband's heart, paying him court and winning his good graces. He looks after his tools, works in his garden, and of an evening, by way of reward, curls himself up in the chimney, behind the babe and the cat. They hear his small voice, just like a cricket's; but they never see much of him, save when a faint glimmer lights a certain cranny in which he loves to stay. Then they see, or think they see, a thin little face; and cry out, "Ah! little one, we have seen you at last!"

In church they are told to mistrust the spirits, for even one that seems innocent, and glides about like a light breeze, may after all be a devil. They take good care not to believe it. His size begets a belief in his innocence. Whilst he is there, they thrive. The husband holds to him as much as the wife, and perhaps more. He sees that the tricksy little elf makes the fortune of the house.

[1] "Trois pas du côté du bane,
     Et trois pas du côté du lit;
     Trois pas du côté du coffre,

Et trois pas --- Revenez ici."
(*Old Song of the Dancing Master.*)

[2] All passages bearing on this point have been gathered together in two learned works by M. Maury (*Les Fées,* 1843; and *La Magie,* 1860). See also Grimm.

[3] A body of tales by the Trouvères of the twelfth and thirteenth centuries. - TRANS.

[4] This loyalty of hers is very touching indeed. In the fifth century the peasants braved persecution by parading the gods of the old religion in the shape of small dolls made of linen or flour. Still the same in the eighth century. The *Capitularies* threaten death in vain. In the twelfth century, Burchard, of Worms, attests their inutility. In 1389, the Sorbonne inveighs against certain traces of heathenism, while in 1400, Gerson talks of it as still a lively superstition.

[5] A. Maury, *Magie,* 159.

[6] This is a favourite haunt of the little rogue's. To this day the Swiss, knowing his tastes, make him a present of some milk. His name among them is troll (*drôle*); among the Germans *kobold, nix.* In France he is called *follet, goblin, lutin;* in England, *Puck, Robin Goodfellow.* Shakespeare says, he does sleepy servants the kindness to pinch them black and blue, in order to rouse them.

Chapter Four - Temptations

I HAVE kept this picture clear of those dreadful shadows of the hour by which it would have been sadly overdarkened. I refer especially to the uncertainty attending the lot of these rural households, to their constant fear and foreboding of some casual outrage which might at any moment descend on them from the castle.

There were just two things which made the feudal rule a hell: on one hand, its *exceeding steadfastness,* man being nailed, as it were, to the ground, and emigration made impossible; on the other, a very great degree of uncertainty about his lot.

The optimist historians who say so much about fixed rents, charters, buying of immunities, forget how slightly all this was guaranteed. So much you were bound to pay the lord, but all the rest he could take if he chose; and this was very fitly called the *right of seizure.* You may work and work away, my good fellow! But while you are in the fields, yon dreaded band from the castle will fall upon your house and carry off whatever they please "for their lord's service."

Look again at that man standing with his head bowed gloomily over the furrow! And thus he is always found, his face clouded, his heart oppressed, as if he were expecting some evil news. Is he meditating some wrongful deed? No; but there are two ideas haunting him, two daggers piercing him in turn. The one is, "In what state shall I find my house this evening?" The other, "Would that the turning up of this sod might bring some treasure to light! that the good spirit would help to buy us free!"

We are assured that, after the fashion of the Etruscan spirit which one day started up from under the ploughshare in the form of a child, a dwarf or gnome of the tiniest stature would sometimes on such an appeal come forth from the ground, and, setting itself on the furrow, would say, "What wantest thou?" But in his amazement the poor man would ask for nothing; he would turn pale, cross himself, and presently go quite away.

Did he never feel sorry afterwards? Said he never to himself, "Fool that you are, you will always be unlucky?" I readily believe he did; but I also think that a barrier of dread invincible stopped him short. I cannot believe with the monks who have told us all things concerning witchcraft, that the treaty with Satan was the light invention of a miser or a man in love. On the contrary, nature and good sense alike inform us that it was only the last resource of an overwhelming despair, under the weight of dreadful outrages and dreadful sufferings.

But those great sufferings, we are told, must have been greatly lightened about the time of St. Louis, who forbade private wars among the nobles. My own opinion is quite the reverse. During the fourscore or hundred years that elapsed between his prohibition and the wars with England (1240-1340), the great lords being debarred from the accustomed sport of burning and plundering their neighbours' lands, became a terror to their own vassals. For the latter such a peace was simply war.

The spiritual, the monkish lords, and others, as shown in the *Journal of Eudes Rigault,* lately published, make one shudder. It is a repulsive picture of profligacy at once savage and uncontrolled. The monkish lords especially assail the nunneries. The austere Rigault, Archbishop of Rouen, confessor of the holy king, conducts a personal inquiry into the state of Normandy. Every evening he comes to e monastery. In all of them he finds the monks leading the life of great feudal lords, wearing arms, getting drunk, fighting duels, keen huntsmen over all the cultivated land; the nuns living among them in wild confusion, and betraying everywhere the fruits of their shameless deeds.

If things are so in the Church, what must the lay lords have been? What like was the inside of those dark towers which the folk below regarded with so much horror? Two tales, undoubtedly historical, namely, *Blue-Beard* and *Griselda,* tell us something thereanent. To his vassals, his serfs, what indeed must have been this devotee of torture who treated his own family in such a way? He is known to us through the only man who was brought to trial for such deeds; and that not earlier than the fifteenth century, Gilles de Retz, who kidnapped children.

Sir Walter Scott's Front de Boeuf, and the other lords of melodramas and romances, are but poor creatures in the face of these dreadful realities. The Templar also in *Ivanhoe*, is a weak artificial conception. The author durst not assay the foul reality of celibate life in the Temple, or within the castle walls.

32

Few women were taken in there, being accounted not worth their keep. The romances of chivalry altogether belie the truth. It is remarkable, indeed, how often the literature of an age expresses the very opposite of its manners, as, for instance, the washy theatre of eclogues after Florian, [1] during the years of the Great Terror.

The rooms in these castles, in such at least as may be seen to-day, speak more plainly than any books. Men-at-arms, pages, footmen, crammed together of nights under low-vaulted roofs, in the daytime kept on the battlements, on narrow terraces, in a state of most sickening weariness, lived only in their pranks down below; in feats no longer of arms on the neighbouring domains, but of hunting, ay, and hunting of men; insults, I may say, without number, outrages untold on families of serfs. The lord himself well knew that such an army of men, without women, could only be kept in order by letting them loose from time to time.

The awful idea of a hell wherein God employs the very guiltiest of the wicked spirits to torture the less guilty delivered over to them for their sport, this lovely dogma of the Middle Ages was exemplified to the last letter. Men felt that God was not among them. Each new raid betokened more and more clearly the kingdom of Satan, until men came to believe that thenceforth their prayers should be offered to him alone.

Up in the castle there was laughing and joking. "The women-serfs were too ugly." There is no question raised as to their beauty. The great pleasure lay in deeds of outrage, in striking and making them weep. Even in the seventeenth century the great ladies died with laughing, when the Duke of Lorraine told them how, in peaceful villages, his people went about harrying and torturing all the women, even to the old.

These outrages fell most frequently, as we might suppose, on families well to do and comparatively distinguished among the serfs; the families, namely, of those serf-born mayors, who already in the twelfth century appear at the head of the village. By the nobles they were hated, jeered, cruelly plagued. Their new-born moral dignity was not to be forgiven. Their wives and daughters were not allowed to be good and wise: they had no right to be held in any respect. Their honour was not their own. *Serfs of the body*, such was the cruel phrase cast for ever in their teeth.

In days to come people will be slow to believe, that the law among Christian nations went beyond anything decreed concerning the olden slavery; that it wrote down as an actual right the most grievous outrage that could ever wound man's heart. The lord spiritual had this foul privilege no less than the lord temporal. In a parish outside Bourges, the parson, as being a lord, expressly claimed the firstfruits of the bride, but was willing to sell his rights to the husband. [2]

It has been too readily believed that this wrong was formal, not real. But the price laid down in certain countries for getting a dispensation, exceeded the means of almost every peasant. In Scotland, for instance, the demand was for "several cows:" a price immense, impossible. So the poor young wife was at their mercy. Besides, the Courts of Béarn openly maintain that this right grew up naturally: "The eldest-born of the peasant is accounted the son of his lord, for he perchance it was who begat him." [3]

All feudal customs, even if we pass over this, compel the bride to go up to the castle, bearing thither the "wedding-dish." Surely it was a cruel thing to make her trust herself amongst such a pack of celibate dogs, so shameless and so ungovernable.

A shameful scene we may well imagine it to have been. As the young husband is leading his bride to the castle, fancy the laughter of cavaliers and footmen, the frolics of the pages around the wretched poor! But the presence of the great lady herself will check them? Not at all. The lady in whose delicate breeding the romances tell us to believe, [4] but who, in her husband's absence, ruled his men, judging, chastising, ordaining penalties, to whom her husband himself was bound by the fiefs she brought him, such a lady would be in no wise merciful, especially towards a girlserf who' happened also to be good-looking. Since, according to the custom of those days, she openly kept her gentleman and her page, she would not be sorry to sanction her own libertinism by that of her husband.

Nothing will she do to hinder the fun, the sport they are making out of you poor trembler who has come to redeem his bride. They begin by bargaining with him; they laugh at the pangs endured by "the miserly peasant;" they suck the very blood and marrow of him. Why all this fury? Because he is neatly clad; is honest, settled; is a man of mark in the village. Why, indeed? Because she is pious, chaste, and pure; because she loves him; because she is frightened and falls a-weeping. Her sweet eyes plead for pity.

In vain does the poor wretch offer all he has, even to her dowry: it is all too little. Angered at such cruel injustice, he will say perhaps that "his neighbour paid nothing." The insolent fellow! he would argue with us! Thereon they gather round him, a yelling mob: sticks and brooms pelt upon him like hail. They jostle him, they throw him down. "You jealous villain, you Lent-faced villain!" they cry; "no one takes your wife from you; you shall have her back tonight, and to enhance the honour done you…your eldest child will be a baron!" Everyone looks out of window at the absurd figure of this dead man in wedding garments. He is followed by bursts of laughter, and the noisy rabble, down to the lowest scullion, give chase to the "cuckold." [5]

The poor fellow would have burst, had he nothing to hope for from the Devil. By himself he returns: is the house empty as well as desolate? No, there is company waiting for him there: by the fireside sits Satan.

But soon his bride comes back, poor wretch, all pale and undone. Alas! alas! for her condition. At his feet she throws herself and craves forgiveness. Then, with a bursting heart, he flings his arms round her neck. He weeps, he sobs, he roars, till the house shakes again.

But with her comes back God. For all her suffering, she is pure, innocent, holy still. Satan for that nonce will get no profit: the treaty is not yet ripe.

Our silly Fabliaux, our absurd tales, assume with regard to this deadly outrage and all its further issues, that the woman sides with her oppressors against her husband; they would have us believe that her brutal treatment by the former makes her happy and transports her with delight. A likely thing indeed! Doubtless she might be seduced by rank, politeness, elegant manners. But no pains are ever taken to that end. Great would be the scoffing at anyone who made true-love's wooing towards a serf. The whole gang of men, to the chaplain, the butler, even the footmen, would think they honoured her by deeds of outrage. The smallest page thought himself a great lord, if he only seasoned his love with insolence and blows.

One day, the poor woman, having just been illtreated during her husband's absence, begins weeping, and saying quite aloud, the while she is tying up her long hair, "Ah, those unhappy saints of the woods, what boots it to offer them my vows? Are they deaf, or have they grown too old? Why have I not some protecting spirit, strong and mighty wicked even, if it need be? Some such I see in stone at the church door; but what do they there? Why do they not go to their proper dwelling, the castle, to carry off and roast those sinners? Oh, who is there will give me power and might? I would gladly give myself in exchange. -Ah, me, what is it I would give? What have I to give on my side? Nothing is left me. Out on this body, out on this soul, a mere cinder now! Why, instead of this useless goblin, have I not some spirit, great, strong, and mighty, to help me?"

"My darling mistress! If I am small, it is your fault; and bigger I cannot grow. And besides, if I were very big, neither you nor your husband would have borne with me. You would have driven me away with your priests and your holy water. I can be strong, however, if you please. For, mistress mine, the spirits in themselves are neither great nor small, neither weak nor strong. For him who wishes it, the smallest can become a giant."

"In what way?"

"Why, nothing can be simpler. To make him a giant, you must grant him only one gift."

"What is that?"

"A lovely woman-soul."

"Ah, wicked one! What then art thou, and what wouldst thou have?"

"Only what you give me every day...Would you be better than the lady up yonder? She has pledged her soul to her husband and to her lover, and yet she yields it whole to her page. I am more than a page to you, more than a servant. In how many matters have I not been your little handmaid! Do not blush, nor be angry. Let me only say, that I am all about you, and already perhaps in you. Else, how could I know your thoughts, even those which you hide from yourself? "Who am I, then? Your little soul, which speaks thus

35

openly to the great one. We are inseparable. Do you know how long I have been with you? Some thousand years, for I belonged to your mother, to hers, to your ancestors. I am the Spirit of the Fireside."

"Tempter! What wilt thou do?"

"Why, thy husband shall be rich, thyself mighty, and men shall fear thee."

"Where am I? Surely thou art the demon of hidden treasures!"

"Why call me demon, if I do deeds of justice, of goodness, of piety? God cannot be everywhere He cannot be always working. Sometimes He likes to rest, leaving us other spirits here to carry on the smaller husbandry, to remedy the ills which his providence passed over, which his justice forgot to handle.

"Of this your husband is an example. Poor, deserving workman, he is killing himself and gaining nought in return. Heaven has had no time to look after him. But I, though rather jealous of him, still love my kind host. I pity him: his strength is going, he can bear up no longer. He will die, like your children, already dead of misery. This winter he was ill; what will become of him the next?"

Thereon, her face in her hands, she wept two, three hours, and even more. And when she had poured out all her tears her bosom still throbbing hard the other said, "I ask nothing: only, I pray, save him."

She had promised nothing, but from that hour she became his.

[1] A writer of eclogues, fables and dramas; in youth a friend of Voltaire, afterwards imprisoned during the Terror. - TRANS.

[2] Lauriere, ii. 100 (on the word Narquette). Michelet, *Origines du Droit,* 264.

[3] When I published my *Origines* in 1837, I could not have known this work, published in 1842.

[4] This delicacy appears in the treatment these ladies inflicted on their poet Jean de Meting, author of the Roman de la Rose.

[5] The old tales are very sportive, but rather monotonous. They turn on three jokes only: the despair of the *cuckold*, the cries of the *beaten*, the wry faces of the *hanged*. The first is amusing, the second laughable, the third, as crown of all, makes people split their sides. And the three have one point in common: it is the weak and helpless who is ill-used.

Chapter Five - Possession

A DREADFUL age was the age of gold; for thus do I call that hard time when gold first came into use. This was in the year 1300, during the reign of that Fair King [1] who never spake a word; the great king who seemed to have a dumb devil, but a devil with mighty arm, strong enough, to burn the Temple, long enough to reach Rome, and with glove of iron to deal the first good blow at the Pope.

Gold thereupon becomes a great pope, a mighty god, and not without cause. The movement began in Europe with the Crusades: the only wealth men cared for was that which having wings could lend itself to their enter-prise; the wealth, namely, of swift exchanges. To strike blows afar off the king wants nothing but gold. An army of gold, a fiscal army, spreads over all the land. The lord, who has brought back with him his dreams of the East, is always longing for its wonders, for damascened armour, carpets, spices, val-uable steeds. For all such things he needs gold. He pushes away with his foot the serf who brings him corn. "That is not all; I want gold!"

On that day the world was changed. Theretofore in the midst of much evil there had always been a harmless certainty about the tax. According as the year was good or bad, the rent followed the course of nature and the meas-ure of the harvest. If the lord said, "This is little," he was answered, "My lord, Heaven has granted us no more."

But the gold, alas! where shall we find it? We have no army to seize it in the towns of Flanders. Where shall we dig the ground to win him his treas-ure? Oh, that the spirit of hidden treasures would be our guide! [2]

While all are desperate, the woman with the goblin is already seated on her sacks of corn in the little neighbouring village. She is alone, the rest being still at their debate in the village.

She sells at her own price. But even when the rest come up, everything favours her, some strange magical allurement working on her side. No one bargains with her. Her husband, before his time, brings his rent in good sounding coin to the feudal elm. "Amazing!" they all say, "but the Devil is in her!"

They laugh, but she does not. She is sorrowful and afraid. In vain she tries to pray that night. Strange prickings disturb her slumber. Fantastic forms appear before her. The small gentle sprite seems to have grown imperious. He waxes bold. She is uneasy, indignant, eager to rise. In her sleep she groans, and feels herself dependent, saying, "No more do I belong to myself!"

"Here is a sensible countryman," says the lord; "he pays beforehand! You charm me: do you know accounts?" "A little." "Well then, you shall reckon with these folk. Every Saturday you shall sit under the elm and receive their money. On Sunday, before mass, you shall bring it up to the castle."

What a change in their condition! How the wife's heart beats when of a Saturday she sees her poor workman, serf though he be, seated like a lord-ling under the baronial shades. At first he feels giddy, but in time accustoms himself to put on a grave air. It is no joking matter, indeed; for the lord com-mands them to show him due respect. When he has gone up to the castle, and the jealous ones look like laughing and designing to pay him off, "You see that battlement," says the lord, "the rope you don't see, but it is also ready. The first man who touches him shall be set up there high and quick."

This speech is repeated from one to another; until it has spread around these two as it were an atmosphere of terror. Everybody doffs his hat to them, bowing very low indeed. But when they pass by, folk stand aloof, and get out of the way. In order to shirk them they turn up cross roads, with backs bended, with eyes turned carefully down. Such a change makes them first savage, but afterwards sorrowful. They walk alone through all the district. The wife's shrewdness marks the hostile scorn of the castle, the trembling hate of those below. She feels herself fearfully isolated between two perils. No one to defend her but her lord, or rather the money they pay him: but then to find that money, to spur on the peasant's slowness, and overcome his sluggish antagonism, to snatch somewhat even from him who has nothing, what hard pressure, what threats, what cruelty, must be employed! This was never in the goodman's line of business. The wife brings him to the mark by dint of much pushing: she says to him, "Be rough; at need be cruel. Strike hard. Otherwise you will fall short of your engagements; and then we are undone."

This suffering by day, however, is a trifle in comparison with the tortures of the night. She seems to have lost the power of sleeping. She gets up, walks to and fro, and roams about the house. All is still; and yet how the house is altered; its old innocence, its sweet security all for ever gone! "Of what is that cat by the hearth a-thinking, as she pretends to sleep, and 'tweenwhiles opens her green eyes upon me? The she-goat with her long beard, looking so discreet and ominous, knows more about it than she can tell. And yon cow which the moon reveals by glimpses in her stall, why does she give me such a sidelong look? All this is surely unnatural!"

Shivering, she returns to her husband's side. "Happy man, how deep his slumber! Mine is over; I cannot sleep, I never shall sleep again." In time, however, she falls off. But oh, what suffering visits her then! The importunate guest is beside her, demanding and giving his orders. If one while she gets rid of him by praying or making the sign of the cross, anon he returns under another form. "Get back, devil! What durst thou? I am a Christian soul. No, thou shalt not touch me!"

In revenge he puts on a hundred hideous forms; twining as an adder about her bosom, dancing as a frog upon her stomach, anon like a bat, sharp-snouted, covering her scared mouth with dreadful kisses. What is it he wants? To drive her into a corner, so that conquered and crushed at last, she may yield and utter the word "Yes." Still she is resolute to say "No." Still she is bent on braving the cruel struggles of every night, the endless martyrdom of that wasting strife.

"How far can a spirit make himself withal a body? What reality can there be in his efforts and approaches? Would she be sinning in the flesh, if she allowed the intrusions of one who was always roaming about her? Would that be sheer adultery?" Such was the sly roundabout way in which sometimes he stayed and weakened her resistance. "If I am only a breath, a smoke, a thin air, as so many doctors call me, why are you afraid, poor fearful soul, and how does it concern your husband?"

It is the painful doom of the soul in. these Middle Ages, that a number of questions which to us would seem idle, questions of pure scholastics, disturb, frighten, and torment it, taking the guise of visions, sometimes of devilish debatings, of cruel dialogues carried on within. The Devil, fierce as he shows himself in the demoniacs, remains always a spirit throughout the days of the Roman Empire, even in the time of St. Martin or the fifth century. With the Barbarian inroads he waxes barbarous, and takes to himself a body. So great a body does he become, that he amuses himself in breaking with stones the bell of the convent of St. Benedict. More and more fleshly is he made to appear, by way of frightening the plunderers of ecclesiastical goods. People are taught to believe that sinners will be tormented not in the spirit only, but even bodily in the flesh; that they will suffer material tortures, not those of ideal flames, but in very deed such exquisite pangs as burning coals, gridirons, and red-hot spits can awaken.

This conception of the torturing devils inflicting material agonies on the souls of the dead, was a mine of gold to the Church. The living, pierced with grief and pity, asked themselves "if it were possible to redeem these poor souls from one world to another; if to these, too, might be applied such forms of expiation, by atonement and compromise, as were practised upon earth?" This bridge between two worlds was found in Cluny, which from its very birth, about 900, became at once among the wealthiest of the monastic orders.

So long as God Himself dealt out his punishments, *making heavy his hand,* or striking *with the sword of the Angel,* according to the grand old phrase, there was much less of horror; if his hand was heavy as that of a judge, it was still the hand of a Father. The Angel who struck remained pure and clean as his own sword. Far otherwise is it when the execution is done by filthy demons, who resemble not the angel that burned up Sodom, but the angel that first went forth therefrom. In that place they stay, and their hell is a kind of Sodom, wherein these spirits, fouler than the sinners yielded into their charge, extract a horrible joy from the tortures they are inflicting. Such was the teaching to be found in the simple carvings hung out at the doors of churches. By these men learned the horrible lesson of the pleasures of pain. On pretence of punishing, the devils wreaked upon their victims the most outrageous whims. Truly an immoral and most shameful idea was this, of a sham justice that befriended the worse side, deepening its wickedness by the present of a plaything, and corrupting the Demon himself!

Cruel times indeed! Think how dark and low a heaven it was, how heavily it weighed on the head of man! Fancy the poor little children from their earliest years imbued with such awful ideas, and trembling within their cradles! Look at the pure innocent virgin believing herself damned for the pleasure infused in her by the spirit! And the wife in her marriage-bed tortured by his attacks, withstanding him, and yet again feeling him within her! - a fearful feeling known to those who have suffered from taenia. You feel in yourself a double life; you trace the monster's movements, now boisterous, anon soft and waving, and therein the more troublesome, as making you fancy yourself on the sea. Then you rush off in wild dismay, terrified at yourself, longing to escape, to die.

Even at such times as the demon was not raging against her, the woman into whom he had once forced his way would wander about as one burdened with gloom. For thenceforth she had no remedy. He had taken fast hold of her, like an impure steam. He is the Prince of the Air, of storms, and not least of the storms within. All this may be seen rudely but forcefully presented under the great doorway of Strasburg Cathedral. Heading the band of *Foolish Virgins,* the wicked woman who lures them on to destruction is filled, blown out by the Devil, who overflows ignobly and passes out from under her skirts in a dark stream of thick smoke.

This blowing-out is a painful feature in the *possession;* at once her punishment and her pride. This proud woman of Strasburg bears her belly well before her, while her head is thrown far back. She triumphs in her size, delights in being a monster.

To this, however, the woman we are following has not yet come. But already she is puffed up with him, and with her new and lofty lot. The earth has ceased to bear her. Plump and comely in these better days, she goes down the street with head upright, and merciless in her scorn. She is feared, hated, admired.

In look and bearing our village lady says, "I ought to be the great lady herself. And what does she up yonder, the shameless sluggard, amidst all those men, in the absence of her lord?" And now the rivalry is set on foot. The village, while it loathes her, is proud thereat. "If the lady of the castle is a baroness, our woman is a queen; and more than a queen, we dare not say what." Her beauty is a dreadful, a fantastic beauty, killing in its pride and pain. The Demon himself is in her eyes.

He has her and yet has her not. She is still *herself,* and preserves *herself.* She belongs neither to the Demon nor to God. The Demon may certainly invade her, may encompass her like a fine atmosphere. And yet he has gained nothing at all; for he has no will thereto. She is *possessed, bedevilled,* and she does not belong to the Devil. Sometimes he uses her with dreadful cruelty, and yet gains nothing thereby. He places a coal of fire on her breast, or within her bowels. She jumps and writhes, but still says, "No, butcher, I will stay as I am."

"Take care! I will lash you with so cruel a scourge of vipers, I will smite you with such a blow, that you will afterwards go. weeping and rending the air with your cries."

The next night he will not come. In the morning it was Sunday her husband went up to the castle. He came back all undone. The lord had said: "A brook that flows drop by drop cannot turn the mill. You bring me a halfpenny at a time, which is good for nought. I must set off in a fortnight. The king marches towards Flanders, and I have not even a warhorse, my own being lame ever since the tourney. Get ready for business: I am in want of a hundred pounds."

"But, my lord, where shall I find them?"

"You may sack the whole village, if you will; I am about to give you men enough. Tell your churls, if the money is not forthcoming they are lost men; yourself especially you shall die. I have had enough of you: you have the heart of a woman; you are slack and sluggish. You shall die you shall pay for your cowardice, your effeminacy. Stay; it makes but very small difference whether you go down now, or whether I keep you here. This is Sunday: right loudly would the folk yonder laugh to see you dangling your legs from my battlements."

All this the unhappy man tells again to his wife; and preparing hopelessly for death, commends his soul to God. She being just as frightened, can neither lie down nor sleep. What is to be done? How sorry she is now to have sent the spirit away! If he would but come back! In the morning, when her husband rises, she sinks crushed upon the bed. She has hardly done so, when she feels on her chest a heavy weight. Gasping for breath, she is like to choke. The weight falls lower till it presses on her stomach, and therewithal on her arms she feels the grasp as of two steel hands.

"You wanted me, and here I am. So, at last, stubborn one, I have your soul at last!"

"But oh, sir, is it mine to give away? My poor husband! you used to love him you said so: you promised -"

"Your husband! You forget. Are you sure your thoughts were always kept upon him? Your soul! I ask for it as a favour; but it is already mine."

"No, sir," she says her pride once more returning to her, even in so dire a strait, "no, sir; that soul belongs to me, to my husband, to our marriage rites."

"Ah, incorrigible little fool! you would struggle Still, even now that you are under the goad! I have seen your soul at all hours; I know it better than you yourself. Day by day did I mark your first reluctances, your pains, and your fits of despair. I saw how disheartened you were when, in a low tone, you said that no one could be held to an impossibility. And then I saw you growing more resigned. You were beaten a little, and you cried out not very loud. As for me, I ask for your soul simply because you have already lost it. Meanwhile, your husband is dying. What is to be done? I am sorry for you: I have you in my power; but I want something more. You must grant it frankly and of free will, or else he is a dead man."

She answered very low, in her sleep, "Ah me! my body and my miserable flesh, you may take them to save my husband; but my heart, never. No one has ever had it, and I cannot give it away."

So, all resignedly she waited there. And he flung at her two words: "Keep them, and they will save you." Therewith she shuddered, felt within her a

41

horrible thrill of fire, and, uttering a loud cry, awoke in the arms of her astonished husband, to drown him in a flood of tears.

She tore herself away by force, and got up, fearing lest she should forget those two important words. Her husband was alarmed; for, without looking even at him, she darted on the wall a glance as piercing as that of Medea. Never was she more handsome. In her dark eye and the yellowish white around it played such a glimmer as one durst not face a glimmer like the sulphurous jet of a volcano.

She walked straight to the town. The first word was *"Green."* Hanging at a tradesman's door she beheld a green gown the colour of the Prince of the World an old gown, which as she put it on became new and glossy. Then she walked, without asking anyone, straight to the door of a Jew, at which she knocked loudly. It was opened with great caution. The poor Jew was sitting on the ground, covered over with ashes. "My dear, I must have a hundred pounds."

"Oh, madam, how am I to get them? The Prince-bishop of the town has just had my teeth drawn to make me say where my gold lies. [3] Look at my bleeding mouth."

"I know, I know; but I come to obtain from you the very means of destroying your Bishop. "When the Pope gets a cuffing, the Bishop will not hold out long."

"Who says so?"

"Toledo." [4]

He hung his head. She spoke and blew: within her was her own soul and the Devil to boot. A wondrous warmth filled the room: he himself was aware of a kind of fiery fountain. "Madam," said he, looking at her from under his eyes, "poor and ruined as I am, I had some pence still in store to sustain my poor children."

"You will not repent of it, Jew. I will swear to you the *great oath* that kills whoso breaks it. "What you are about to give me, you shall receive back in a week, at an early hour in the morning. This I swear by your *great oath* and by mine, which is yet greater: '*Toledo.*'"

A year went by. She had grown round and plump; had made herself one mass of gold. Men were amazed at her power of charming. Every one admired and obeyed her. By some devilish miracle the Jew had grown so generous as to lend at the slightest signal. By herself she maintained the castle, both through her own credit in the town, and through the fear inspired in the village by her rough extortion. The all-powerful green gown floated to and fro, ever newer and more beautiful. Her own beauty grew, as it were, colossal with success and pride. Frightened at a result so natural, everyone said, "At her time of life how tall she grows!"

Meanwhile we have some news: the lord is coming home. The lady, who for a long time had not dared to come forth, lest she might meet the face of

42

this other woman down below, now mounted her white horse. Surrounded by all her people, she goes to meet her husband; she stops and salutes him.

And, first of all, she says, "How long I have been looking for you! Why did you leave your faithful wife so long a languishing widow? And yet I will not take you in to-night, unless you grant me a boon."

"Ask it, ask it, fair lady" says the gentlemen laughing; "but make haste, for I am eager to embrace you. How beautiful you have grown!"

She whispered in his ear, so that no one knew what she said. Before going up to the castle the worthy lord dismounts by the village church, and goes in. Under the porch, at the head of the chief people, he beholds a lady, to whom without knowing her he offers a low salute. With matchless pride she bears high over the men's heads the towering horned bonnet *(hennin)* [5] of the period; the triumphal cap of the Devil, as it was often called, because of the two horns wherewith it was embellished. The real lady, blushing at her eclipse, went out looking very small. Anon she muttered, angrily, "There goes your serf. It is all over: everything has changed places: the ass insults the horse."

As they are going off, a bold page, a pet of the lady's, draws from his girdle a well-sharpened dagger, and with a single turn cleverly cuts the fine robe along her loins. [6] The crowd was astonished, but began to make it out when it saw the whole of the Baron's household going off in pursuit of her. Swift and merciless about her whistled and fell the strokes of the whip. She flies, but slowly, being already grown somewhat heavy. She has hardly gone twenty paces when she stumbles; her best friend having put a stone in her way to trip her up. Amidst roars of laughter she sprawls yelling on the ground. But the ruthless pages flog her up again. The noble handsome grey-hounds help in the chase and bite her in the tenderest places. At last, in sad disorder, amidst the terrible crowd, she reaches the door of her house. It is shut. There with hands and feet she beats away, crying, "Quick, quick, my love, open the door for me?" There hung she, like the hapless screech-owl whom they nail up on a farm-house door; and still as hard as ever rained the blows. Within the house all is deaf. Is the husband there? Or rather, being rich and frightened, does he dread the crowd, lest they should sack his house?

And now she has borne such misery, such strokes, such sounding buffets, that she sinks down in a swoon. On the cold stone threshold she finds herself seated, naked, half-dead, her bleeding flesh covered with little else than the waves of her long hair. Some one from the castle says, "No more now! We do not want her to die."

They leave her alone, to hide herself. But in spirit she can see the merriment going on at the castle. The lord however, somewhat dazed, said that he was sorry for it. But the chaplain says, in his meek way, "If this woman is *bedevilled,* as they say, my lord, you owe it to your good vassals, you owe it to the whole country, to hand her over to Holy Church. Since all that business with the Templars and the Pope, what way the Demon' is making! Nothing but fire will do for him." Upon which a Dominican says, "Your reverence has spoken right well. This devilry is a heresy in the highest degree. The bedevilled, like the heretic, should be burnt. Some of our good fathers, however, do not trust themselves now even to the fire. "Wisely they desire that, before all things, the soul may be slowly purged, tried, subdued by fastings; that it may not be burnt in its pride, that it shall not triumph at the stake. If you, madam, in the greatness of your piety, of your charity, would take the trouble to work upon this woman, putting her for some years *in pace* in a safe cell, of which you only should have the key, by thus keeping up the chastening process you might be doing good to her soul, shaming the Devil, and giving herself up meek and humble into the hands of the Church."

[1] Philip the Fair of France, who put down the Templar in Paris, and first secured the liberties of the Gallican Church. - TRANS.
[2] The devils trouble the world all through the Middle Ages; but not before the thirteenth century does Satan put on a settled shape. *"Compacts"* says M. Maury, "are very rare before that epoch;" and I believe him. How could they treat with one who as yet had no real existence I Neither of the treating parties was yet ripe for the contract. Before the will could be reduced to the dreadful pass of selling itself for ever, it must be made thoroughly desperate. It is not the unhappy who falls into despair, but the truly wretched, who being quite conscious of his misery, and having yet more to suffer, can find no escape therefrom. The wretched in this way are the men of the fourteenth century, from whom they ask a thing so impossible as payments in gold. In this and the following chapter I have touched on the circumstances, the feelings, the growing despair, which brought about the enormity of *compacts,* and, worse still than these, the dreadful character of the Witch. If the name was freely used, the thing itself was then rare, being no less than a marriage and a kind of priesthood. For ease of illustration, I have joined together the details of so delicate a scrutiny by a thread of fiction. The outward body of it matters little. The essential point is to remember that such things were not caused, as they try to persuade us, by *human fickleness, by the inconstancy of our fallen nature, by the chance persuasions of desire.* There was needed the deadly pressure of an age of iron, of cruel needs: it was needful that Hell itself should seem a shelter, an asylum, by contrast with the hell below.
[3] This was a common way of extracting help from the Jews. King John Lackland often tried it.
[4] Toledo seems to have been the holy city of Wizards, who in Spain were numberless. These relations with the civilized Moors, with the Jews so learned and paramount in Spain, as managers of the royal revenues, had given them a very high degree of culture, and in Toledo they formed a kind of University. In the sixteenth century, it was christianised, remodelled, reduced to mere *white magic.* See the *Deposition of the Wizard Achard, Lord of Beaumont, a Physician of Poitou. Lancre, Incredulité,* p. 781.
[5] The absurd head-dress of the -women, with its one and often two horns sloping back from the head, in the fourteenth century. - TRANS.
[6] Such cruel outrages were common in those days. By the French and Anglo-Saxon laws, lewdness was thus punished. Grimm, 679, 711. Sternhook, 19, 326. Ducange, iii. 52. Michelet, *Origines,* 386, 389. By and by, the same rough usage is dealt out to hon-

est women, to citizen's wives, whose pride the nobles seek to abase. We know the kind of ambush into which the tyrant Hagenbach drew the honourable ladies of the chief burghers in Alsace, probably in scorn of their rich and royal costume, all silks and gold. In my *Origines* I have also related the strange claim made by the Lord of Pace, in Anjou, on the pretty (and honest) women of the neighbourhood. They were to bring to the castle fourpence and a chaplet of flowers, and to dance with his officers: a dangerous trip, in which they might well fear some such affronts as those offered by Hagenbach. They were forced to obey by the threat of being stripped and pricked with a goad bearing the impress of the lord's arms.

Chapter Six - The Covenant

NOTHING was wanting but the victim. They knew that to bring this woman before her was the most charming present she could receive. Tenderly would she have acknowledged the devotion of anyone who would have given her so great a token of his love, by delivering that poor bleeding body into her hands.

But the prey was aware of the hunters. A few minutes later and she would have been carried off, to be for ever sealed up beneath the stone. Wrapping herself in some rags found by chance iu the stable, she took to herself wings of some kind, and before midnight gained some out-of-the-way spot on a lonely moor all covered with briars and thistles. It was on the skirts of a wood, where by the uncertain light she might gather a few acorns, to swallow them like a beast. Ages had elapsed since evening; she was utterly changed. Beauty and queen of the village no more, she seemed with the change in her spirit to have changed her postures also. Among her acorns she squatted like a boar or a monkey. Thoughts far from human circled within her as she heard, or seemed to hear the hooting of an owl, followed by a burst of shrill laughter. She felt afraid, but perhaps it was the merry mockbird mimicking all those sounds, according to its wonted fashion.

But the laughter begins again: whence comes it? She can see nothing. Apparently it comes from an old oak. Distinctly, however, she hears these words: "So, here you are at last! You have come with an ill grace; nor would you have come now, if you had not tried the full depth of your last need. You were fain first to run the gauntlet of whips; to cry out and plead for mercy, haughty as you were; to be mocked, undone, forsaken, unsheltered even by your husband. Where would you have been this night, if I had not been charitable enough to show you the *in pace* getting ready for you in the tower? Late, very late, you are in coming to me, and only after they have called you the *old woman*. In your youth you did not treat me well, when I was your wee goblin, so eager to. serve you, Now take your turn, if so I wish it, to serve me and kiss my feet.

"You were mine from birth through your inborn wickedness, through those devilish charms of yours. I was your lover, your husband. Your own has shut his door against you: I will not shut mine. I welcome you to my domains, my free prairies, my woods. How am I the gainer, you may say? Could I not long since have had you at any hour? Were you not invaded, possessed, filled with my flame? I changed your blood and renewed it: not a vein in your body where I do not flow. You know not yourself how utterly you are mine. But our wedding has yet to be celebrated with all the forms. I have some manners, and feel rather scrupulous. Let us be one for everlasting."

"Oh! sir, in my present state, what should I say? For a long, long while back have I felt, too truly felt, that you were all my fate. With evil intent you caressed me, loaded me with favours, and made me rich, in order at length to cast me down. Yesterday, when the black greyhound bit my poor naked flesh, its teeth scorched me, and I said, '' Tis he!' At night when that daughter of Herodias with her foul language scared the company, somebody put them up to the promising her my blood; and that was you!"

"True; but 'twas I who saved you and brought you hither. I did everything, as you have guessed. I ruined you, and why? That I might have you all to myself. To speak frankly, I was tired of your husband. You took to haggling and pettifogging: far otherwise do I go to work; I want all or none. This is why I have moulded and drilled you, polished and ripened you, for my own behoof. Such, you see, is my delicacy of taste. I don't take, as people imagine, those foolish souls who would give themselves up at once. I prefer the choicer spirits, who have reached a certain dainty stage of fury and despair. Stop: I must let you know how pleasant you look at this moment. You are a great beauty, a most desirable soul. I have loved you ever so long, but now I am hungering for you.

"I will do things on a large scale, not being one of those husbands who reckon with their betrothed. If you wanted only riches, you should have them in a trice. If you wanted to be queen in the stead of Joan of Navarre, that too, though difficult, should be done, and the King would not lose much thereby in the matter of pride and haughtiness. My wife is greater than a queen. But, come, tell me what you wish."

"Sir, I ask only for the power of doing evil."

"A delightful answer, very delightful! Have I not cause to love you? In reality those words contain all the law and all the prophets. Since you have made so good a choice, all the rest shall be thrown in, over and above. You shall learn all my secrets. You shall see into the depths of the earth. The whole world shall come and pour out gold at thy feet. See here, my bride, I give you the true diamond, *Vengeance*. I know you, rogue; I know your most hidden desires. Ay, our hearts on that point understand each other well! Therein at least shall I have full possession of you. You shall behold your enemy on her knees at your feet, begging and praying for mercy, and only too happy to earn her release by doing whatever she has made you do. She will burst into tears; and you will graciously say, *No*: whereon she will cry, 'Death and damnation!' ...Come, I will make this my special business."

46

"Sir, I am at your service. I was thankless indeed, for you have always heaped favours on me. I am yours, my master, my god! None other do I desire. Sweet are your endearments, and very mild your service."

And so she worships him, tumbling on all-fours. At first she pays him, after the forms of the Temple, such homage as betokens the utter abandonment of the will. Her master, the Prince of this World, the Prince of the Winds, breathes upon her in his turn, like an eager spirit. She receives at once the three sacraments, in reverse order baptism, priesthood, and marriage. In this new Church, the exact opposite of the other, everything must be done the wrong way. Meekly, patiently, she endures the cruel initiation, [1] borne up by that one word, "Vengeance!"

Far from being crushed or weakened by the infernal thunderbolt, she arose with an awful vigour and flashing eyes. The moon, which for a moment had chastely covered herself, took flight on seeing her again. Blown out to an amazing degree by the hellish vapour, filled with fire, with fury, and with some new ineffable desire, she grew for a while enormous with excess of fulness, and displayed a terrible beauty. She looked around her, and all nature was changed. The trees had gotten a tongue, and told of things gone by. The herbs became simples. The plants which yesterday she trod upon as so much hay, were now as people discoursing on the art of medicine.

She awoke on the morrow far, very far, from her enemies, in a state of thorough security. She had been sought after, but they had only found some scattered shreds of her unlucky green gown. Had she in her despair flung herself headlong into the torrent? Or had she been carried off alive by the Devil? No one could tell. Either way she was certainly damned, which greatly consoled the lady for having failed to find her.

Had they seen her they would hardly have known her again, she was so changed. Only the eyes remained, not brilliant, but armed with a very strange and a rather deterring glimmer. She herself was afraid of frightening: she never lowered them, but looked sideways, so that the full force of their beams might be lost by slanting them. From the sudden browning of her hue people would have said that she had passed through the flame. But the more watchful felt that the flame was rather in herself, that she bore about her an impure and scorching heat. The fiery dart with which Satan had pierced her was still there, and, as through a baleful lamp, shot forth a wild, but fearfully witching sheen. Shrinking from her, you would yet stand still, with a strange trouble filling your every sense.

She saw herself at the mouth of one of those troglodyte caves, such as you find without number in the hills of the Centre and the West of France. It was in the borderland, then wild, between the country of Merlin and the country of Melusina. Some moors stretching out of sight still tear witness to the ancient wars, the unceasing havoc, the many horrors, which prevented the country being peopled again. There the Devil was in his home. Of the few inhabitants most were his zealous worshippers. Whatever attractions he might have found in the rough brakes of Lorraine, the black pine-forests of the Jura, or the briny deserts of Burgos, his preferences lay, perhaps, in our western marches. There might be found not only the visionary shepherd, that Satanic union of the goat and the goatherd, but also a closer conspiracy with nature, a deeper insight into remedies and poisons, a mysterious connection, whose links we know not, with Toledo the learned, the University of the Devil.

The winter was setting in: its breath having first stripped the trees, had heaped together the leaves and small boughs of dead wood. All this she found prepared for her at the mouth of her gloomy den. By a wood and moor, half a mile across, you came down within reach of some villages, which had grown up beside a watercourse. "Behold your kingdom!" said the voice within her. "To-day a beggar, to-morrow you shall be queen of the whole land."

[1] This will be explained further on. We must guard against the pedantic additions of the sixteenth century writers.

Chapter Seven - The King of the Dead

AT first she was not much affected by promises like these. A lonely hermitage without God, amidst the great monotonous breezes of the West, amidst memories all the more ruthless for that mighty solitude, of such heavy losses, such sharp affronts; a widowhood so hard and sudden, away from the husband who had left her to her shame all this was enough to bow her down. Plaything of fate, she seemed like the wretched weed upon the moor, having no root, but tossed to and fro, lashed and cruelly cut by the north-east winds; or rather, perhaps, like the grey, many-cornered coral, which only sticks fast to get more easily broken. The children trampled on her; the people said, with a laugh, "She is the bride of the winds."

Wildly she laughed at herself when she thought on the comparison. But, from the depth of her dark cave, she heard, -

"Ignorant and witless, you know not what you say. The plant thus tossing to and fro may well look down upon the rank and vulgar herbs. If it tosses, it is, at least, all self-contained itself both flower and seed. Do thou be like it; be thine own root, and even in the whirlwind thou wilt still bear thy blossom: our own flowers for ourselves, as they come forth from the dust of tombs and the ashes of volcanoes.

"To thee, first flower of Satan, do I this day grant the knowledge of my former name, my olden power. I was, I am, the *King of the Dead*. Ay, have I not been sadly slandered? 'Tis I who alone can make them reappear; a boon untold, for which I surely deserved an altar."

To pierce the future and to call up the past, to forestal and to live again the swift-flying moments, to enlarge the present with that which has been and that which will be these are the two things forbidden to the Middle Ages; but forbidden in vain. Nature is invincible; nothing can be gained in such a quarter. He who thus errs is *a man*. It is not for him to be rooted to his furrow, with eyes cast down, looking no where beyond the steps he takes behind his oxen. No: we will go forward with head upraised, looking further and looking deeper! This earth that we measure out with so much care, we kick our feet upon withal, and keep ever saying to it, "What dost thou hold in thy bowels? What secrets lie therein? Thou givest us back the grain we entrust to thee; but not that human seed, those beloved dead, we have lent into thy charge. Our friends, our loves, that lie there, will they never bud again? Oh, that we might see them, if only for one hour, if only for one moment!

"Some day we ourselves shall reach the unknown land, whither they have already gone. But shall we see them again there? Shall we dwell with them? Where are they, and what are they doing? They must be kept very close prisoners, these dear dead of mine, to give me not one token! And how can I make them hear me? My father, too, whose only hope I was, who loved me with so mighty a love, why comes he never to me? Ah, me! on either side is bondage, imprisonment, mutual ignorance; a dismal night, where we look in vain for one glimmer!" [1]

These everlasting thoughts of Nature, from having in olden times been simply mournful, became in the Middle Ages painful, bitter, weakening, and the heart thereby grew smaller. It seems as if they had reckoned on flattening the soul, on pressing and squeezing it down to the compass of a bier. The burial of the serf between four deal boards was well suited to such an end: it haunted one with the notion of being smothered. A person thus enclosed, if ever he returned in one's dreams, would no longer appear as a thin luminous shadow encircled by a halo of Elysium, but only as the wretched sport of some hellish griffin-cat. What a hateful and impious idea, that my good, kind father, my mother so revered by all, should become the plaything of such a beast! You may laugh now, but for a thousand years it was no laughing matter: they wept bitterly. And even now the heart swells with wrath, the very pen grates angrily upon the paper, as one writes down these blasphemous doings.

Moreover, it was surely a cruel device to transfer the Festival of the Dead from the Spring, where antiquity had placed it, to November. In May, where it fell at first, they were buried among the flowers. In March, wherein it was afterwards placed, it became the signal for labour and the lark. The dead and the seed of corn entered the earth together with the same hope. But in November, when all the work is done, the weather close and gloomy for many days to come; when the folk return to their homes; when a man, reseating himself by the hearth, looks across on that place for evermore empty ah, me! at such a time how great the sorrow grows! Clearly, in choosing a moment already in itself so funereal, for the obsequies of Nature, they feared that a man would not find cause enough of sorrow in himself!

49

The coolest, the busiest of men, however taken up they be with life's distracting cares, have, at least, their sadder moments. In the dark wintry morning, in the night that comes on so swift to swallow us up in its shadow, ten years, nay, twenty years hence, strange feeble voices will rise up in your heart: "Good morning, dear friend, 'tis we! You are alive, are working as hard as ever. So much the better! You do not feel our loss so heavily, and you have learned to do without us; but we cannot, we never can, do without you. The ranks are closed, the gap is all but filled. The house that was ours is full, and we have blessed it. All is well, is better than when your father carried you about; better than when your little girl said, in her turn, to you, 'Papa, carry me.' But, lo! you are in tears. Enough, till we meet again!"

Alas, and are they gone? That wail was sweet and piercing: but was it just? No. Let me forget myself a thousand times rather than I should forget them! And yet, cost what it will to say so, say it we must, that certain traces are fading off, are already less clear to see; that certain features are not indeed effaced, but grown paler and more dim. A hard, a bitter, a humbling thought it is, to find oneself so weak and fleeting, wavering as unremembered water; to feel that in time one loses that treasure of grief which one had hoped to preserve for ever. Give it me back, I pray: I am too much bounden to so rich a fountain of tears. Trace me again, I implore you, those features I love so well. Could you not help me at least to dream of them by night?

More than one such prayer is spoken in the month of November. And amidst the striking of the bells and the dropping of the leaves, they clear out of church, saying one to another in low tones: "I say, neighbour; up there lives a woman of whom folk speak well and ill. For myself, I dare say nothing; but she has power over the world below. She calls up the dead, and they come. Oh, if she might without sin, you know, without angering God make my friends come to me! I am alone, as you must know, and have lost everything in this world. But who knows what this woman is, whether of hell or heaven? I won't go (he is dying of curiosity all the while); I won't. I have no wish to endanger my soul: besides, the wood yonder is haunted. Many's the time that things unfit to see have been found on the moor. Haven't you heard about Jacqueline, who was there one evening looking for one of her sheep? Well, when she returned, she was crazy. I won't go."

Thus unknown to each other, many of the men at least went thither. For as yet the women hardly dared so great a risk. They remark the dangers of the road, ask many questions of those who return therefrom. The new Pythoness is not like her of Endor, who raised up Samuel at the prayer of Saul. Instead of showing you the ghosts, she gives you cabalistic words and powerful potions to bring them back in your dreams. Ah, how many a sorrow has recourse to these! The grandmother herself, tottering with her eighty years, would behold her grandson again. By an unwonted effort, yet not without a pang of shame at sinning on the edge of the grave, she drags herself to the spot. She is troubled by the savage look of a place all rough with yews and

50

thorns, by the rude, dark beauty of that relentless Proserpine. Prostrate, trembling, grovelling on the ground, the poor old woman weeps and prays. Answer there is none. But when she dares to lift herself up a little, she sees that Hell itself has been a-weeping.

It is simply Nature recovering herself. Proserpine blushes self-indignantly thereat. "Degenerate soul!" she calls herself, "why this weakness? You came hither with the firm desire of doing nought but evil. Is this your master's lesson? How he will laugh at you for this!"

"Nay! Am I not the great shepherd of the shades, making them come and go, opening unto them the gate of dreams? Your Dante, when he drew my likeness, forgot my attributes. When he gave me that useless tail, he did not see that I held the shepherd's staff of Osiris; that from Mercury I had inherited his caduceus. In vain have they thought to build up an insurmountable wall between the two worlds; I have wings to my heels, I have flown over. By a kindly rebellion of that slandered Spirit, of that ruthless monster, succour has been given to those who mourned; mothers, lovers, have found comfort. He has taken pity on them in defiance of their new god."

The scribes of the Middle Ages, being all of the priestly class, never cared to acknowledge the deep but silent changes of the popular mind. It is clear that from thenceforth compassion goes over to Satan's side. The Virgin herself, ideal as she is of grace, makes no answer to such a want of the heart. Neither does the Church, who expressly forbids the calling up of the dead. While all books delight in keeping up either the swinish demon of earlier times, or the griffin butcher of the second period, Satan has changed his shape for those who cannot write. He retains somewhat of the ancient Pluto; but his pale nor wholly ruthless majesty, that permitted the dead to come back, the living once more to see the dead, passes ever more and more into the nature of his father, or his grandfather, Osiris, the shepherd of souls.

Through this one change come many others. Men with their mouths acknowledge the hell official and the boiling caldrons; but in their hearts do they truly believe therein? Would it be so easy to win these infernal favours for hearts beset with hateful traditions of a hell of torments? The one idea neutralizes without wholly effacing the other, and between them grows up a vague mixed image, resembling more and more nearly the hell of Virgil. A mighty solace was here offered to the human heart. Blessed above all was the relief thus given to the poor women, whom that dreadful dogma about the punishment of their loved dead had kept drowned in tears and inconsolable. The whole of their lifetime had been but one long sigh.

The Sibyl was musing over her master's words, when a very light step became audible. The day has scarcely dawned: it is after Christmas, about the first day of the new year. Over the crisp and rimy grass approaches a small, fair woman, all a-trembling, who has no sooner reached the spot, than she swoons and loses her breath. Her black gown tells plainly of her widowhood.

51

To the piercing gaze of Medea, without moving or speaking, she reveals all. there is no mystery about her shrinking figure. The other says. to her with a loud voice: "You need not tell me, little dumb creature, for you would never get to the end of it. I will speak for you. Well, you are dying of love!" Recovering a little, she clasps her hands together, and sinking almost on her knees, tells everything, making a full confession. She had suffered, wept, prayed, and would have silently suffered on. But these winter feasts, these family reunions, the ill-concealed happiness of other women who, without pity for her, showed off their lawful loves, had driven the burning arrow again into her heart. Alas, what could she do? If he might but return and comfort her for one moment! "Be it even at the cost of my life; let me die, but only let me see him once more!"

"Go back to your house: shut the door carefully: put up the shutter even against any curious neighbour. Throw off your mourning, and put on your wedding clothes; place a cover for him on the table; but yet he will not come. You will sing the song he made for you, and sang to you so often, but yet he will not come. Then you shall draw out of your box the last dress he wore, and, kissing it, say, 'So much the worse for thee if thou wilt not come!' And presently when you have drunk this wine, bitter, but very sleepful, you will lie down as a wedded bride. Then assuredly he will come to you."

The little creature would have been no woman, if next morning she had not shown her joy and tenderness by owning the miracle in whispers to her best friend. "Say nought of it, I beg. But he himself told me, that if I wore this gown and slept a deep sleep every Sunday, he would return."

A happiness not without some danger. Where would the rash woman be, if the Church learned that she was no longer a widow; that re-awakened by her love, the spirit came to console her?

But strange to tell, the secret is kept. There is an understanding among them all, to hide so sweet a mystery. For who has no concern therein? Who has not lost and mourned? Who would not gladly see this bridge created between two worlds? "O thou beneficent Witch! Blessed be thou, spirit of the nether world!"

[1] The glimmer shines forth in Dumesnil's *Immortalité,* and *La Foi Nouvelle,* in the *Ciel et Terre* of Reynaud, Henry Martin. &c.

Chapter Eight - The Prince of Nature

HARD is the long sad winter of the North-west. Even after its departure it renews its visits, like a drowsy sorrow which ever and again comes back and rages afresh. One morning everything wakes up decked with bright needles. In this cruel mocking splendour that makes one shiver through and through, the whole vegetable world seems turned mineral, loses its sweet diversity, and freezes into a mass of rough crystals.

The poor Sibyl, as she sits benumbed by her hearth of leaves, scourged by the flaying north-east winds, feels at her heart a cruel pang, for she feels herself all alone. But that very thought again brings her relief. With returning pride returns a vigour that warms her heart and lights up her soul. Intent, quick, and sharp, her sight becomes as piercing as those needles; and the world, the cruel world that caused her suffering, is to her transparent as glass. Anon she rejoices over it, as over a conquest of her making.

For is she not a queen, a queen with courtiers of her own? The crows have clearly some connection with her. In grave, dignified body they come like ancient augurs, to talk to her of passing things. The wolves passing by salute her timidly with sidelong glances. The bear, then oftener seen than now, would sometimes, in his heavily good-natured way, seat himself awkwardly at the threshold of her den, like a hermit calling on a fellow-hermit, just as we often see him in the Lives of the Desert Fathers.

All those birds and beasts with whom men only made acquaintance in hunting or slaying them, were outlawed as much as she. With all these she comes to an understanding; for Satan as the chief outlaw, imparts to his own the pleasures of natural freedom, the wild delight of living in a world sufficient unto itself.

Rough freedom of loneliness, all hail! The whole earth seems still clothed in a white shroud, held in bondage by a load of ice, of pitiless crystals, so uniform, sharp, and agonizing. After the year 1200 especially, the world is shut in like a transparent tomb, wherein all things look terribly motionless, hard, and stiff.

The Gothic Church has been called a "crystallization;" and so it truly is. About 1300, architecture gave up all its old variety of form and living fancies, to repeat itself for evermore, to vie with the monotonous prisms of Spitzbergen, to become the true and awful likeness of that hard crystal city, in which a dreadful dogma thought to bury all life away.

But for all the props, buttresses, flying-buttresses, that keep the monument up, one thing there is that makes it totter. There is no loud battering from without, but a certain softness in the very foundations, which attacks the crystal with an imperceptible thaw. What thing do I mean? The humble stream of warm tears shed by a whole world, until they have become a very sea of wailings. What do I call it? A breath of the future, a stirring of the natural life, which shall presently rise again in irresistible might. The fantastic building of which more than one side is already sinking, says, not without terror, to itself, "It is the breath of Satan."

Beneath this Heela-glacier lies a volcano which has no need of bursting out; a mild, slow, gentle heat, which caresses it from below, and, calling it nearer, says in a whisper, "Come down."

The Witch has something to laugh at, if from the gloom she can see how utterly Dante and St. Thomas, [1] in the bright light yonder, ignore the true position of things. They fancy that the Devil wins his way by cunning or by terror. They make him grotesque and coarse, as in his childhood, when Jesus could still send him into the herd of swine. Or else they make him subtle as a logician of the schools, or a fault-finding lawyer. If he had been no better than this compound of beast and disputant, if he had only lived in the mire or on fine-drawn quibbles about nothing, he would very soon have died of hunger.

People were too ready to crow over him, when he was shewn by Bartolus [2] pleading against the woman--that is, the Virgin who gets him nonsuited and condemned with costs. At that time, indeed, the very contrary was happening on earth. By a master-stroke of his he had won over the plaintiff herself, his fair antagonist, the Woman; had seduced her, not indeed by verbal pleadings, but by arguments not less real than they were charming and irresistible. He put into her hands the fruits of science and of nature.

No need for controversies, for pleas of any kind: he simply shows himself. In the East, the new-found Paradise, he begins to work. From that Asian world, which men had thought to destroy, there springs forth a peerless day-dawn, whose beams travel afar until they pierce the deep winter of the West. There dawns on us a world of nature and of art, accursed of the ignorant indeed, but now at length come forward to vanquish its late victors in a pleasant war of love and motherly endearments. All are conquered, all rave about it; they will have nothing but Asia herself. With her hands full she comes to meet us. Her tissues, shawls, her carpets so agreeably soft, so wondrously harmonized, her bright and well-wrought blades, her richly damascened arms, make us aware of our own barbarism. Moreover, little as that may seem, these accursed lands of the "miscreant," ruled by Satan, are visibly blessed with the fairest fruits of nature, that elixir of the powers of God; with *the first of vegetables*, coffee; with *the first of beasts,* the Arab horse. "What am I saying? with a whole world of treasures, silk, sugar, and a host of herbs all-powerful to relieve the heart, to soothe and lighten our sufferings.

All this breaks upon our view about the year 1300. Spain herself, whose brain is wholly fashioned out of Moors and Jews, for all that she is again subdued by the barbarous children of the Goth, bears witness in behalf of those *miscreants.* Wherever the Mussulman children of the Devil are at work, all is prosperous, the springs well forth, the ground is covered with flowers. A right worthy and harmless travail decks it with those wondrous vineyards, through which men recruit themselves, drowning all care, and seeming to drink in draughts of very goodness and heavenly compassion.

To whom does Satan bring the foaming cup of life? In this fasting world, which has so long been fasting from reason, what man was there strong enough to take all this in without growing giddy, without getting drunken and risking the loss of his wits?

Is there yet a brain so far from being petrified or crystallized by the teaching of St. Thomas, as to remain open to the living world, to its vegetative forces? Three magicians, Albert the Great, Roger Bacon, Arnaud of Villeneuve. [3] by strong efforts make their way to Nature's secrets; but those lusty intellects lack flexibility and popular power, Satan falls back on his own Eve. The woman is still the most natural thing in the world; still keeps her hold on those traits of roguish innocence one sees in a kitten or a child of very high spirit. Besides, she figures much better in that world-comedy, that mighty game wherewith the universal Proteus disports himself.

But being light and changeful, she is all the less liable to be carked and hardened by pain! This woman, whom we have seen outlawed from the world, and rooted on her wild moor, affords a case in point. Have we yet to learn whether, bruised and soured as she is, with her heart full of hate, she will re-enter the natural world and the pleasant paths of life? Assuredly her return thither will not find her in good tune, will happen mainly through a round of ill. In the coming and going of the storm she is all the more scared and violent for being so very weak.

When in the mild warmth of spring, from the air, the depths of the earth, from the flowers and their languages, a new revelation rises round her on every side, she is taken dizzy at the first. Her swelling bosom overflows. The Sibyl of science has her tortures, like her of Cumae or of Delphi. The schoolmen find their fun in saying, "It is the wind and nought else that blows her out. Her lover, the Prince of the Air, fills her with dreams and delusions, with wind, with smoke, with emptiness." Foolish irony! So far from this being the true cause of her drunkenness, it is nothing empty, it is a real, a substantial thing, which has loaded her bosom all too quickly.

Have you ever seen the agave, that hard wild African shrub, so sharp, bitter, and tearing, with huge bristles instead of leaves? Ten years through it loves and dies. At length one day the amorous shoot, which has so long been gathering in the rough thing, goes off with a noise like gunfire, and darts skyward. And this shoot becomes a whole tree, not less than thirty feet high, and bristling with sad flowers.

Some such analogy does the gloomy Sibyl feel, when one morning of a spring-time, late in coming, and therefore impetuous at the last, there takes place all around her a vast explosion of life.

And all things look at her, and all things bloom for her. For every thing that has life says softly, "Whoso understands me, I am his."

What a contrast! Here is the wife of the desert and of despair, bred up in hate and vengeance, and lo! all these innocent things agree to smile upon her! The trees, soothed by the south wind, pay her gentle homage. Each herb of the field, with its own special virtue of scent, or remedy, or poison very often the three things are one offers itself to her, saying, "Gather me."

All things are clearly in love. "Are they not mocking me? I had been readier for hell than for this strange festival. spirit, art thou indeed that spirit of dread whom once I knew, the traces of whose cruelty I bear about me what am I saying, and where are my senses? the wound of whose dealing scorches me still?

55

"Ah, no! 'Tis not the spirit whom I hoped for in my rage; *'he who always says, No!'* This other one utters a yes of love, of drunken dizziness. What ails him? Is he the mad, the dazed soul of life?

"They spoke of the great Pan as dead. But here he is in the guise of Bacchus, of Priapus, eager with long-delayed desire, threatening, scorching, teeming. No, no! Be this cup far from me! Trouble only should I drink from it, who knows? A despair yet sharper than my past despairs."

Meanwhile wherever the woman appears, she becomes the one great object of love. She is followed by all. and for her sake all despise their own proper kind. What they say about the black he-goat, her pretended favourite, may be applied to all. The horse neighs for her, breaking everything and putting her in danger. The awful king of the prairie, the black bull, bellows with grief, should she pass him by at a distance. And, behold, yon bird despondingly turns away from his hen, and with whirring wings hastes to convince the woman of his love!

Such is the new tyranny of her master, who, by the funniest hap of all, foregoes the part accredited to him as king of the dead, to burst forth a very king of life.

"No!" she says; "leave me to my hatred: I ask for nothing more. Let me be feared and fearful! The beauty I would have, is only that which dwells in these black serpents of my hair, in this countenance furrowed with grief, and the scars of thy thunderbolt." But the Lord of Evil replies with cunning softness: "Oh, but you are only the more beautiful, the more impressible, for this fiery rage of yours! Ay, call out and curse on, beneath one and the same goad! 'Tis but one storm calling another. Swift and smooth is the passage from wrath to pleasure."

Neither her fury nor her pride would have saved her from such allurements. But she is saved by the boundlessness of her desire. There is nought will satisfy her. Each kind of life for her is all too bounded, wanting in power. Away from her, steed and bull and loving bird! Away, ye creatures all! for one who desires the Infinite, how weak ye are!

She has a woman's longing; but for what? Even for the whole, the great all-containing whole. Satan did not foresee that no one creature would content her. That which he could not do, is done for her in some ineffable way. Overcome by a desire so wide and deep, a longing boundless as the sea, she falls asleep. At such a moment, all else forgot, no touch of hate, no thought of vengeance left in her, she slumbers on the plain, innocent in her own despite, stretched out in easy luxuriance like a sheep or a dove.

She sleeps, she dreams; a delightful dream! It seemed as if the wondrous might of universal life had been swallowed up within her; as if life and death and all things thenceforth lay fast in her bowels; as if in return for all her suffering, she was teeming at last with Nature herself.

[1] St. Thomas Aquinas, the "Angelic Doctor," who died in 1274. - TRANS.
[2] Bartolus or Bartoli, a lawyer and law-writer of the fourteenth century. - TRANS.

Three eminent schoolmen of the thirteenth century, whose scientific researches pointed the way to future discoveries. - TRANS.

Chapter Nine - The Devil A Physician

THAT still and dismal scene of the Bride of Corinth, is repeated literally from the thirteenth to the fifteenth century. While it was yet night, just before the daybreak, the two lovers, Man and Nature, meet again, embrace with rapture, and, at that same moment horrible to tell! behold themselves attacked by fearful plagues. "We seem still to hear the loved one saying to her lover, "It is all over: thy hair will be white to-morrow. I am dead, and thou too wilt die."

Three dreadful blows happen in these three centuries. In the first we have a loathsome changing of the outer man, diseases of the skin, above all, leprosy. In the second, the evil turns inwards, becomes a grotesque excitement of the nerves, a fit of epileptic dancing. Then all grows calm, but the blood is changed, and ulcers prepare the way for syphilis, the scourge of the fifteenth century.

Among the chief diseases of the Middle Ages, so far as one can look therein, to speak generally, had been hunger, weakness, poverty of blood, that kind of consumption which is visible in the sculptures of that time. The blood was like clear water, and scrofulous ailments were rife everywhere. Barring the well-paid doctors, Jew or Arab, of the kings, the art of medicine was practised only with holy water at the church door. Thither on Sundays, after the service, would come a crowd of sick, to whom words like these were spoken: "You have sinned and God has afflicted you. Be thankful: so much the less will you suffer in the next world. Resign yourselves to suffer and to die. The Church has prayers for the dead." Weak, languishing, hopeless, with no desire to live, they followed this counsel faithfully, and let life go its way. A fatal discouragement, a wretched state of things, that would have prolonged without end these ages of lead, and debarred them from all progress! Worst of all things is it to resign oneself so readily, to welcome death with so much docility, to have strength for nothing, to desire nothing. Of more worth was that new era, that close of the Middle Ages, which at the cost of cruel sufferings first enabled us to regain our former energy; namely, *the resurrection of desire.*

Some Arab writers have asserted that the widespread eruption of skin-diseases which marks the thirteenth century, was caused by the taking of certain stimulants to re-awaken and renew the defaults of passion. Undoubtedly the burning spices brought over from the East, tended somewhat to such an issue. The invention of distilling and of divers fermented drinks may also have worked in the same direction.

But a greater and far more general fermentation was going on. During the sharp inward struggle between two worlds and two spirits, a third surviving silenced both. As the fading faith and the newborn reason were disputing together, somebody stepping between them caught hold of man. You ask who? A spirit unclean and raging, the spirit of sour desires, bubbling painfully within.

Debarred from all outlet, whether of bodily enjoyment, or the free flow of soul, the sap of life thus closely rammed together, was sure to corrupt itself. Bereft of light, of sound, of speech, it spoke through pains and ominous excrescences. Then happened a new and dreadful thing. The desire put off without being diminished, finds itself stopped short by a cruel enchantment, a shocking metamorphosis. [1] Love was advancing blindly with open arms. It recoils groaning; but in vain would it flee: the fire of the blood keeps raging; the flesh eats itself away in sharp titillations, and sharper within rages the coal of fire, made fiercer by despair.

What remedy does Christian Europe find for this twofold ill? Death and captivity; nothing more. When the bitter celibacy, the hopeless love, the passion irritable and ever-goading, bring you into a morbid state; when your blood is decomposing, then you shall go down into an *In pace*, or build your hut in the desert. You must live with the handbell in your hand, that all may flee before you. "No human being must see you: no consolation may be yours. If you come near, "'tis death."

Leprosy is the last stage, the *apogee* of this scourge; but a thousand other ills, less hideous but still cruel, raged everywhere. The purest and the most fair were stricken with sad eruptions, which men regarded as sin made visible, or the chastisement of God. Then people did what the love of life had never made them do: they forsook the old sacred medicine, the bootless holy water, and went off to the Witch. From habit and fear as well, they still repaired to church; but thenceforth their true church was with her, on the moor, in the forest, in the desert. To her they carried their vows.

Prayers for healing, prayers for pleasure. On the first effervescing of their heated blood, folk went to the Sibyl, in great secrecy, at uncertain hours. "What shall I do? and what is this I feel within me? I burn: give me some lenitive. I burn: grant me that which causes my intolerable desire."

A bold, a blameable journey, for which they reproach themselves at night. Let this new fatality be never so urgent, this fire be never so torturing, the Saints themselves never so powerless; still, have not the indictment of the Templars and the proceedings of Pope Boniface unveiled the Sodom lying hid beneath the altar? But a wizard Pope, a friend of the Devil, who also carried him away, effects a change in all their ideas. Was it not with the Demon's help that John XXII., the son of a shoemaker, a Pope no more of Home, succeeded in amassing in his town of Avignon more gold than the Emperor and all the kings? As the Pope is, so is the bishop. Did not Guichard, Bishop of Troyes, procure from the Devil the death of the King's daughters? No death we ask

58

for we; but pleasant things for life, for health, for beauty, and for pleasure: the things of God which God refuses. What shall we do? Might we but win them through the grace of the *Prince of this World!*

When the great and mighty doctor of the Renaissance, Paracelsus, cast all the wise books of ancient medicine into the fire, Latin, and Jewish, and Arabic, all at once, he declared that he had learned none but the popular medicine, that of the *good women,* [2] the *shepherds,* and the *headsmen,* the latter of whom made often good horse-doctors and clever surgeons, resetting bones broken or put out of joint.

I make no doubt but that his admirable and masterly work on *The Diseases of Women* the first then written on a theme so large, so deep, so tender came forth from his special experience of those women to whom others went for aid; of the witches, namely, who always acted as the midwives: for never in those days was a male physician admitted to the woman's side, to win her trust in him, to listen to her secrets. The witches alone attended her, and became, especially for women, the chief and only physician.

"What we know for surest with regard to their medicinal practice is, that for ends the most different, alike to stimulate and to soothe, they made use of one large family of doubtful and very dangerous plants, called, by reason of the services they rendered, *The Comforters,* or Solaneae. [2]

A vast and popular family, many kinds of which abound to excess under our feet, in the hedges, everywhere a family so numerous that of one kind alone we have eight hundred varieties. [4] There is nothing easier, nothing more common, to find. But these plants are mostly dangerous in the using. It needs some boldness to measure out a dose, the boldness, perhaps, of genius.

Let us, step by step, mount the ladder of their powers. [5] The first are simply pot-herbs, good for food, such as the mad-apples and the tomatoes, miscalled "love-apples." Other, of the harmless kinds, are sweetness and tranquillity itself, as the white mullens, or lady's fox-gloves, so good for fomentations.

Going higher up, you come on a plant already suspicious, which many think a poison, a plant which at first seems like honey and afterwards tastes bitter, reminding one of Jonathan's saying, "I have eaten a little honey, and therefore shall I die." But this death is serviceable, a dying away of pain. The "bittersweet" should have been the first experiment of that bold homoeopathy which rose, little by little, up to the most dangerous poisons. The slight irritation and the tingling which it causes might point it out as a remedy for the prevalent diseases of that time, those, namely, of the skin.

The pretty maiden who found herself woefully adorned with uncouth red patches, with pimples, or with ringworm, would come crying for such relief. In the case of an elder woman the hurt would be yet more painful. The bosom, most delicate thing in nature, with its innermost vessels forming a matchless flower, becomes, through its injective and congestive tendencies,

59

the most perfect instrument for causing pain. Sharp, ruthless, restless are the pains she suffers. Gladly would she accept all kinds of poison. Instead of bargaining with the Witch, she only puts her poor hard breast between her hands.

From the bittersweet, too weak for such, we rise to the dark nightshades, which have rather more effect. For a few days the woman is soothed. Anon she comes back weeping. "Very well, to-night you may come again. I will fetch you something, as you wish me; but it will be a strong poison."

It was a heavy risk for the Witch. At that time they never thought that poisons could act as remedies, if applied outwardly or taken in very weak doses. The plants they compounded together under the name of *witches' herbs,* seemed to be but ministers of death. Such as were found in her hands would have proved her, in their opinion, a poisoner or a dealer in accursed charms. A blind crowd, all the more cruel for its growing fears, might fell her with a shower of stones, or make her undergo the trial by water the noyade. Or even most dreadful doom of all! they might drag her with a rope round her neck to the churchyard, where a pious festival was held and the people edified by seeing her thrown to the flames.

However, she runs the risk, and fetches home the dreadful plant. The other woman comes back to her abode by night or morning, whenever she is least afraid of being met. But a young shepherd, who saw her there, told the village, "If you had seen her as I did, gliding among the rubbish of the ruined hut, looking about her on all sides, muttering I know not what! Oh, but she has frightened me very much! If she had seen me, I was a lost man. She would have changed me into a lizard, a toad, or a bat. She took a paltry herb the paltriest I ever saw of a pale sickly yellow, with red and black marks, like the flames, as they say, of hell. The horror of the thing is, that the whole stalk was hairy like a man, with long, black, sticky hairs. She plucked it roughly, with a grunt, and suddenly I saw her no more. She could not have run away so quick; she must have flown. What a dreadful thing that woman is! How dangerous to the whole country!"

Certainly the plant inspires dread. It is the henbane, a cruel and dangerous poison, but a powerful emollient, a soft sedative poultice, which melts, unbends, lulls to sleep the pain, often taking it quite away.

Another of these poisons the Belladonna, so called, undoubtedly, in thankful acknowledgment, had great power in laying the convulsions that sometimes supervened in childbirth, and added a new danger, a new fear, to the danger and the fear of that most trying moment. A motherly hand instilled the gentle poison, casting the mother herself into a sleep, and smoothing the infant's passage, after the manner of the modern chloroform, into the world. [6]

Belladonna cures the dancing-fits while making you dance. A daring homoeopathy this, which at first must frighten: it is *medicine reversed,* contrary in most things to that which alone the Christians studied, which alone they valued, after the example of the Jews and Arabs.

How did men come to this result? Undoubtedly by the simple effect of the great Satanic principle, that *everything must be done the wrong way*, the very opposite way to that followed by the holy people. These latter have a dread of poisons. Satan uses them and turns them into remedies. The Church thinks by spiritual means, by sacraments and prayers, to act even on the body. Satan, on the other hand, uses material means to act even upon the soul, making you drink of forgetfulness, love, reverie, and every passion. To the blessing of the priest he opposes the magnetic passes made by the soft hands of women, who cheat you of your pains.

By a change of system, and yet more of dress, as in the substitution Of linen for wool, the skin-diseases lost their intensity. Leprosy abated, but seemed to go inwards and beget deeper ills. The fourteenth century wavered between three scourges the epileptic dancings, the plague, and the sores which, according to Paracelsus, led the way to syphilis.

The first danger was not the least. About 1350 it broke out in a frightful manner with the dance of St. Guy, and was singular especially in this, that it did not act upon each person separately. As if carried on by one same galvanic current, the sick caught each other by the hand, formed immense chains, and spun and spun round till they died. The spectators, who laughed at first, presently catching the contagion, let themselves go, fell into the mighty current, increased the terrible choir.

What would have happened if the evil had held on as long as leprosy did even in its decline?

It was the first step, as it were, towards epilepsy. If that generation of sufferers had not been cured, it would have begotten another decidedly epileptic. What a frightful prospect! Think of Europe covered with fools, with idiots, with raging madmen! We are not told how the evil was treated and checked. The remedy prescribed by most, the falling upon these jumpers with kicks and cuffings, was entirely fitted to increase the frenzy and turn it into downright epilepsy. [7] Doubtless there was some other remedy, of which people were loth to speak. At the time when witchcraft took its first great flight, the wide-spread use of the *Solaneae*, above all, of belladonna, vulgarized the medicine which really checked those affections. At the great popular gatherings of the Sabbath, of which we shall presently speak, the *witches' herb*, mixed with mead, beer, cider, [8] or perry (the strong drinks of the West), set the multitude dancing a dance luxurious indeed, but far from epileptic.

But the greatest revolution caused by the witches, the greatest step *the wrong way* against the spirit of the Middle Ages, was what may be called the reënfeoffment of the stomach and the digestive organs. They had the boldness to say, "There is nothing foul or unclean." Thenceforth the study of matter was free and boundless. Medicine became a possibility.

That this principle was greatly abused, we do not deny; but the principle is none the less clear. There is nothing foul but moral evil. In the natural world all things are pure: nothing may be withheld from our studious regard, nothing be forbidden by an idle spiritualism, still less by a silly disgust.

It was here especially that the Middle Ages showed themselves in their true light, as *anti-natural,* out of Nature's oneness drawing distinctions of castes, of priestly orders. Not only do they count the spirit *noble*, and the body *ignoble*; but even parts of the body are called noble, while others are not, being evidently plebeian. In like manner heaven is noble, and hell is not;jbut why? - "Because heaven is high up." But in truth it is neither high, nor low, being above and beneath alike. And what is hell? Nothing at all. Equally foolish are they about the world at large an the smaller world of men.

This world is all one piece: each thing in it is attached to all the rest. If the stomach is servant of the brain and feeds it, the brain also works none the less for the stomach, perpetually helping to prepare for it the digestive *sugar*. [9]

There was no lack of injurious treatment. The witches were called filthy, indecent, shameless, immoral. Nevertheless, their first steps on that road may be accounted as a happy revolution in things most moral, in charity and kindness. With a monstrous perversion of ideas the Middle Ages viewed the flesh in its representative, woman, accursed since the days of Eve as a thing impure. The Virgin, exalted as *Virgin* more than as *Our Lady*, far from lifting up the real woman, had caused her abasement, by setting men on the track of a mere scholastic puritanism, where they kept rising higher and higher in subtlety and falsehood.

Woman herself ended by sharing in the hateful prejudice and deeming herself unclean. She hid herself at the hour of childbed. She blushed at loving and bestowing happiness on others. Sober as she mostly was in comparison with man, living as she mostly did on herbs and fruits, sharing through her diet of milk and vegetables the purity of the most innocent breeds, she almost besought forgiveness for being born, for living, for carrying out the conditions of her life.

The medical art of the Middle Ages busied itself peculiarly about the man, a being noble and pure, who alone could become a priest, alone could make God at the altar. It also paid some attention to the beasts, beginning indeed with them; but of children it thought seldom: of women not at all.

The romances, too, with their subtleties portray the converse of the world. Outside the courts and highborn adulterers, which form the chief topic of these romances, the woman is always a poor Griselda, born to drain the cup of suffering, to be often beaten, and never cared for.

In order to mind the woman, to trample these usages under foot, and to care for her in spite of herself, nothing less would serve than the Devil, woman's old ally, her trusty friend in Paradise, and the "Witch, that monster who deals with everything the wrong way, exactly contrariwise to that of the holier people. The poor creature set such little store by herself. She would shrink back, blushing, and loth to say a word. The Witch being clever and evil-hearted, read her to the inmost depths. Ere long she won her to speak out, drew from her her little secret, overcame her refusals, her modest, humble hesitations. Rather than undergo the remedy, she was willing almost to die. But the cruel sorceress made her live.

[1] Leprosy has been traced to Asia and the Crusades; but Europe had it in herself. The war declared by the Middle Ages against the flesh and all cleanliness bore its fruits. More than one saint boasted of having never washed even his hands. And how much did the rest wash? To have stripped for a moment would have been sinful. The worldlings carefully follow the teaching of the monks. This subtle and refined society, which sacrificed marriage and seemed inspired only with the poetry of adultery, preserved a strange scruple on a point so harmless. It dreaded all cleansing, as so much defilement. There was no bathing for a thousand years!
[2] The name given in fear and politeness to the witches.
[3] Man's ingratitude is painful to see. A thousand other plants have come into use: a hundred exotic vegetables have become the fashion. But the good once done by these poor *Comforters* is clean forgotten! - Nay, who now remembers or even acknowledges the old debt of humanity to harmless nature? The *Asclepias acida, Sarcostemma,* or flesh-plant, which for five thousand years was the *Holy Wafer* of the East, its very palpable God, eaten gladly by five hundred millions of men, this plant, in the Middle Ages called the Poison-queller (*vince-venenum*), meets with not one word of historical comment in our books of Botany. Perhaps two thousand years hence they will forget the wheat. See Langlois on the Soma of India and the Horn of Persia. *Mem. de l'Academie des Inscriptions,* xix. 326.
[4] M. d'Orbigny's *Dictionary of Natural History,* article *Morelles.*
[5] I have found this ladder nowhere else. It is the more important, because the witches who made these essays at the risk of passing for poisoners, certainly began with the weakest, and rose gradually to the strongest. Each step of power thus gives its relative date, and helps us in this dark subject to set up a kind of chronology. I shall complete it in the following chapters, when I come to speak of the Mandragora and the Datura. I have chiefly followed Pouchet's Solanées and Botanique Générale.
[6] Madame La Chapelle and M. Chaussier have renewed to good purpose these practices of the older medicine. Pouchet, *Solanées.*
[7] We should think that few physicians would quite agree with M. Michelet. - TRANS.
[8] Cider was first made in the twelfth century.
[9] This great discovery was made by Claude Bernard.

Chapter Ten - Charms and Philtres

LET no one hastily conclude from the foregoing chapter that I attempt to whiten, to acquit entirely, the dismal bride of the Devil. If she often did good, she could also do no small amount of ill. There is no great power which is not abused. And this one had three centuries of actual reigning, in the interlude between two worlds, the older dying and the new struggling painfully to begin. The Church, which in the quarrels of the sixteenth century will regain some of her strength, at least for fighting, in the fourteenth is down in the mire. Look at the truthful picture drawn by Clémangis. The nobles, so proudly arrayed in their new armour, fall all the more heavily at Crécy, Poitiers, Agincourt. All who survive end by being prisoners in England. What a theme for ridicule! The citizens, the very peasants make merry and shrug their shoulders. This general absence of the lords gave, I fancy, no small encouragement to the Sabbath gatherings which had always taken place, but at this time might first have grown into vast popular festivals.

How mighty the power thus wielded by Satan's sweetheart, who cures, foretells, divines, calls up the souls of the dead; who can throw a spell upon you, turn you into a hare or wolf, enable you to find a treasure, and, best of all, ensure your being beloved! It is an awful power which combines all others. How could a stormy soul, a soul most commonly gangrened, and sometimes grown utterly wayward, have helped employing it to wreak her hate and revenge; sometimes even out of a mere delight in malice and uncleanness?

All that once was told the confessor, is now imparted to her: not only the sins already done, but those also which folk purpose doing. She holds each by her shameful secret, by the avowal of her uncleanest desires. To her they entrust both their bodily and mental ills; the lustful heats of a blood inflamed and soured; the ceaseless prickings of some sharp, urgent, furious desire.

To her they all come: with her there is no shame. In plain blunt words they beseech her for life, for death, for remedies, for poisons. Thither comes a young woman, to ask through her tears for the means of saving her from the fruits of her sin. Thither comes the step-mother a common theme in the Middle Ages to say that the child of a former marriage eats well and lives long. Thither comes the sorrowing wife whose children year by year are born only to die. And now, on the other hand, comes a youth to buy at any cost the burning draught that shall trouble the heart of some haughty dame, until, forgetful of the distance between them, she has stooped to look upon her little page.

In these days there are but two types, two forms of marriage, both of them extreme and outrageous.

The scornful heiress of a fief, who brings her husband a crown or a broad estate, an Eleanor of Guyenne for instance, will, under her husband's very eyes, hold her court of lovers, keeping herself under very slight control. Let us leave romances and poems, to look at the reality in its dread march onward to the unbridled rage of the daughters of Philip the Fair, of the cruel Isabella, who by the hands of her lovers impaled Edward II. The insolence of the feudal women breaks out diabolically in the triumphant two-horned bonnet and other brazen-faced fashions.

But in this century, when classes are beginning to mingle slightly, the woman of a lower rank, when she marries a lord, has to fear the hardest trials. So says the truthful history of the humble, the meek, the patient Griselda. In a more popular form it becomes the tale of *Blue-Beard,* a tale which seems to me quite earnest and historical. The wife so often killed and replaced by him could only have been his vassal. He would have reckoned wholly otherwise with the daughter or sister of a baron, who might avenge her. If I am not misled by a specious conjecture, we must believe that this tale is of the fourteenth century, and not of those preceding, in which the lord would never have deigned to take a wife below himself.

Specially remarkable in the moving tale of *Griselda* is the fact, that throughout her heavy trials, she never seeks support in being devout or in loving another. She is evidently faithful, chaste, and pure. It never comes into her mind to love elsewhere.

Of the two feudal women, the Heiress and Griselda, it is peculiarly the first who has her household of gentlemen, her courts of love, who shows favour to the humblest lovers, encouraging them, delivering, as Eleanor did, the famous sentence, soon to become quite classical: "There can be no love between married folk."

Thereupon a secret hope, but hot and violent withal, arises in more than one young heart. If he must give himself to the Devil, he will rush full tilt on this adventurous intrigue. Let the castle be never so surely closed, one fine opening is still left for Satan. In a game so perilous, what chance of success reveals itself? Wisdom answers, None. But what if Satan said, Yes?

We must remember how great a distance feudal pride set between the nobles themselves. Words are misleading: one *cavalier* might be far below another.

The knight banneret, who brought a whole army of vassals to his king's side, would look with utter scorn from, one end of his long table on the poor *lackland* knights seated at the other. How much greater his scorn for the simple varlets, grooms, pages, &c., fed upon his leavings! Seated at the lowermost end of the table, close to the door, they scraped the dishes sent down to them, often empty, from the personages seated above beside the hearth. It never would cross the great lord's mind, that those below would dare to lift eyes of fancy towards their lovely mistress, the haughty heiress of a fief, sitting near her mother, "crowned by a chaplet of white roses." Whilst he bore with wondrous patience the love of some stranger knight, appointed by his lady to bear her colours, he would have savagely punished the boldness of any servant who looked so high. Of this kind was the raging jealousy shown by the Lord of Fayel, who was stirred to deadly wrath, not because his wife had a lover, but because that lover was one of his household, the castellan or simple constable of his castle of Coucy.

The deeper and less passable seemed the gulf between the great heiress, lady of the manor, and the groom or page who, barring his shirt, had nothing, not even his coat, but what belonged to his master, the stronger became love's temptation to overleap that gulf.

The youth was buoyed up by the very impossibility. At length, one day that he managed to get out of the tower, he ran off to the Witch and asked her advice. Would a philtre serve as a spell to win her? Or, failing that, must he make an express covenant? He never shrank at all from the dreadful idea of yielding himself to Satan. "We will take care for that, young man: but hie thee up again; you will find some change already."

The change, however, is in himself. He is stirred by some ineffable hope, that escapes in spite of him from a deep downcast eye, scored by an ever-darting flame. Somebody, we may guess who, having eyes for him alone, is moved to throw him, as she passes, a word of pity. Oh, rapture! Kind Satan! Charming, adorable Witch!

He cannot eat nor drink until he has been to see the latter again. Respectfully kissing her hand, he almost falls at her feet. Whatever she may ask him, whatever she may bid him do, he will obey her. That moment, if she wishes it, he will give her his golden chain, will give her the ring upon his finger, though he had it from a dying mother. But the Witch, in her native malice, in her hatred of the Baron, feels an especial comfort in dealing him a secret blow.

Already a vague anxiety disturbs the castle. A dumb tempest, without lightning or thunder, broods over it, like an electric vapour on a marsh. All is silence, deep silence; but the lady is troubled. She suspects that some supernatural power has been at work. For why indeed be thus drawn to this youth, more than to some one else, handsomer, nobler, renowned already for deeds of arms? There is something toward, down yonder! Has that woman cast a spell upon her, or worked some hidden charm? The more she asks herself these questions, the more her heart is troubled.

The Witch has something to wreak her malice upon at last. In the village she was a queen; but now the castle comes to her, yields itself up to her on that side where its pride ran the greatest risk. For us this passion has a peculiar interest, as the rush of one soul towards its ideal against every social barrier, against the unjust decree of fate. To the Witch, on her side, it holds out the deep, keen delight of humbling the lady's pride, and revenging perhaps her own wrongs; the delight of serving the lord as he served his vassals, of levying upon him, through the boldness of a mere child, the firstfruits of his outrageous wedding-rights. Undoubtedly, in these intrigues where the Witch had to play her part, she often acted from a depth of levelling hatred natural to a peasant.

Already it was something gained to have made the lady stoop to love a menial. We should not be misled by such examples as John of Saintré and Cherubin. The serving-boy filled the lowest offices in the household. The footman proper did not then exist, while on the other hand, few, if any maid-servants lived in military strongholds. Young hands did everything, and were not disgraced thereby. The service, specially the body-service of the lord and lady, honoured and raised them up. Nevertheless, it often placed the high-born page in situations sorrowful enough, prosaic, not to say ridiculous. The lord never distresses himself about that. And the lady must indeed be charmed by the Devil, not to see what every day she saw, her well-beloved employed in servile and unsuitable tasks.

In the Middle Ages the very high and the very low are continually brought together. That which is hidden by the poems, we can catch a glimpse of otherwhere. With those ethereal passions, many gross things were clearly blended.

All we know of the charms and philtres used by the witches is very fantastic, not seldom marked by malice, and recklessly mixed up with things that seem to us the least likely to have awakened love. By these methods they went a long way without the husband's perceiving in his blindness the game they made of him.

These philtres were of various kinds. Some were for exciting and troubling the senses, like the stimulants so much abused in the East. Others were dangerous, and often treacherous draughts to whose illusions the body would yield itself without the will. Others again were employed as tests when the passion was defied, when one wished to see how far the greediness of desire might derange the senses, making them receive as the highest and holiest of favours, the most disagreeable services done by the object of their love.

The rude way in which a castle was constructed, with nothing in it but large halls, led to an utter sacrifice of the inner life. It was long enough before they took to building in one of the turrets a closet or recess for meditation and the saying of prayers. The lady was easily watched. On certain days set or waited for, the bold youth would attempt the stroke, recommended him by the Witch, of mingling a philtre with her drink.

This, however, was a dangerous matter, not often tried. Less difficult was it to purloin from the lady things which escaped her notice, which she herself despised. He would treasure up the very smallest paring of a nail; he would gather up respectfully one or two beautiful hairs that might fall from her comb. These he would carry to the Witch, who often asked, as our modern sleep-wakers do, for something very personal and strongly redolent of the person, but obtained without her leave; as, for instance, some threads torn out of a garment long worn and soiled with the traces of perspiration. With much kissing, of course, and worshipping, the lover was fain reluctantly to throw these treasures into the fire, with a view to gathering up the ashes afterwards. By and by, when she came to look at her garment, the fine lady would remark the rent, but guessing at the cause, would only sigh and hold her tongue. The charm had already begun to work.

Even if she hesitated from regard for her marriage-vow, certain it is that life in a space so narrow, where they were always in each other's sight, so near and yet so far, became a downright torment. And even when she had once shown her weakness, still before her husband and others equally jealous the moments of happiness would assuredly be rare. Hence sprang many a foolish outbreak of unsatisfied desire. The less they came together, the more deeply they longed to do so. A disordered fancy sought to attain that end by means grotesque, unnatural, utterly senseless. So by way of establishing a means of secret correspondence between the two, the Witch had the letters of the alphabet pricked on both their arms. If one of them wanted to send a thought to the other, he brightened and brought out by sucking the blood-red letters of the wished-for word. Immediately, so it is said, the corresponding letters bled on the other's arm.

Sometimes in these mad fits they would drink each of the other's blood, so as to mingle their souls, it was said, in close communion. The devouring of Coucy's heart, which the lady "found so good that she never ate again," is the most tragical instance of these monstrous vows of loving cannibalism. But when the absent one did not die, but only the love within him, then the lady would seek counsel of the Witch, begging of her the means of holding him, of bringing him back.

The incantations used by the sorceress of Theocritus and Virgil, though employed also in the Middle Ages, were seldom of much avail. An attempt was made to win back the lover by a spell seemingly copied from antiquity, by means of a cake, of a *confarreatio* [1] like that which, both in Asia and Europe, had always been the holiest pledge of love. But in this case it is not the soul only, it is the flesh also they seek to bind; there must be so true an identity established between the two, that, dead to all other women, he shall live only for her. It was a cruel ceremony on the woman's side. "No haggling, madam," says the Witch. Suddenly the proud dame grows obedient, even to letting herself be stripped bare: for thus indeed it must be.

What a triumph for the Witch! And if this lady were the same as she who had once made her "run the gauntlet," how meet the vengeance, how dread the requital now! But it is not enough to have stripped her thus naked. About her loins is fastened a little shelf, on which a small oven is set for the cooking of the cake. "Oh, my dear, I cannot bear it longer! Make haste, and relieve me."

"You must bear it, madam; you must feel the heat. When the cake is done, he will be warmed by you, by your flame."

It is over; and now we have the cake of antiquity, of the Indian and the Roman marriage, but spiced and warmed up by the lecherous spirit of the Devil. She does not say with Virgil's wizard, [2]

"Ducite ab urbe domum, mea carmina, ducite Daphnin!"

But she takes him the cake, steeped, as it were, in the other's suffering, and kept warm by her love. He has hardly bitten it when he is overtaken by an odd emotion, by a feeling of dizziness. Then as the blood rushes up to his heart he turns red and hot. Passion fastens anew on him, and inextinguishable desire. [3]

[1] One form of wedding among the Romans, in which the bride-cake was broken between the pair, in token of their union. TRANS.
[2] "Hither, ye spells of mine, bring Daphnis home from the city!" - *Virgil,* Eclogue viii.
[3] I am wrong in saying inextinguishable. Fresh philtres were often needed; and the blame of this must lie with the lady, from whom the Witch in her mocking, malignant rage exacted the most humiliating observances.

Chapter Eleven - The Rebels' Communion, Sabbaths, The Black Mass

WE must now speak of the *Sabbaths;* a word which at different times clearly meant quite different things. Unhappily, we have no detailed accounts of these gatherings earlier than the reign of Henry IV. [1] By that time they were nothing more than a great lewd farce carried on under the cloak of witchcraft. But these very descriptions of a thing so greatly corrupted are marked by certain antique touches that tell of the successive periods and the different forms through which it had passed.

We may set out with this firm idea that, for many centuries, the serf led the life of a wolf or a fox; that he was *an animal of the night,* moving about, I may say, as little as possible in the daytime, and truly living in -the night alone.

Still, up to the year 1000, so long as the people made their own saints and legends, their daily life was not to them uninteresting. Their nightly Sabbaths were only a slight relic of paganism. They held in fear and honour the Moon, so powerful over the good things of earth. Her chief worshippers, the old women, burn small candles to *Dianom* - the Diana of yore, whose other names were Luna and Hecate. The Lupercal (or wolf-man) is always following the women and children, disguised indeed under the dark face of ghost Hallequin (Harlequin). The Vigil of Venus was kept as a holiday precisely on the first of May. On Midsummer Day they kept the Sabaza by sacrificing the he-goat of Bacchus Sabasius. In all this there was no mockery; nothing but a harmless carnival of serfs. But about the year 3000 the church is well-nigh shut against the peasant through the difference between his language and hers. By 1100 her services became quite unintelligible. Of the mysteries played at the church-doors, he has retained chiefly the comic side, the ox and the ass, &c. On these he makes Christmas carols, which grow ever more and more burlesque, forming a true Sabbatic literature.

Are we to suppose that the great and fearful risings of the twelfth century had no influence on these mysteries, on this night-life of the *wolf,* the *game bird*, the *wild quarry.* The great sacraments of rebellion among the serfs, when they drank of each other's blood, or ate of the ground by way of solemn pledge, [2] may have been celebrated at the Sabbaths. The "Marseillaise" of that time, sung by night rather than day, was perhaps a Sabbatic chant:

> "Nous sommes hommes commes ils sont!
> Tout aussi grand coeur nous avons!
> Tout autant souffrir nous pouvons!" [3]

But the tombstone falls again in 1200. Seated thereon the Pope and the King, with their enormous weight, have sealed up man. Has he now his old life by night? More than ever. The old pagan dances must by this time have waxed furious. Our negroes of the Antilles, after a dreadful day of heat and hard work, would go and dance away some four leagues off. So it was with the serf too. But with his dances there must have mingled a merriment born of revenge, satiric farces, burlesques and caricatures of the baron and the priest: a whole literature of the night indeed, that knew not one word of the literature of the day, that knew little even of the burgher Fabliaux.

Of such a nature were the Sabbaths before 1300. Before they could take the startling form of open warfare against the God of those days, much more was needed still, and especially these two things: not only a descending into the very depths of despair, but also *an utter losing of respect for anything.*

To this pass they do not come until the fourteenth century, under the Avignon popes, and during the Great Schism; when the Church with two heads seems no longer a church; when the king and all his nobles, being in shameful captivity to the English, are extorting the means of ransom from their oppressed and outraged people. Then do the Sabbaths take the grand and horrible form of the *Black Mass,* of a ritual upside down, in which Jesus is defied and bidden to thunder on the people if He can. In the thirteenth century this devilish drama was still impossible, through the horror it would have caused. And later again, in the fifteenth, when everything, even suffering itself, had become exhausted, so fierce an outburst could not have issued forth; so monstrous an invention no one would have essayed. It could only have belonged to the age of Dante.

It took place, I fancy, at one gush; an explosion as it were of genius raving, bringing impiety up to the height of a great popular passion-fit. To understand the nature of these bursts of rage, we must remember that, far from imagining the fixedness of God's laws, a people brought up by their own clergy to believe and depend on miracles, had for ages past been hoping and waiting for nothing else than a miracle which never came. In vain they demanded one in the desperate hour of their last worst strait. Heaven thenceforth appeared to them as the ally of their savage tormentors, nay, as itself a tormentor too.

Thereon began the *Black Mass* and the Jacquerie. [4]

In the elastic shell of the Black Mass, a thousand variations of detail may afterwards have been inserted; but the shell itself was strongly made and, in my opinion, all of one piece.

This drama I succeeded in reproducing in my "History of France." in the year 1857. There was small difficulty in casting it anew in its four acts. Only at that time I left in it too many of the grotesque adornments which clothed the Sabbath of a later period; nor did I clearly enough define what belonged to the older shell, so dark and dreadful.

Its date is strongly marked by certain savage tokens of an age accursed, and yet more by the ruling place therein assigned to woman, a fact most characteristic of the fourteenth century.

It is strange to mark how, at that period, the woman who enjoys so little freedom still holds her royal sway in a hundred violent fashions. At this time she inherits fiefs, brings her kingdoms to the king. On the lower levels she has still her throne, and yet more in the skies. Mary has supplanted Jesus. St. Francis and St. Dominic have seen the three worlds in her bosom. By the immensity of her grace she washes away sin; ay, and sometimes helps the sinner, as in the story of a nun whose place the Virgin took in the choir, while she herself was gone to meet her lover.

Up high, and down very low, we see the woman Beatrice reigns in heaven among the stars, while John of Meung in the *Romaunt of the Rose* is preaching the community of women. Pure or sullied, the woman is everywhere. We might say of her what Raymond Lulle said of God: "What part has He in the world? The whole."

But alike in heaven and in poetry the true heroine is not the fruitful mother decked out with children; but the Virgin, or some barren Beatrice, who dies young.

A fair English damsel passed over into France, it is said, about the year 1300, to preach the redemption of women. She looked on herself as their Messiah.

In its earliest phase the Black Mass seemed to betoken this redemption of Eve, so long accursed of Christianity. The woman fills every office in the Sabbath. She is priestess, altar, pledge of holy communion, by turns. Nay, at bottom, is she not herself as God?

Many popular traits may be found herein, and yet it comes not wholly from the people. The peasant who honoured strength alone, made small account of the woman; as we see but too clearly in our old laws and customs. From him the woman would not have received the high place she holds here. It is by her own self the place is won.

I would gladly believe that the Sabbath in its then shape was woman's work, the work of such a desperate woman as the Witch was then. In the fourteenth century she saw open before her a horrible career of torments lighted up for three or four hundred years by the stake. After 1300 her medical knowledge is condemned as baleful, her remedies are proscribed as if they were poisons. The harmless drawing of lots, by which lepers then thought to better their luck, brought on a massacre of those poor wretches. Pope John XXII. ordered the burning of a bishop suspected of Witchcraft. Under a system of such blind repression there was just the same risk in daring little as in daring much. Danger itself made people bolder; and the Witch was able to dare anything.

Human brotherhood, defiance of the Christian heaven, a distorted worship of nature herself as God such was the purport of the Black Mass.

They decked an altar to the arch-rebel of serfs, *to Him who had been so wronged*, the old outlaw, unfairly hunted out of heaven, "the Spirit by whom earth was made, the Master who ordained the budding of the plants." Such were the names of honour given him by his worshippers, the *Luciferians*, and also, according to a very likely opinion, by the Knights of the Temple.

The greatest miracle of those unhappy times is, the greater abundance found at the nightly communion of the brotherhood, than was to be found elsewhere by day. By incurring some little danger the Witch levied her contributions from those who were best off, and gathered their offerings into a common fund. Charity in a Satanic garb grew very powerful, as being a crime, a conspiracy, a form of rebellion. People would rob themselves of their food by day for the sake of the common meal at night.

Figure to yourself, on a broad moor, and often near an old Celtic cromlech, at the edge of a wood, this twofold scene: on one side a well-lit moor and a great feast of the people; on the other, towards yon wood, the choir of that church whose dome is heaven. What I call the choir is a hill commanding somewhat the surrounding country. Between these are the yellow flames of torch-fires, and some red brasiers emitting a fantastic smoke. At the back of all is the Witch, dressing up her Satan, a great wooden devil, black and shaggy. By his horns, and the goat-skin near him, he might be Bacchus; but his manly attributes make him a Pan or a Priapus. It is a darksome figure, seen differently by different eyes; to some suggesting only terror, while others are touched by the proud melancholy wherein the Eternally Banished seems absorbed. [5]

Act First. The magnificent *In troit* taken by Christendom from antiquity, that is, from those ceremonies where the people in long train streamed under the colonnades on their way to the sanctuary, is now taken back for himself by the elder god upon his return to power. The *Lavabo*, likewise borrowed from the heathen lustrations, reappears now. All this he claims back by right of age.

His priestess is always called, by way of honour, the Elder; but she would sometimes have been young. Lancre tells of a witch of seventeen, pretty, and horribly savage.

The Devil's bride was not to be a child: she must be at least thirty years old, with the form of a Medea, with the beauty that comes of pain; an eye deep, tragic, lit up by a feverish fire, with great serpent tresses waving at their will: I refer to the torrent of her black untamable hair. On her head, perhaps, you may see the crown of vervein, the ivy of the tomb, the violets of death.

When she has had the children taken off to their meal, the service begins: "I will come before thine altar; but save me, Lord, from the faithless and violent man (from the priest and the baron)."

Then come the denial of Jesus, the paying of homage to the new master, the feudal kiss, like the greetings of the Temple, when all was yielded without reserve, without shame, or dignity, or even purpose; the denial of an olden god being grossly aggravated by a seeming preference for Satan's back.

It is now his turn to consecrate his priestess. The wooden deity receives her in the manner of an olden Pan or Priapus. Following the old pagan form she sits a moment upon him in token of surrender, like the Delphian seeress on Apollo's tripod. After receiving the breath of his spirit, the sacrament of his love, she purifies herself with like formal solemnity. Thenceforth she is a living altar.

The Introit over, the service is interrupted for the feast. Contrary to the festive fashion of the nobles, who all sit with their swords beside them, here, in this feast of brethren, are no arms, not even a knife.

As a keeper of the peace, each has a woman with him. Without a woman no one is admitted. Be she a kinswoman or none, a wife or none; be she old or young, a woman he must bring with him.

What were the drinks passed round among them? Mead, or beer, or wine; strong cider or perry? The last two date from the twelfth century.

The illusive drinks, with their dangerous admixture of belladonna, did they already appear at that board? Certainly not. There were children there. Besides, an excess of commotion would have prevented the dancing.

This whirling dance, the famous *Sabbath-round,* was quite enough to complete the first stage of drunkenness. They turned back to back, their arms behind them, not seeing each other, but often touching each other's back. Gradually no one knew himself, nor whom he had by his side. The old wife then was old no more. Satan had wrought a miracle. She was still a woman, desirable, after a confused fashion beloved.

Act Second. Just as the crowd, grown dizzy together, was led, both by the attraction of the women and by a certain vague feeling of brotherhood, to imagine itself one body, the service was resumed at the *Gloria.* The altar, the host, became visible. These were represented by the woman herself. Prostrate, in a posture of extreme abasement, her long black silky tresses lost in the dust; she, this haughty Proserpine, offered up herself. On her back a demon officiated, saying the *Credo,* and making the offering. [6]

At a later period this scene came to be immodest. But at this time, amidst the calamities of the fourteenth century, in the terrible days of the -Black Plague, and of so many a famine, in the days of the Jacquerie and those hateful brigands, the Free Lances, on a people thus surrounded by danger, the effect was more than serious. The whole assembly had much cause to fear a surprise. The risk run by the Witch in this bold proceeding was very great, even tantamount to the forfeiting of her life. Nay, more; she braved a hell of suffering, of torments such as may hardly be described. Torn by pincers, and broken alive; her breasts torn out; her skin slowly singed, as in the case of the wizard bishop of Cahors; her body burned limb by limb on a small fire of red-hot coal, she was like to endure an eternity of agony.

Certainly all were moved when the prayer was spoken, the harvest-offering made, upon this devoted creature who gave herself up so humbly. Some wheat was offered to the *Spirit of the Earth*, who made wheat to grow. A flight of birds, most likely from the woman's bosom, bore to the *God of Freedom* the sighs and prayers of the serfs. What did they ask? Only that we, their distant descendants, might become free. [7]

What was the sacrament she divided among them? Not the ridiculous pledge we find later in the reign of Henry IV., but most likely; that *confarreatio* which we saw in the case of the philtres, the hallowed pledge of love, a cake baked on her own body, on the victim who, perhaps, to-morrow would herself be passing through the fire. It was her life, her death, they ate there. One sniffs already the scorching flesh.

Last of all they set upon her two offerings, seemingly of flesh; two images, one of *the latest dead,* the other of the newest-born in the district. These shared in the special virtue assigned to her who acted as altar and Host in one, and on these the assembly made a show of receiving the communion. Their Host would thus be threefold, and always human. Under a shadowy likeness of the Devil the people worshipped none other than its own self.

The true sacrifice was now over and done. The woman's work was ended, when she gave herself up to be eaten by the multitude. Rising from her former posture, she would not withdraw from the spot until she had proudly stated, and, as it were, confirmed the lawfulness of her proceedings by an appeal to the thunderbolt, by an insolent defiance of the discrowned God.

In mockery of the *Agnus Dei,* and the breaking of the Christian Host, she brought a toad dressed up, and pulled it to pieces. Then rolling her eyes about in a frightful way she raised them to heaven, and beheading the toad, uttered these strange words: "Ah, *Philip,* [8] if I had you here, you should be served in the same manner!"

No answer being outwardly given to her challenge, no thunderbolt hurled upon her head, they imagine that she has triumphed over the Christ. The nimble band of demons seized their moment to astonish the people with various small wonders which amazed and overawed the more credulous. The toads, quite harmless in fact, but then accounted poisonous, were bitten and torn between their dainty teeth. They jumped over large fires and pans of live coal, to amuse the crowd and make them laugh at the fires of Hell.

Did the people really laugh after a scene so tragical, so very bold? I know not. Assuredly there was no laughing on the part of her who first dared all this. To her these fires must have seemed like those of the nearest stake. Her business rather lay in forecasting the future of that devilish monarchy, in creating the Witch to be.

[1] The least bad of these is by Lancre, a man of some wit, whose evident connection with some young witches gave him something to say. The accounts of the Jesuit Del Rio and the Dominican Michaëlis are the absurd productions of two credulous and silly pedants.
[2] At the battle of Courtray. See also Grimm and my *Origines.*
[3] "We are fashioned of one clay:
  Big as theirs our hearts are aye:
  We can bear as much as they." - TRANS.
[4] The Peasants' war which raged in France in 1364.
[5] This is taken from Del Rio, but is not, I think, peculiar to Spain. It is an ancient trait, and marked by the primitive inspiration.
[6] This important fact of the woman being her own altar, is known to us by the trial of La Voisin, which M. Ravaisson, Sen., is about to publish with the other *Papers of the Bastille.*
[7] This grateful offering of wheat and birds is peculiar to France. In Lorraine, and no doubt in Germany, black beasts were offered, as the black cat, the black goat, or the black bull.
[8] Lancre, 136. Why "Philip," I cannot say. By Satan Jesus is always called John or *Janicot* (Jack). Was she speaking of Philip of Valois, who brought on the wasting hundred years' war with England?

Chapter Twelve - The Sequel Love and Death Satan Disappears

AND now the multitude is made free, is of good cheer. For some hours the serf reigns in short-lived freedom. His time indeed is scant enough. Already the sky is changing, the stars are going down. Another moment, and the cruel dawn remits him to his slavery, brings him back again under hostile eyes, under the shadow of the castle, beneath the shadow of the church; back again to his monotonous toiling, to the old unending weariness of heart, governed as it were by two bells, whereof one keeps saying "Always," the other "Never." Anon they will be seen coming each out of his own house, heavily, humbly, with an air of calm composure.

Let them at least enjoy the one short moment! Let each of these disinherited, for once fulfil his fancy, for once indulge his musings. What soul is there so all unhappy, so lost to all feeling, as never to have one good dream, one fond desire; never to say, "If this would only happen!"

The only detailed accounts we have, as I said before, are modern, belonging to a time of peace and well-doing, when France was blooming afresh, in the latter years of Henry VI., years of thriving luxury, entirely different from that dark age when the Sabbath was first set going.

No thanks to Mr. Lancre and others, if we refrain from portraying the Third Act as like the Church-Fair of Rubens, a very miscellaneous orgie, a great burlesque ball, which allowed of every kind of union, especially between near kindred. According to those authors, who would make us groan with horror, the main end of the Sabbath, the explicit doctrine taught by Satan, was incest; and in those great gatherings, sometimes of two thousand souls, the most startling deeds were done before the whole world.

This is hard to believe; and the same writers tell of other things which seem quite opposed to a view so cynical. They say that people went to those meetings only in pairs, that they sat down to the feast by twos, that even if one person came alone, she was assigned a young demon, who took charge of her, and did the honours of the feast. They say, too, that jealous lovers were not afraid to go thither in company with the curious fair.

We also find that the most of them came by families, children and all. The latter were sent off only during the first act, not during the feast, nor the services, nor yet while this third act was going on; a fact which proves that some decency was observed. Moreover, the scene was twofold. The household groups stayed on the moor in a blaze of light. It was only beyond the fantastic curtain of torch-smoke that the darker spaces, where people could roam in all directions, began.

The judges, the inquisitors, for all their enmity, are fain to allow the existence here of a general spirit of peace and mildness. Of the three things that startle us in the feasts of nobles, there is not one here; no swords, no duels, no tables reeking blood. No faithless gallantries here bring dishonour on some intimate friend. Unknown, unneeded here, for all they say, is the unclean brotherhood of the Temple; in the Sabbath, woman is everything.

The question of incest needs explaining. All alliances between kinsfolk, even those most allowable in the present day, were then regarded as a crime. The modern law, which is charity itself, understands the heart of man and the well-being of families. [1] It allows the widower to marry his wife's sister, the best mother his children could have. Above all, it allows a man to wed his cousin, whom he knows and may trust fully, whom he has loved perhaps from childhood, his playfellow of old, regarded by his mother with special favour as already the adopted of her own heart. In the Middle Ages all this was incestuous.

The peasant being fondest of his own family was driven to despair. It was a monstrous thing for him to marry a cousin, even in the sixth degree. It was impossible for him to get married in his own village where the question of kinship stood so much in his way. He had to look for a wife elsewhere, afar off. But in those days there was not much intercourse or acquaintance between different places, and each hated its own neighbours. On feast days one village would fight another without knowing the reason why, as may sometimes still be seen in countries never so thinly peopled. No one durst go seek a wife in the very spot where men had been fighting together, where he himself would have been in great danger.

There was another difficulty. The lord of the young serf forbade his marrying in the next lordship. Becoming the serf of his wife's lord he would have been wholly lost to his own. Thus he was debarred by the priest from his cousin, by the lord from a stranger; and so it happened that many did not marry at all.

The result was just what they pretended to avoid. In the Sabbath the natural sympathies sprang forth again. There the youth found again her whom he had known and loved at first, her whose "little husband" he had been called at ten years old. Preferring her as he certainly did, he paid but little heed to canonical hindrances.

When we come to know the Medieval Family better, we give up believing the declamatory assumptions of a general mingling together of the people forming so great a crowd. On the contrary, we feel that each small group is so closely joined together, as to be utterly barred to the entrance of a stranger.

The serf was not jealous towards his own kin, but his poverty and wretchedness made him exceedingly afraid of worsening his lot by multiplying children whom he could not support. The priest and the lord on their part wished to increase the number of their serfs wanted the woman to be always bearing; and the strangest sermons were often delivered on this head, [2] varied sometimes with threats and cruel reproaches. All the more resolute was the prudence of the man. The woman, poor creature, unable to bear children fit to live on such conditions, bearing them only to her sorrow, had a horror of being made big. She never would have ventured to one of these night festivals without being first assured, again and again, that no woman ever came away pregnant. [3]

They were drawn thither by the banquet, the dancing, the lights, the amusements; in nowise by carnal pleasure. The last thing they cared for was to heighten their poverty, to bring one more wretch into the world, to give another serf to their lord.

* * *

Cruel indeed was the social system of those days. Authority bade men marry, but rendered marriage nearly impossible, at once by the excessive misery of most, and the senseless cruelty of the canonical prohibitions.

The result was quite opposed to the purity thus preached. Under a show of Christianity existed the patriarchate of Asia alone.

Only the firstborn married. The younger brothers and sisters worked under him and for him. In the lonely farms of the mountains of the South, far from all neighbours and every woman, brothers and sisters lived together, the latter serving and in all ways belonging to the former; a way of life analogous to that in Genesis, to the marriages of the Parsees, to the customs still obtaining in certain shepherd tribes of the Himalayas.

The mother's fate was still more revolting. She could not many her son to a kinswoman, and thus secure to herself a kindly-affected daughter-in-law. Her son married, if he could, a girl from a distant village, an enemy often, whose entrance proved baneful either to the children of a former marriage, or to the poor mother, who was often driven away by the stranger wife. You may not think it, but the fact is certainly so. At the very least she was ill-used; banished from the fireside, from the very table.

There is a Swiss law forbidding the removal of the mother from her place by the chimney-corner.

She was exceedingly afraid of her son's marrying. But her lot was little happier if he did not marry. None the less servant was she of the young master of the house, who succeeded to all his father's rights, even to that of beating her. This impious custom I have seen still followed in the South: a son of five-and-twenty chastising his mother when she got drunk.

How much greater her suffering in those days of savagery! Then it was rather he who came back from the feast half-drunken, hardly knowing what he was about. But one room, but one bed, was all they had between them. She was by no means free from fear. He had seen his friends married, and felt soured thereat. Thenceforth her way is marked by tears, by utter weakness, by a woeful self-surrender. Threatened by her only God, her son, heartbroken at finding herself in a plight so unnatural, she falls desperate. She tries to drown all her memories in sleep. At length comes an issue for which neither of them can fairly account, an issue such as nowadays will often happen in the poorer quarters of large towns, where some poor woman is forced, frightened, perhaps beaten, into bearing every outrage. Thus conquered, and, spite of her scruples, far too resigned, she endured thenceforth a pitiable bondage; a life of shame and sorrow, and abundant anguish, growing with the yearly widening difference between their several ages. The woman of six-and-thirty might keep watch over a son of twenty years: but at fifty, alas! or still later, where would he be? From the great Sabbath where thronged the people of far villages, he would be bringing home a strange woman for his youthful mistress, a woman hard, heartless, devoid of ruth, who would rob her of her son, her seat by the fire, her bed, of the very house which she herself had made.

To believe Lancre and others, Satan accounted the son for praiseworthy, if he kept faithful to his mother, thus making a virtue of a crime. If this be true, we must assume that the woman was protected by a woman, that the Witch sided with the mother, to defend her hearth against a daughter-in-law who, stick in hand, would have sent her forth to beg.

Lancre further maintains that "never was good Witch, but she sprang from the love of a mother for her son." In this way, indeed, was born the Persian soothsayer, the natural fruit, they say, of so hateful a mystery; and thus the secrets of the magical art were kept confined to one family which constantly renewed itself.

An impious error led them to imitate the harmless mystery of the husbandman, the unceasing vegetable round whereby the corn resown in the furrow, brings forth its corn.

The less monstrous unions of brother with sister, so common in the East, and in Greece, were cold and rarely fruitful. They were wisely abandoned; nor would people ever have returned to them, but for that rebellious spirit which, being aroused by absurd restrictions, flung itself foolishly into the opposite extreme. Thus from unnatural laws, hatred begot unnatural customs.

A cruel, an accursed time, a time big with despair!

We have been long discoursing; but the dawn is well-nigh come. In a moment the hour will strike for the spirits to take themselves away. The Witch feels her dismal flowers already withering on her brow. Farewell, her royalty, perhaps her life! Where would they be, if the day still found her there?

Of Satan, what shall she make? A flame, a cinder? He asks for nothing better; knowing well, in his craftiness, that the only way to live and to be born again, is first to die.

And will he die, he who as the mighty summoner of the dead, granted to them that mourn their only joy on earth, the love they had lost, the dream they had cherished? Ah, no! he is very sure to live.

Will he die, he that mighty spirit who, finding Creation accurst, and Nature lying cold upon the ground, flung thither like a dirty foster-child from off the Church's garment, gathered her up and placed her on his bosom? In truth it cannot be.

Will he die, he the one great physician of the Middle Ages, of a world that, falling sick, was saved by his poisons and bidden, poor fool, to live?

As the gay rogue is sure of living, he dies wholly at his ease. He shuffles out of himself, cleverly burns up his fine goatskin, and disappears in a blaze of dawn.

But *she* who made Satan, who made all things, good or ill, whose countenance was given to so many forms of love, of devotion, and of crime, to what end will she come? Behold her all lonely on her waste moorland.

She is not, as they say, the dread of all. Many will bless her. More than one have found her beautiful, would sell their share in Paradise to dare be near her. But all around her is a wide gulf. They who admire, are none the less afraid of this all-powerful Medea, with her fair deep eyes, and the thrilling adders of her dark overflowing hair.

To her thus lonely for ever, for evermore without love, what is there left? Nothing but the Demon who had suddenly disappeared.

"'Tis well, good Devil, let us go. I am utterly loath to stay here any more. Hell itself is far preferable. Farewell to the world!"

She must live but a very little longer, to play out the dreadful drama she had herself begun. Near her, ready saddled by the obedient Satan, stood a huge black horse, the fire darting from his eyes and nostrils. She sprang upon him with one bound.

They follow her with their eyes. The good folk say with alarm, "What is to become of her?" With a frightful burst of laughter, she goes off, vanishing swift as an arrow. They would like much to know what becomes of the poor woman, but that they never will. [4]

[1] Of course the allusion here, as shown in the next following sentence, is to French law in particular. As for the marriage of cousins, there is much to say on both sides of the question. - TRANS.

[2] The ingenious M. Génin has very recently collected the most curious information on this point.

[3] Boguet, Lancre, and other authors, are agreed on this question.

[4] See the end of the Witch of Berkeley, as told by William of Malmesbury.

Book Two

Chapter One - The Witch in Her Decline Satan Multiplied and Made Common

THE Devil's delicate fondling, the lesser Witch, begotten of the Black Mass after the greater one's disappearance, came and bloomed in all her malignant cat-like grace. This woman is quite the reverse of the other: refined and sidelong in manner, sly and purring demurely, quick also at setting up her back. There is nothing of the Titan about her, to be sure. Far from that, she is naturally base; lewd from her cradle and full of evil daintinesses. Her whole life is the expression of those unclean thoughts which sometimes in a dream by night may assail him who would shrink with horror from any such by day.

She who is born with such a secret in her blood, with such instinctive mastery of evil, she who has looked so far and so low down, will have no religion, no respect for anything or person in the world; none even for Satan, since he is a spirit still, while she has a particular relish for all things material.

In her childhood she spoiled everything. Tall and pretty she startled all by her slovenly habits. With her Witchcraft becomes a mysterious cooking up of some mysterious chemistry. From an early date she delights to handle repulsive things, to-day a drug, tomorrow an intrigue. Among diseases and love-affairs she is in her element. She will make a clever go-between, a bold and skilful empiric. War will be made against her as a fancied murderer, as a woman who deals in poisons. And yet she has small taste for such things, is far from murderous in her desires. Devoid of goodness, she yet loves life, loves to work cures, to prolong others' lives. She is dangerous in two ways: on the one hand by selling receipts for barrenness, and even for abortion; while on the other, her headlong libertine fancy leads her to compass a woman's fall with her cursed potions, to triumph in the wicked deeds of love.

Different, indeed, is this one from the other! She is a manufacturer: the other was the ungodly one, the demon, the great rebellion, the wife, we might almost say, the mother of Satan; for out of her and her inward strength he grew up. But this one is the Devil's daughter notwithstanding. Two things she derives from him, her uncleanness, her love of handling life. These are her allotted walk, in these she is quite an artist; an artist already trading in her lore, and we are admitted into the business.

It was said that she would perpetuate herself by-the incest from which she sprang. But she has no need of that: numberless little ones will she beget without help from another. In less than fifty years, at the opening of the fifteenth century, under Charles VI., a mighty contagion was spread abroad. Whoever thought he had any secrets or any receipts, whoever fancied himself a seer, whoever dreamed and travelled in his dreams, would call himself a pet of Satan. Every moonstruck woman adopted the awful name of Witch!

A perilous, profitable name, cast at her in their hatred by people who alternately insult and implore the unknown power. It is none the less accepted, nay, is often claimed. To the children who follow her, to the woman who, with threatening fists, hurl the name at her like a stone, she turns round, saying proudly, "'Tis true, you have said well!"

The business improves, and men are mingled in it. Hence another fall for the art. Still the least of the witches retains somewhat of the Sibyl. Those other frowsy charlatans, those clownish jugglers, molecatchers, ratkillers, who throw spells over beasts, who sell secrets which they have not, defiled these times with the stench of a dismal black smoke, of fear and foolery. Satan grows enormous, gets multiplied without end. 'Tis a poor triumph, however, for him. He grows dull and sick at heart. Still the people keep flowing towards him, bent on having no other God than he. Himself only is to himself untrue.

In spite of two or three great discoveries, the fifteenth century is, to my thinking, none the less a century tired out, a century of few ideas.

It opened right worthily with the Sabbath Royal of St. Denis, the wild and woeful ball given by Charles VI. in the abbey so named, to commemorate the burial of Du Guesclin, which had taken place so many years before. For three days and nights was Sodom wallowing among the graves. The foolish king, not yet grown quite an idiot, compelled his royal forefathers to share in the ball, by making their dry bones dance in their biers. Death, becoming a go-between whether he would or no, lent a sharp spur to the voluptuous revel. Then broke out those unclean fashions of an age when ladies made themselves taller by wearing the Devil's horned-bonnet, and gloried in dressing as if they were all with child. [1] To this fashion they clung for the next forty years. The younger folk on their side, not to be behind in shamelessness, eclipsed them in the display of naked charms. The woman wore Satan on her forehead in the shape of a horned headdress: on the feet of the bachelor and the page he was visible in the tapering scorpion-like tips of their shoes. Under the mask of animals they represented the lowest side of brute nature. The famous child stealer, Retz, here took his first flight in villany. The great feudal ladies, unbridled Jezebels, with less sense of shame in them than the men, scorned all disguise whatever; displayed themselves with face uncovered. In their sensual rages, in their mad parade of debauchery, the king, the whole company might see the bottomless pit itself yawning for the life, the feeling, the body, and the soul of each.

Out of such doings come forth the conquered of Agincourt, a poor generation of effete nobles, in whose miniatures you shiver to see the falling away of their sorry limbs, as shown through the treacherous tightness of their clothes. [2]

Much to be pitied is the Witch who, when the great lady came home from that royal feast, became her bosom-counsellor and agent charged with the doing of impossible things.

In her own castle, indeed, the lady is almost, if not all alone, amidst a crowd of single men. To judge from romances you would think she delighted in girding herself with an array of fair girls. Far otherwise are we taught by history and common sense. Eleanor is not so silly as to match herself against Rosamond. With all their own rakishness, those queens and great ladies could be frightfully jealous; witness she who is said by Henry Martin to have caused the death of a girl admired by her husband, under the outrageous handling of his soldiery. The power wielded by the lady's love depends, we repeat, on her being alone. Whatever her age and figure, she becomes the dream of all. The Witch takes mischievous delight in making her abuse her goddesship, in tempting her to make game of the men she humbles and be-fools. She goes to all lengths of boldness, even treating them like very beasts. Look at them being transformed! Down on all fours they tumble, like fawning monkeys, absurd bears, lewd dogs, or swine eager to follow their contemptuous Circé.

Her pity rises thereat? Nay, but she grows sick of it all, and kicks those crawling beasts with her foot. The thing is impure, but not heinous enough. An absurd remedy is found for her complaint. These others being so nought, she is to have something yet more nought namely, a little sweetheart. The advice is worthy of the Witch. Love's spark shall be lighted before its time in some young innocent, sleeping the pure sleep of childhood! Here you have the ugly tale of little John of Saintré, pink of cherubim, and other paltry puppets of the Age of Decay.

Through all those pedantic embellishments and sentimental moralizings, one clearly marks the vile cruelty that lies below. The fruit was killed in the flower. Here, in a manner, is the very "eating of children," which was laid so often to the Witch's charge. Anyhow, she drained their lives. The fair lady who caresses one in so tender and motherly a way, what is she but a vampire, draining the blood of the weak? The upshot of such atrocities we may gather from the tale itself. Saintré becomes a perfect knight, but so utterly frail and weak as to be dared and defied by the lout of a peasant priest, in whom the lady, become better advised, has seen something that will suit her best.

Such idle whimsies heighten the surfeit, the mad rage of an empty mind. Circe among her beasts grows so weary and heartsick that she would be a beast herself. She fancies herself wild, and locks herself up. From her tower she casts an evil eye towards the gloomy forest. She fancies herself a prisoner, and rages like a wolf chained fast. "Let the old woman come this moment: I want her. Run!" Two minutes later again: "What! is she not come yet?"

At last she is come. "Hark you: I have a sore longing invincible, as you know to choke you, to drown you, or to give you up to the bishop, who already claims you. You have but one way of escape, that is, to satisfy another longing of mine by changing me into a wolf. I feel wretchedly bored, weary of keeping still. I want, by night at least, to run free about the forest. Away with stupid servants, with dogs that stun me with their noise, with clumsy horses that kick out and shy at a thicket."

"But if you were caught, my lady."

"Insolent woman! You would rather die, then?" "At least you have heard the story of the woman-wolf, whose paw was cut-off. [3] But, oh! how sorry I should be."

"That is my concern. I will hear nothing more, I am in a hurry have been barking already. What happiness, to hunt all by myself in the clear moonlight; by myself to fasten on the hind, or man likewise if he comes near me; to attack the tender children, and, above all, to set my teeth in the women; ay, the women, for I hate them all – not one like yourself. Don't start, I won't bite you – you are not to my taste, and besides, you have no blood in you! 'Tis blood I crave – blood!"

She can no longer refuse. "Nothing easier, my lady. To-night, at nine o'clock, you will drink this. Lock yourself up, and then turning into a wolf, while they think you are still here, you can scour the forest."

It is done; and next morning the lady finds herself worn out and depressed. In one night she must have travelled some thirty leagues. She has been hunting and slaying until she is covered with blood. But the blood, perhaps, comes from her having torn herself among the brambles.

A great triumph and danger also for her who has wrought this miracle. From the lady, however, whose command provoked it, she receives but a gloomy welcome. "Witch, 'tis a fearful power you have; I should never have guessed it. But now I fear and dread you. Good cause, indeed, they have to hate you. A happy day will it be when you are burnt. I can ruin you when I please. One word of mine about last night, and my peasants would this evening whet their scythes upon you. Out, you black-looking, hateful old hag!"

The great folk, her patrons, launch her into strange adventures. For what can she refuse to her terrible protectors, when nothing but the castle saves her from the priest, from the faggot? If the baron, on his return from a crusade, being bent on copying the manners of the Turks, sends for her, and orders her to steal him a few children, what can she do? Raids such as those grand ones in which two thousand pages were sometimes carried off from Greek ground to enter the seraglio, were by no means unknown to the Christians; were known from the tenth century to the barons of England, at a later date to the knights of Rhodes and Malta. The famous Giles of Retz, the only one brought to trial, was punished, not for having stolen his small serfs, a crime not then uncommon, but for having sacrificed them to Satan. She who actually stole them, and was ignorant, doubtless, of their future lot, found herself between two perils: on the one hand the peasant's fork and scythe; on the other, those torments which awaited her, when recusant, within the tower. Retz's terrible Italian would have made nothing of pounding her in a mortar. [4]

On all sides the perils and the profits went together. A position more frightfully corrupting could not have been found. The Witches themselves didn't deny the absurd powers imputed to them by the people. They averred that by means of a doll stuck over with needles they could weave their spells around whomever they pleased, making him waste away until he died. They averred that mandragora, torn from beneath the gallows by the teeth of a dog, who invariably died therefrom, enabled them to pervert the understanding; to turn men into beasts, to give women over to idiocy and madness. Still more dreadful was the furious frenzy caused by the Thorn-apple, or Datura, which made men dance themselves to death, and go through a thousand shameful antics, without their own knowledge or remembrance. [5]

Hence there grew up against them a feeling of boundless hatred, mingled with as extreme a fear. Sprenger, who wrote the *Hammer for Witches,* relates with horror how, in a season of snow, when all the roads were broken up, he saw a wretched multitude, wild with terror, and spell-bound by evils all too real, fill up all the approaches to a little German town. "Never," says he, "did you behold so mighty a pilgrimage to our Lady of Grace, or her of the wilderness. All these people, who hobbled, crawled, and stumbled among the quagmires, were on their way to the Witch, to beseech the grace of the Devil upon themselves. How proud and excited must the old woman have felt at seeing so large a concourse prostrate before her feet!" [6]

[1] Even in a very mystic theme, in a work of such genius as the *Lamb* of Van Eyck (says John of Bruges), all the Virgins seem big. It was only the quaint fashion of the fifteenth century.

[2] This wasting away of a used-up, enervated race, mars the effect of all those splendid miniatures of the Court of Burgundy, the Duke of Berry, &c. No amount of clever handling could make good works of art out of subjects so very pitiable.

[3] Among the great ladies imprisoned in their castles, this dreadful fancy was not rare. They hungered and thirsted for freedom, for savage freedom. Boguet mentions how, among the hills of Auvergne, a hunter one night drew his sword upon a she-wolf, but missing her, cut off her paw. She fled away limping. He came to a neighbouring castle to seek the hospitality of him who dwelt there. The gentleman, on seeing him, asked if he had had good sport. By way of answer he thought to draw out of his pouch the she-wolfs paw; but what was his amazement to find instead of the paw a hand, and on one of the fingers a ring, which the gentleman recognized as belonging to his wife! Going at once in search of her, he found her hurt and hiding her fore-arm. To the arm which had lost its hand he fitted that which the hunter had brought him, and the lady was fain to own that she it was, who in the likeness of a wolf had at-

85

tacked the hunter, and afterwards saved herself by leaving a paw on the battle-field. The husband had the cruelty to give her up to justice, and she was burnt.

[4] See my *History of France,* and still more the learned and careful account by the lamented Armand Gueraud: *Notice sur Gilles de Rais,* Nantes, 1855. We there find that the purveyors of that horrible child's charnel-house were mostly men.

[5] Pouchet, on the *Solaneae and General Botany.* Nysten, *Dictionary of Medicine,* article *Datura.* The robbers employed these potions but too often. A butcher of Aix and his wife, whom they wanted to rob of their money, were made to drink of some such, and became so maddened thereby, that they danced all one night naked in a cemetery.

[6] The Witch delighted in causing the noble and the great to undergo the most outrageous trials of their love. We know that queens and ladies of rank (in Italy even to the last century) held their court at times the most forbidding, and exacted the most unpleasant services from their favourites. There was nothing too mean, too repulsive, for the domestic brute the cicisbeo, the priest, the half-witted page to undergo, in the stupid belief that the power of a philtre increased with its Hastiness. This was sad enough when the ladies were neither young, nor beautiful, nor witty. But what of that other astounding fact, that a Witch, who was neither a great lady, nor young, nor fair, but poor, and perhaps a serf, clad only in dirty rags, could still by her malice, by the strange power of her raging lewdness, by some bewitchingly treacherous spell, stupefy the gravest personages, and abase them to so low a depth? Some monks of a monastery on the Rhine, wherein, as in many other German convents, none but a noble of four hundred years' standing could gain admission, sorrowfully owned to Sprenger that they had seen three of their brethren bewitched in turn, and a fourth killed by a woman, who boldly said, "I did it, and will do so again: they cannot escape me, for they have eaten," &c. (Sprenger, *Malleus maleficarum, quaestio,* vii. p. 84.) "The worst of it is," says Sprenger, "that we have no means of punishing or examining her: *so she lives still.*"

Chapter Two - The Hammer for Witches

THE witches took small care to hide their game. Rather they boasted of it; and it was, indeed, from their own lips that Sprenger picked up the bulk of the tales that grace his hand-book. It is a pedantic work, marked out into the absurd divisions and subdivisions employed by the followers of St. Thomas Aquinas; but a work sincere withal, and frank -spoken, written by a man so thoroughly frightened by this dreadful duel between God and the Devil, wherein God *generally* allows the Devil to win, that the only remedy he can discern is to pursue the latter fire in hand, and burn with all speed those bodies which he had chosen for his dwelling-place.

Sprenger's sole merit is the fact of his having written a complete book, which crowns a mighty system, a whole literature. To the old *Penitentiaries,* handbooks of confessors for the inquisition of sin, succeeded the *Directories* for the inquisition of heresy, the greatest sin of all. But for Witchcraft, the greatest of all heresies, special hand-books or directories were appointed.

Hammers for Witches, to wit. These handbooks, continually enriched by the zeal of the Dominicans, attained perfection in the *Malleus* of Sprenger, the book by which he himself was guided during his great mission to Germany, and which for a century after served as a guide and light for the courts of the Inquisition.

How was Sprenger led to the study of these things? lie tells us that being in Rome, at a refectory where the monks were entertaining some pilgrims, he saw two from Bohemia; one a young priest, the other his father. The father sighing prayed for a successful journey. Touched with a kindly feeling Sprenger asked him why he sorrowed. Because his son was *possessed*: at great cost and with much trouble he had brought him to the tomb of the saints, at Rome.

"Where is this son of yours?" said the monk.

"By your side."

"At this answer I shrank back alarmed. I scanned the young priest's figure, and was amazed to see him. eat with so modest an air, and answer with so much gentleness. He informed me that, on speaking somewhat sharply to an old woman, she had laid him under a spell, and that spell was under a tree. What tree? The Witch steadily refused to say."

Sprenger's charity led him to take the possessed from church to church, from relic to relic. At every halting-place there was an exorcism, followed by furious cries, contortions, jabbering in every language, and gambols without number: all this before the people, who followed the pair with shuddering admiration.

The devils, so abundant in Germany, were scarcer among the Italians. For some days Rome talked of nothing else. The noise made by this affair doubt-less brought the Dominican into public notice. He studied, collected all the *Mallei,* and other manuscript handbooks, and became a first-rate authority in the processes against demons. His *Malleus* was most likely composed during the twenty years between this adventure and the important mission entrust-ed to Sprenger by Pope Innocent VIII., in 1484.

For that mission to Germany a clever man was specially needed; a man of wit and ability, who might overcome the dislike of honest German folk for the dark system it would be his care to introduce. In the Low Countries Home had suffered a rude check, which brought the Inquisition into vogue there, and consequently closed France against it: Toulouse alone, as being the old Albigensian country, having endured the Inquisition. About the year 1460 a Penitentiary [1] of Rome, being made Dean of Arras, thought to strike an awe-inspiring blow at the *Chambers of Rhetoric*, literary clubs which had be-gun to handle religious questions. He had one of these Rhetoricians burnt for a wizard, and along with him some wealthy burgesses, and even a few knights. The nobles were angry at this near approach to themselves: the pub-lic voice was raised in violent outcry. The Inquisition was cursed and spat upon, especially in France. The Parliament of Paris roughly closed its doors upon it; and thus by her awkwardness did Rome lose her opportunity of establishing that Reign of Terror throughout the North.

About 1484 the time seemed better chosen. The Inquisition had grown to so dreadful a height in Spain, setting itself even above the king, that it seemed already confirmed as a conquering institution, able to move forward alone, to make its way everywhere, and seize upon everything. In Germany, indeed, it was hindered by the jealous antagonism of the spiritual princes, who, having courts of their own, and holding inquisitions by themselves, would never agree to accept that of Rome. But the position of these princes towards the popular movements by which they were then so greatly disquieted, soon rendered them more manageable. All along the Rhine, and throughout Swabia, even on the eastern side towards Salzburg, the country seemed to be undermined. At every moment, burst forth some fresh revolt of the peasantry. A vast underground volcano, an invisible lake of fire, showed itself, as it were, from place to place, in continual spouts of flame. More dreaded than that of Germany, the foreign Inquisition appeared at a most seasonable hour for spreading terror through the country, and crushing the rebellious spirits, by roasting, as the wizards of to-day, those who might else have been the insurgents of to-morrow. It was a beautiful *derivative,* an excellent popular weapon for putting down the people. This time the storm got turned upon the Wizards, as in 1349, and on many other occasions it had been launched against the Jews.

Only the right man was needed. He who should be the first to set up his judgment-seat in sight of the jealous courts of Mentz and Cologne, in presence of the mocking mobs of Strasburg or Frankfort, must indeed be a man of ready wit. He would need great personal cleverness to atone for, to cause a partial forgetfulness of his hateful mission. Rome, too, has always plumed herself on choosing the best men for her work. Caring little for questions, and much for persons, she thought rightly enough that the successful issue of her affairs depended on the special character of her several agents abroad. "Was Sprenger the right man? He was a German to begin with, a Dominican enjoying beforehand the support of that dreaded order through all its convents, through all its schools. Need was there of a worthy son of the schools, a good disputant, of a man well skilled in the *Sum,* [2] grounded firm in his St. Thomas, able at any moment to quote texts. All this Sprenger certainly was: and best of all, he was a fool.

"It has been often said that *diabolus* comes from *dia*, 'two,' and *bolus*, 'a pill or ball,' because devouring alike soul and body, he makes but one pill, one mouthful of the two. But" - he goes on to say with the gravity of *Sganarelle* - "in Greek etymology *diabolus* means 'shut up in a house of bondage,' or rather 'flowing down' (Teufel?), that is to say, falling, because he fell from heaven."

"Whence comes the word sorcery (*maléfice*)? From *maleficiendo*, which means *male de fide sentiendo*. [3] A curious etymology, but one that will hold a great deal. Once trace a resemblance between witchcraft and evil opinions, and every wizard becomes a heretic, every doubter a wizard. All who think wrongly can be burnt for wizards. This was done at Arras; and they long to establish the same rule, little by little, everywhere else.

Herein lies the once, sure merit of Sprenger. A fool, but a fearless one, he boldly lays down the most unwelcome theses. Others would have striven to shirk, to explain away, to diminish, the objections that might be made. Not he, however. From the first page he puts plainly forward, one by one, the natural manifest reasons for not believing in the Satanic miracles. To these he coldly adds: *"They are but so many heretical mistakes."* And without stopping to refute those reasons, he copies you out the adverse passages found in the Bible, St. Thomas, in books of legends, in the canonists, and the scholiasts. Having first shown you the right interpretation, he grinds it to powder by dint of authority.

He sits down satisfied, calm as a conqueror; seeming to say, "Well, what say you now? Will you dare use your reason again? Go and doubt away then; doubt, for instance, that the Devil delights in setting himself between wife and husband, although the Church and all the canonists repeatedly admit this reason for a divorce!

Of a truth this is unanswerable: nobody will breathe so much as a whisper in reply. Since Sprenger heads his handbook for judges by declaring the slightest doubt *heretical,* the judge stands bound accordingly; he feels that he cannot stumble, that if unhappily he should ever be tempted by an impulse of doubt or humanity, he must begin by condemning himself and delivering his own body to the flames.

The same method prevails everywhere: first the sensible meaning, which is then confronted openly, without reserve, by the negation of all good sense. Some one, for instance, might be tempted to say that as love is in the soul, there is no need to account for it by the mysterious working of the Devil. That is surely specious, is it not?

"By no means," says Sprenger.

"I mark a difference. He who cuts wood does not cause it to burn: he only does so indirectly. The woodcutter is Love; see Denis the Areopagite, Origen, John of Damascus. Therefore, love is but the indirect cause of love."

"What a thing, you see, to have studied! No weak school could have turned out such a man. Only Paris, Louvain, or Cologne, had machinery fit to mould the human brain. The school of Paris was mighty: for dog-Latin who can be matched with the *Janotus* of Gargantua? [4] But mightier yet was Cologne, glorious queen of darkness, whence Hutten drew the type of his *Obscuri viri,* that thriving and fruitful race of obscurantists and ignoramuses. [5]

This massive logician, so full of words, so devoid of meaning, sworn foe of nature as well as reason, takes his seat with a proud reliance on his books and gown, on his dirt and dust. On one side of his judgement-table lies the *Sum,* on the other the *Directory.* Beyond these he never goes: at all else he only smiles. On such a man as he there is no imposing: he is not the man to utter anent astrology or alchemy nonsense not so foolish but that others might be led thereby to observe truly. And yet Sprenger is a freethinker: he is sceptical about old receipts! Albert the Great may aver, that some sage in a spring of water will suffice to raise a storm, but Sprenger only shakes his head. Sage indeed! Tell that to others, I beg. For all my little experience, I see herein the craft of One who would put us on the wrong scent, that cunning Prince of the Air; but he will fare ill, for he has to deal with a doctor more subtle than the Subtle One himself.

I should have liked to see face to face this wonderful specimen of a judge, and the people who were brought before him. The creatures that God might bring together from two different worlds would not be more unlike, more strange to each other, more utterly wanting in a common language. The old hag, a skeleton in tatters, with an eye flashing forth evil things, a being thrice cooked in hell-fire; and the ill-looking hermit shepherd of the Black Forest or the upper Alpine wastes such are the savages offered to the leaden gaze of a scholarling, to the judgement of a schoolman.

Not long will they let him toil in his judgment-seat. They will tell all without being tortured. Come the torture will indeed, but afterwards, by way of complement and crown to the law-procedure. They explain and relate to order whatever they have done. The Devil is the Witch's bedfellow, the shepherd's intimate friend. She, for her part, smiles triumphantly, feels a manifest joy in the horror of those around.

Truly, the old woman is very mad, and equally so the shepherd. Are they foolish? Not at all, but far otherwise. They are refined, subtle, skilled in growing herbs, and seeing through walls. Still more clearly do they see those monumental ass's ears that overshadow the doctor's cap. Clearest of all is the fear he has of them, for in vain does he try to bear him boldly; he does nought but tremble. He himself owns that, if the priest who adjures the demon does not take care, the Devil will change his lodging only to pass into the priest himself, feeling all the more proud of dwelling in a body dedicated to God. Who knows but these simple Devils of Witches and shepherds might even aspire to inhabit an inquisitor? He is far from easy in mind when in his loudest voice he says to the old woman, "If your master is so mighty, why do I not feel his blows?"

"And, indeed I felt them but too strongly," says the poor man in his book. "When I was in Ratisbon, how often he would come knocking at my window-panes! How often he stuck pins in my cap! A hundred visions too did I have of dogs, monkeys," &c.

The dearest delight of that great logician, the Devil, is, by the mouth of the seeming old woman, to push the doctor with awkward arguments, with crafty questions, from which he can only escape by acting like the fish who saves himself by troubling the water and turning it black as ink. For instance, "The Devil does no more than God allows him: why, then, punish his tools?"

Or again, "We are not free. As in the case of Job, the Devil is allowed by God to tempt and beset us, to urge us on by blows. Should we, then, punish him who is not free?" Sprenger gets out of that by saying, "We are free beings." Here come plenty of texts. "You are made serfs only by covenant with the Evil One." The answer to this would be but too ready: "If God allows the Evil One to tempt us into making covenants, he renders covenants possible," &c.

"I am very good," says he, "to listen to yonder folk. He is a fool who argues with the Devil." So say all the rest likewise. They all cheer the progress of the trial: all are strongly moved, and show in murmurs their eagerness for the execution. They have seen enough of men hanged. As for the Wizard and the Witch, 'twill be a curious treat to see those two faggots crackling merrily in the flames.

The judge has the people on his side, so he is not embarrassed. According to his *Directory* three witnesses would be enough. Are not three witnesses readily found, especially to witness a falsehood? In every slanderous town, in every envious village teeming with the mutual hate of neighbours, witnesses abound. Besides, the *Directory* is a superannuated book, a century old. In that century of light, the fifteenth, all is brought to perfection. If witnesses are wanting, we are content with the *public voice*, the general clamour. [6]

A genuine outcry, born of fear; the piteous cry of victims, of the poor bewitched. Sprenger is greatly moved thereat. Do not fancy him one of those unfeeling schoolmen, the lovers of a dry abstraction. He has a heart: for which very reason he is so ready to kill. He is compassionate, full of loving-kindness. He feels pity for yon weeping woman, but lately pregnant, whose babe the witch had smothered by a look. He feels pity for the poor man whose land she wasted with hail. He pities the husband, who though himself no wizard, clearly sees his wife to be a witch, and drags her with a rope round her neck before Sprenger, who has her burnt.

From a cruel judge escape was sometimes possible; but from our worthy Sprenger it was hopeless. His humanity is too strong: it needs great man-agement, a very large amount of ready wit, to avoid a burning at his hands. One day there was brought before him the plaint of three good ladies of Strasburg who, at one same hour of the same day, had been struck by an arm unseen. Ah, indeed! They are fain to accuse a man of evil aspect, of having laid them under a spell. On being brought before the inquisitor, the man vows and swears by all the saints that he knows nothing about these ladies, has never so much as seen them. The judge is hard of believing: nor tears nor oaths avail aught with him. His great compassion for the ladies made him inexorable, indignant at the man's denials. Already he was rising from his seat. The man would have been tortured into confessing his guilt, as the most innocent often did. He got leave to speak, and said: "I remember, indeed, hav-ing struck some one yesterday at the hour named; but whom? No Christian beings, but only three cats which came furiously biting at my legs." The judge, like a shrewd fellow, saw the whole truth of the matter; the poor man was innocent; the ladies were doubtless turned on certain days into cats, and the Evil One amused himself by sending them at the legs of Christian folk, in order to bring about the ruin of these latter by making them pass for wizards.

A judge of less ability would never have hit upon this. But such a man was not always to be had. It was needful to have always handy on the table of the Inquisition a good fool's guide, to reveal to simple and inexperienced judges the tricks of the Old Enemy, the best way of baffling him, the clever and deep-laid tactics employed with such happy effect by the great Sprenger in his campaigns on the Rhine. To that end the *Malleus,* which a man was required to carry in his pocket, was commonly printed in small 18mo, a form at that time scarce. It would not have been seemly for a judge in difficulties to open a folio on the table before his audience. But his handbook of folly he might easily squint at from the corner of his eye, or turn over its leaves as he held it under the table.

This *Malleus* (or Mallet), like all books of the same class, contains a singular avowal, namely, that the Devil is gaining ground; in other words, that God is losing it; that mankind, after being saved by Christ, is becoming the Devil's prey. Too clearly indeed does he step forward from legend to legend. What a way he has made between the time of the Gospels, when he was only too glad to get into the swine, and the days of Dante, when, as lawyer and divine, he argues with the saints, pleads his cause, and by way of closing a successful syllogism, bears away the soul he was fighting for, saying, with a triumphant laugh, "You didn't know that I was a logician!"

In the earlier days of the Middle Ages he waits till the last pangs to seize the soul and beat I it off. Saint Hildegarde, about 1100, thinks that "*he cannot enter the body of a living man*, for else his limbs would fly off in all directions: it is but the shadow and the smoke of the Devil which pass therein." That last gleam of good sense vanishes in the twelfth century. In the thirteenth we find a suppliant so afraid of being caught alive that he has himself watched day and night by two hundred armed men.

Then begins a period of increasing terror, in which men trust themselves less and ever less to God's protection. The Demon is no longer a stealthy sprite, no longer a thief by night, gliding through the gloom. He becomes the fearless adversary, the daring ape of Heaven, who in broad daylight mimics God's creation under God's own sun. Is it the legends tell us this? Nay, it is the greatest of the doctors. "The Devil," says Albert the Great, "transforms all living things." St. Thomas goes yet further. "All changes that may occur naturally by means of seeds, can be copied by the Devil." What an astounding concession, which coming from the mouth of so grave a personage, means nothing short of setting up one Creator face to face with another! "But in things done without the germinal process," he adds, "such as the changing of men into beasts or the resurrection of the dead, there the Devil can do nothing." Thus to God is left the smaller part of His work! He may only perform miracles, a kind of action alike singular and infrequent. But the daily miracle of life is not for Him alone: His copyist, the Devil, shares with Him the world of nature!

For man himself, whose weak eyes see no difference between nature as sprung from God and nature as made by the Devil, here is a world split in twain! A dreadful uncertainty hangs over everything. Nature's innocence is gone. The clear spring, the pale flower, the little bird, are these indeed of God, or only treacherous counterfeits, snares laid out for man? Back! all things look doubtful! The better of the two creations, being suspiciously like the other, becomes eclipsed and conquered. The shadow of the Devil covers up the day, spreads over all life. To judge by appearances and the fears of men, he has ceased to share the world; he has taken it all to himself.

So matters stand in the days of Sprenger. His book teems with saddest avowals of God's weakness. "These things," he says, "are done with God's leave." To permit an illusion so entire, to let people believe that God is nought and the Devil everything, is more than mere *permission*; is tantamount to decreeing the damnation of countless souls whom nothing can save from such an error. No prayers, no penances, no pilgrimages, are of any avail; nor even, so it is said, the sacrament of the altar. Strange and mortifying avowal! The very nuns who have just confessed themselves, declare *while the host is yet in their mouths,* that even then they feel the infernal lover troubling them without fear or shame, troubling and refusing to leave his hold. And being pressed with further questions, they add, through their tears, that he has a body *because he has a soul.*

The Manichees of old, and the more modern Albigenses, were charged with believing in the Power of Evil struggling side by side with Good, with making the Devil equal to God. Here, however, he is more than equal; for if God through His holy sacrament has still no power for good, the Devil certainly seems superior.

I am not surprised at the wondrous sight then offered by the world. Spain with a darksome fury, Germany with the frightened pedantic rage certified in the *Malleus,* assail the insolent conqueror through the wretches in whom he chooses to dwell. They burn, they destroy the dwellings in which he has taken up his abode. Finding him too strong for men's souls, they try to hunt him out of their bodies. But what is the good of it all? You burn one old woman and he settles himself in her neighbour. Nay, more; if Sprenger may be trusted, he fastens sometimes on the exorcising priest, and triumphs over his very judge.

Among other expedients, the Dominicans advised recourse to the intercession of the Virgin, by a continual repeating of the *Ave Maria*. Sprenger, for his part, always averred that such a remedy was but a momentary one. You might be caught between two prayers. Hence came the invention of the rosary, the chaplet of beads, by means of which any number of aves might be mumbled through, whilst the mind was busied elsewhere. "Whole populations adopted this first essay of an art thereafter to be used by Loyola in his attempt to govern the world, an art of which his *Exercises* furnish the ingenious groundwork.

All this seems opposed to what was said in the foregoing chapter as to the decline of Witchcraft. The Devil is now popular and everywhere present. He seems to have come off conqueror: but has he gained by his victory? What substantial profit has he reaped therefrom?

Much, as beheld in his new phase of a scientific rebellion which is about to bring forth the bright Renaissance. None, if beheld under his old aspect, as the gloomy Spirit of Witchcraft. The stories told of him in the sixteenth century, if more numerous, more widespread than ever, readily swing towards the grotesque. People tremble, but they laugh withal. [7]

[1] Officer charged with the absolution of penitents. TRANS.
[2] A mediaeval text-book on theology. TRANS.
[3] "Thinking ill of the faith." TRANS.
[4] A character in Rabelais. "Date nobis clochas nostras, &c." - *Gargantua,* ch. 19. - TRANS.
[5] Ulrich von Hutten, friend of Luther, and author of the witty *Epistolae obscurorum virorum.* - TRANS.
[6] Faustin Hélie, in his learned and luminous *Traité de l'Instruction Criminelle* (vol. i. p. 398), has clearly explained the manner in which Pope Innocent III., about 1200, suppressed the safeguards theretofore required in any prosecution, especially the risk incurred by prosecutors of being punished for slander. Instead of these were established the dismal processes of *Denunciation and Inquisition.* The frightful levity of these latter methods is shown by Soldan. Blood was shed like water.
[7] See my *Memoirs of Luther,* concerning the Kilcrops, &c.

Chapter Three - Century of Toleration in France: Reaction

THE Church forfeited the wizard's property to the judge and the prosecutor. Wherever the Canon Law was enforced the trials for witchcraft waxed numerous, and brought much wealth to the clergy. Wherever the lay tribunals claimed the management of these trials they grew scarce and disappeared, at least for a hundred years in France, from 1450 to 1550.

The first gleam of light shot forth from France in the middle of the fifteenth century. The inquiry made by Parliament into the trial of Joan of Arc, and her after reinstalment, set people thinking on the intercourse of spirits, good and bad; on the errors, also, of the spiritual courts. She whom the English, whom the greatest doctors of the Council of Basil pronounced a Witch, appeared to Frenchmen a saint and sibyl. Her reinstalment proclaimed to France the beginning of an age of toleration. The Parliament of Paris likewise reinstalled the alleged Waldenses of Arras. In 1498 it discharged as mad one who was brought before it as a wizard. None such were condemned in the reigns of Charles VIII., Louis XII., and Francis I.

On the contrary, Spain, under the pious Isabella (1506) and the Cardinal Ximenes, began burning witches. In 1515, Geneva, being then under a Bishop, burned five hundred in three months. The Emperor Charles V., in his German Constitutions, vainly sought to rule, that "Witchcraft, as causing damage to goods and persons, is a question for *civil*, not ecclesiastic law." In vain did he do away the right of confiscation, except in cases of treason. The small prince-bishops, whose revenues were largely swelled by trials for witchcraft, kept on burning at a furious rate. In one moment, as it were, six hundred persons were burnt in the infinitesimal bishopric of Bamberg, and nine hundred in that of Wurtzburg. The way of going to work was very simple. Begin by using torture against the witnesses; create witnesses for the prosecution by means of pain and terror; then, by dint of excessive kindliness, draw from the accused a certain avowal, and believe that avowal in the teeth of proven facts. A witch, for instance, owns to having taken from the graveyard the body of an infant lately dead, that she might use it in her magical compounds. Her husband bids them go the graveyard, for the child is there still. On being disinterred, the child is found all right in his coffin. But against the witness of his own eyes the judge pronounces it *an appearance*, a cheat of the Devil. He prefers the wife's confession to the fact itself; and she is burnt forthwith. [1]

So far did matters go among these worthy prince bishops, that after a while, Ferdinand II., the most bigoted of all emperors, the emperor of the Thirty Years' War, was fain to interfere, to set up at Bamberg an imperial commissary, who should maintain the law of the empire, and see that the episcopal judge did not begin the trial with tortures which settled it beforehand, which led straight to the stake.

Witches were easily caught by their confessions, sometimes without the torture. Many of them were half mad. They would own to turning themselves into beasts. The Italian women often became cats, and gliding under the doors, sucked, they said, the blood of children. In the land of mighty forests, in Lorraine and on the Jura, the women, of their own accord, became wolves, and, if you could believe them, devoured the passers-by, even when nobody had passed by. They were burnt. Some girls, who swore they had given themselves to the Devil, were found to be maidens still. They, too, were burnt. Several seemed in a great hurry, as if they wanted to be burnt. Sometimes it happened from raging madness, sometimes from despair. An Englishwoman being led to the stake, said to the people, "Do not blame my judges. I wanted to put an end to my own self. My parents kept aloof from me in their dread. My husband had disowned me. I could not have lived on without disgrace. I longed for death, and so I told a lie."

The first words of open toleration against silly Sprenger, his frightful Handbook, and his Inquisitors, were spoken by Molitor, a lawyer of Constance. He made this sensible remark, that the confessions of witches should not be taken seriously, because it was the very Father of Lies who spoke by their mouths. He laughed at the miracles of Satan, affirming them to be all illusory. In an indirect way, such jesters as Hutten and Erasmus dealt violent blows at the Inquisition, through their satires on the Dominican idiots. Cardan [2] said, straightforwardly, "In order to obtain forfeit property, the same persons acted as accusers and judges, and invented a thousand stories in proof."

That apostle of toleration, Chatillon, who maintained against Catholics and Protestants both, that heretics should not be burnt, though he said nothing about wizards, put men of sense in a better way. Agrippa, [3] Lavatier, above all, Wyer, [4] the illustrious physician of Cleves, rightly said that if those wretched witches were the Devil's plaything, we must lay the blame on the Devil, not on them; must cure, instead of burning them. Some physicians of Paris soon pushed incredulity so far as to maintain that the possessed and the witches were simply knaves. This was going too far. Most of them were sufferers under the sway of an illusion.

The dark reign of Henry II. and Diana of Poitiers ends the season of toleration. Under Diana, they burn heretics and wizards again. On the other hand, Catherine of Medici, surrounded as she was by astrologers and magicians, would have protected the latter. Their numbers increased amain. The wizard Trois-Echelles, who was tried in the reign of Charles IX., reckons them at a hundred thousand, declaring all France to be one Witch.

Agrippa and others affirm, that all science is contained in magic. In white magic undoubtedly. But the fears of fools and their fanatic rage, put little difference between them. In spite of Wyer, in spite of those true philosophers, Light and Toleration, a strong reaction towards darkness set in from a quarter whence it was least expected. Our magistrates, who for nearly a century, had shown themselves enlightened and fair-dealing, now threw themselves into the Spanish Catholicon [5] and the fury of the Leaguists, [6] until they waxed more priest-like than the priests themselves. While scouting the Inquisition from France, they matched, and well-nigh eclipsed it by their own deeds: the Parliament of Toulouse alone sending four hundred human bodies at one time to the stake. Think of the horror, the black smoke of all that flesh, of the frightful melting and bubbling of the fat amidst those piercing shrieks and yells! So accursed, so sickening a sight had not been seen, since the Albigenses were broiled and roasted.

But this is all too little for Bodin, lawyer of Angers, and a violent adversary to Wyer. He begins by saying that the wizards in Europe are numerous enough to match Xerxes' army of eighteen hundred thousand men. Then, like Caligula, he utters a prayer, that these two millions might be gathered together, so as he, Bodin, could sentence and burn them all at one stroke.

The new rivalry makes matters worse. The gentry of the Law begin to say that the priest, being too often connected with the wizard, is no longer a safe judge. In fact, for a moment, the lawyers seem to be yet more trustworthy. In Spain, the Jesuit pleader, Del Rio; in Lorraine, Remy (1596); Boguet (1602) on the Jura; Leloyer (1605) in Anjou; are all matchless persecutors, who would have made Torquemada [7] himself die of envy.

In Lorraine there seemed to be quite a dreadful plague of wizards and visionaries. Driven to despair by the constant passing of troops and brigands, the multitude prayed to the Devil only. They were drawn on by the wizards. A number of villagers, frightened by a twofold dread of wizards on the one hand, and judges on the other, longed to leave their homes and nee elsewhither, if Remy, Judge of Nancy, may be believed. In the work he dedicated (1596) to the Cardinal of Lorraine, he owns to having burnt eight hundred witches, in sixteen years. "So well do I deal out judgements," he says, "that last year sixteen slew themselves to avoid passing through my hands."

The priests felt humbled. Could they have done better than the laity? Nay, even the monkish lords of Saint Claude asked for a layman, honest Boguet, to sit in judgment on their own people, who were much given to witchcraft. In that sorry Jura, a poor land of firs and scanty pasturage, the serf in his despair yielded himself to the Devil. They all worshipped the Black Cat.

Boguet's book had immense weight. This Golden Book, by the petty judge of Saint Claude, was studied as a handbook by the worshipful members of Parliament. In truth, Boguet is a thorough lawyer, is even scrupulous in his own way. He finds fault with the treachery shown in these prosecutions; will not hear of barristers betraying their clients, of judges promising pardon only to ensure the death of the accused. He finds fault with the very doubtful tests to which the witches were still exposed. "Torture," he says, "is needless: it never makes them yield." Moreover, he is humane enough to have them strangled before throwing them to the flames, always except the werewolves, "whom you must take care to burn alive." He cannot believe that Satan would make a compact with children: "Satan is too sharp; knows too well that, under fourteen years, any bargain made with a minor, is annulled by default of years and due discretion." Then the children are saved? Not at all; for he contradicts himself, and holds, moreover, that such a leprosy cannot be purged away without burning everything, even to the cradles. Had he lived, he would have come to that. He made the country a desert: never was there a judge who destroyed people with so fine a conscience.

But it is to the Parliament of Bourdeaux that the grand hurrah for lay jurisdiction is sent up in Lancre's book on *The Fickleness of Demons.* The author, a man of some sense, a counsellor in this same Parliament, tells with a triumphant air of his fight with the Devil in the Basque country, where, in less than three months, he got rid of I know not how many witches, and, better still, of three priests. He looks compassionately on the Spanish Inquisition, which at Logrofio, not far off, on the borders of Navarre and Castille, dragged on a trial for two years, ending in the poorest way by a small *auto-da-fé,* and the release of a whole crowd of women.

[1] For this and other facts regarding Germany, see Soldan.
[2] A famous Italian physician, who lived through the greater part of the sixteenth century. -TRANS.
[3] Cornelius Agrippa, of Cologne, born in 1486, sometime Secretary of the Emperor Maximilian, and author of two works famous in their day, *Vanity of the Sciences*, and *Occult Philosophy.* - TRANS.
[4] A friend of Sir Philip Sydney, who seat for him when dying. - TRANS.
[5] Catholicon, or purgative panacea: *i.e.* the Inquisition. TRANS.
[6] The wars of the Catholic League against Henry of Navarre began in 1576. - TRANS.
[7] The infamous Spanish Inquisitor, who died at the close of the fifteenth century, after sixteen years of untold atrocities against the heretics of Spain. TRANS.

Chapter Four - The "Witches of the Basque Country: 1609

[1]

THAT strong-handed execution of the priests shows M. Lancre to have been a man of independent spirit. In politics he is the same. In his book on *The Prince* (1617), he openly declares "the law to be above the King."

Never was the Basque character better drawn than in his book on *The Fickleness of Demons.* In France, as in Spain, the Basque people had privileges which almost made them a republic. On our side they owed the King no service but that of arms: at the first beat of drum they were bound to gather two thousand armed men commanded by Basque captains. They were not oppressed by their clergy, who seldom prosecuted wizards, being wizards themselves. The priests danced, wore swords, and took their mistresses to the Witches' Sabbath. These mistresses acted as their sextonesses or *bénédictes,* to keep the churches in order. The parson quarrelled with nobody, offered the White Mass to God by day, the Black by night to the Devil, and sometimes, according to Lancre, in the same church.

The Basques of Bayonne and St. Jean de Luz, a race of men quaint, venturesome, and fabulously bold, left many widows, from their habit of sailing out into the roughest seas to harpoon whales. Leaving their wives to God or the Devil, they threw themselves in crowds into the Canadian settlements of Henry IV. As for the children, these honest worthy sailors would have thought about them more, if they had been clear as to their parentage. But on their return home they would reckon up the months of their absence, and they never found the reckoning right.

The women, bold, beautiful, imaginative, spent their day seated on tombs in the grave-yards, talking of the Sabbath, whither they expected to go in the evening. This was their passion, their craze.

They are born witches, daughters of the sea and of enchantment. They sport among the billows, swimming like fish. Their natural master is the Prince of the Air, King of Winds and Dreams, the same who inspired the Sibyl and breathed to her the future.

The judge who burns them is charmed with them, nevertheless. "When you see them pass" says he, "their hair flowing in the breeze about their shoulders, they walk so trim, so bravely armed in that fair head-dress, that the sun playing through it as through a cloud, causes a mighty blaze which shoots forth hot lightning-flashes. Hence the fascination of their eyes, as dangerous in love as in witchcraft."

This amiable Bordeaux magistrate, the earliest sample of those worldly judges who enlivened the gown in the seventeenth century, plays the lute between whiles, and even makes the witches dance before sending them to the stake. And he writes well, far more clearly than anyone else. But for all that, one discovers in his work a new source of obscurity, inherent to those times. The witches being too numerous for the judge to burn them all, the most of them have a shrewd idea that he will show some indulgence to those who enter deepest into his thoughts and passions! What passions? you ask. First, his love of the frightfully marvellous, a passion common enough; the delight of feeling afraid; and also, if it must be said, the enjoyment of unseemly pleasures. Add to these a touch of vanity: the more dreadful and enraged those clever women show the Devil to be, the greater the pride taken by the judge in subduing so mighty an adversary. He arrays himself as it were in his victory, enthrones himself in his foolishness, triumphs in his senseless twaddling.

The prettiest thing of this kind is the report of the procedure in the Spanish *auto-da-fé* of Logroño, as furnished to us by Llorente. Lancre, while quoting him jealously and longing to disparage him, owns to the surpassing charm of the festival, the splendour of the sight, the moving power of the music. On one platform were the few condemned to the flames, on another a crowd of reprieved criminals. The confession of a repentant heroine who had dared all things, is read aloud. Nothing could be wilder. At the Sabbaths they ate children made into hash, and by way of second course, the bodies of wizards disentombed. Toads dance, and talk and complain lovingly of their mistresses, getting them scolded by the Devil. The latter politely escorts the witches home, lighting them with the arm of a child who died unchristened, &c.

Among our Basques witchcraft put on a less fantastic guise. It seems that at this time the Sabbath was only a grand feast to which all, the nobles included, went for purposes of amusement. In the foremost line would be seen persons in veils and masks, by some supposed to be princes. "Once on a time," says Lancre, "none but idiots of the Landes appeared there: now people of quality are seen to go." To entertain these local grandees, Satan sometimes created a *Bishop of the Sabbath*. Such was the title he gave the young lord Lancinena, with whom the Devil in person was good enough to open the ball.

So well supported, the witches held their sway, wielding over the land an amazing terrorism of the fancy. Numbers regarded themselves as victims, and became in fact seriously ill. Many were stricken with epilepsy, and barked like dogs. In one small town of Acqs were counted as many as forty of these barkers. The Witch had so fearful a hold upon them, that one lady being called as witness, began barking with uncontrollable fury as the Witch, unawares to herself, drew near.

Those to whom was ascribed so terrible a power lorded it everywhere. No one would dare shut his door against them. One magistrate, the criminal assessor of Bayonne, allowed the Sabbath to be held in his own house. Urtubi, Lord of Saint Pé, was forced to hold the festival in his castle. But his head was shaken to that degree, that he imagined a witch was sucking his blood. Emboldened, however, by his fear, he, with another gentleman, repaired to Bordeaux, and persuaded the Parliament to obtain from the King the commissioning of two of its members, Espagnet and Lancre, to try the wizards in the Basque country. This commission, absolute and without appeal, worked with unheard-of vigour; in four months, from May to August, 1609, condemned sixty or eighty witches, and examined five hundred more, who, though equally marked with the sign of the Devil, figured in the proceedings as witnesses only.

It was no safe matter for two men and a few soldiers to carry on these trials amongst a violent, hotheaded people, a multitude of wild and daring sailors' wives. Another source of danger was in the priests, many of whom were wizards, needing to be tried by the lay commissioners, despite the lively opposition of the clergy.

When the judges appeared, many persons saved themselves in the hills. Others boldly remained, saying, it was the judges who would he burnt. So little fear had the witches themselves, that before the audience they would sink into the Sabbatic slumber, and affirm on awaking that, even in court, they had enjoyed the blessedness of Satan. Many said, they only suffered from not being able to prove to him how much they burned to suffer for his sake.

Those who were questioned said they could not speak. Satan rising into their throats blocked up their gullets. Lancre, who wrote this narrative, though the younger of the commissioners, was a man of the world. The witches guessed that, with a man of his sort, there were means of saving themselves. The league between them was broken. A beggar-girl of seventeen, La Murgui, or Margaret, who had found witchcraft gainful, and, while herself almost a child, had brought away children as offerings to the Devil, now betook herself, with another girl, Lisalda, of the same age, to denouncing all the rest. By word of mouth or in writing she revealed all; with the liveliness, the noise, the emphatic gestures of a Spaniard, entering truly or falsely into a hundred impure details. She frightened, amused, wheedled her judges, drawing them after her like fools. To this corrupt, wanton, crazy girl, they entrusted the right of searching about the bodies of girls and boys, for the spot whereon Satan had set his mark. This spot discovered itself by a certain numbness, by the fact that you might stick needles into it without causing pain. While a surgeon thus tormented the elder ones, she took in hand the young, who, though called as witnesses, might themselves be accused, if she pronounced them to bear the mark. It was a hateful thing to see this brazen-faced girl made sole mistress of the fate of those wretched beings, commissioned to prod them all over with needles, and able at will to assign those bleeding bodies to death!

She had gotten so mighty a sway over Lancre, as to persuade him that, while he was sleeping in Saint Pe, in his own house, guarded by his servants and his escort, the Devil came by night into his room, to say the Black Mass; while the witches getting inside his very curtains, would have poisoned him, had he not been well protected by God Himself. The Black Mass was offered by the Lady of Lancinena, to whom Satan made love in the very bedroom of the judge. We can guess the likely aim of this wretched tale: the beggar bore a grudge against the lady, who was good-looking, and, but for this slander, might have come to bear sway over the honest commissioner.

Lancre and his colleague taking fright, went forward; never dared to draw back. They had their royal gallows set up on the very spots where Satan had held a Sabbath. People were alarmed thereat, deeming them strongly backed by the arm of royalty. Impeachments hailed about them. The women all came in one Ions: string to accuse each other. Children were brought forward to impeach their mothers. Lancre gravely ruled that a child of eight was a good, sufficient, reputable witness!

M. d'Espagnet could give but a few moments to this matter, having speedily to show himself in the Estates of Beam. Lancre being pushed unwittingly forward by the violence of the younger informers, who would have fallen into great danger, if they had failed to get the old ones burnt, threw the reins on the neck of the business, and hurried it on at full gallop. A due amount of witches were condemned to the stake. These, too, on finding themselves lost, ended by impeaching others. When the first batch were brought to the stake, a frightful scene took place. Executioner, constables, and sergeants, all thought their last hour was come. The crowd fell savagely upon the carts, seeking to force the wretches to withdraw their accusations. The men put daggers to their throats: their furious companions were like to finish them with their nails.

Justice, however, got out of the scrape with some credit; and then the commissioners went on to the harder work of sentencing eight priests whom they had taken up. The girls' confessions had brought these men to light. Lancre speaks of their morals like one who knew all about them of himself. He rebukes them, not only for their gay proceedings on Sabbath nights, but, most of all, for their sextonesses and female churchwardens. He even repeats certain tales about the priests having sent off the husbands to Newfoundland, and brought back Devils from Japan who gave up the wives into their hands.

The clergy were deeply stirred: the Bishop of Bayonne would have made resistance. His courage failing him, he appointed his vicar-general to act as judge-assistant in his own absence. Luckily the Devil gave the accused more help than their Bishop. He opened all the doors, so that one morning five of the eight were found missing. The commissioners lost no time in burning the three still left to them.

This happened about August, 1609. The Spanish inquisitors at Logrolio did not crown their proceedings with an *auto-da-fé*, before the 8th November, 1610. They had met with far more trouble than our own countrymen, owing to the frightful number of persons accused. How burn a whole people? They sought advice of the Pope, of the greatest doctors in Spain. The word was given to draw back. Only the wilful who persisted in denying their guilt, were to be burnt; while they who pleaded guilty should be let go. The same method had already been used to rescue priests in trials for loose living. According to Llorente, it was deemed sufficient, if they owned their crime, and went through a slight penance.

The Inquisition, so deadly to heretics, so cruel to Moors and Jews, was much less so to wizards. These, being mostly shepherds, had no quarrel with the Church. The rejoicings of goatherds were too low, if not too brutish, to disturb the enemies of free thought.

Lancre wrote his book mainly to show how much the justice of French Parliaments and laymen excelled the justice of the priests. It is written lightly, merrily, with flowing pen. It seems to express the joy felt by one who has come creditably out of a great risk. It is a gasconading, an over-boastful joy. He tells with pride how, the Sabbath following the first execution of the witches, their children went and wailed to Satan, who replied that their mothers had not been burnt, but were alive and happy. From the midst of the crowd the children thought they heard their mothers' voices saying how thoroughly blest they were. Satan was frightened nevertheless. He absented himself for four Sabbaths, sending a small commonplace devil in his stead. He did not show himself again till the 22nd July. When the wizards asked him the reason of his absence, he said, "I have been away, pleading your cause against *Little John*," the name by which he called Jesus. "I have won the suit, and they who are still in prison will not be burnt."

The lie was given to the great liar. And the conquering magistrate avers that, while the last witch was burning, they saw a swarm of toads come out of her head. The people fell on them with stones, so that she was rather stoned

102

than burnt. But for all their attacks, they could not put an end to one black toad which escaped from flames, sticks, and stones, to hide, like the Devil's imp it was, in some spot where it could never be found. [2]

[1] The Basques of the Lower Pyrenees, the Aquitani of Caesar, belonged to the old Iberian race which peopled Western Europe before the Celtic era. - TRANS.
[2] For a more detailed account of these Basque Witches, the English reader may turn to Wright's *Narratives of Sorcery and Magic*. Bentley, 1851. - TRANS.

Chapter Five - Satan Turns Priest

WHATEVER semblance of Satanic fanaticism was still preserved by the witches, it transpires from the narratives of Lancre and other writers of the seventeenth century, that the Sabbath then was mainly an affair of money. They raised contributions almost by force, charged something for right of entrance, and extracted fines from those who stayed away. At Brussels and in Picardy, they had a fixed scale of payment for rewarding those who brought new members into the brotherhood.

In the Basque country no mystery was kept up. The gatherings there would amount to twelve thousand persons, of all classes, rich or poor, priests and gentlemen. Satan, himself a gentleman, wore a hat upon his three horns, like a man of quality. Finding his old seat, the druidic stone, too hard for him, he treats himself to an easy well-gilt arm-chair. Shall we say he is growing old? More nimble now than when he was young, he frolics about, cuts capers, and leaps from the bottom of a large pitcher. He goes through the service head downwards, his feet in the air.

He likes everything to go off quite respectably, and spares no cost in his scenic arrangements. Besides the customary flames, red, yellow, and blue, which entertain the eye, as they show forth or hide the flickering shadows, he charms the ear with strange music, mainly of little bells that tickle the nerves with something like the searching vibrations of musical-glasses. To crown this splendour Satan bids them bring out his silver plate. Even his toads give themselves airs, become fashionable, and, like so many lordlings, go about in green velvet.

The general effect is that of a large fair, of a great masked ball with very transparent disguises. Satan, who understands his epoch, opens the ball with the Bishop of the Sabbath, or the King and Queen: offices devised in compliment to the great personages, wealthy or well-born, who honour the meeting by their presence.

Here may be seen no longer the gloomy feast of rebels, the baleful orgie of serfs and boors, sharing by night the sacrament of love, by day the sacrament of death. The violent Sabbath-round is no more the one only dance of the evening. Thereto are now added the Moorish dances, lively or languishing, but always amorous and obscene, in which girls dressed up for the purpose, like *La Murgui* or *La Lisalda,* feigned and showed off the most provoking characters. Among the Basques these dances formed, we are told, the invincible charm which sent the whole world of women, wives, daughters, widows the last in great numbers headlong into the Sabbath.

Without such amusements and the accompanying banquet, one could hardly understand this general rage for these Sabbaths. It is a kind of love without love; a feast of barrenness undisguised. Boguet has settled that point to a nicety. Differing in one passage, where he dismisses the women as afraid of coming to harm, Lancre is generally at one with Boguet, besides being more sincere. The cruel and foul researches he pursues on the very bodies of witches, show clearly that he deemed them barren, and that a barren passive love underlay the Sabbath itself.

The feast ought therefore to have been a dismal one, if the men had owned the smallest heart.

The silly girls who went to dance and eat were victims in every way. But they were resigned to everything save the prospect of bearing children. They bore indeed a far heavier load of wretchedness than the men. Sprenger tells of the strange cry, which even in his day burst forth in the hour of love, "May the Devil have the fruits!" In his day, moreover, people could live for two *sous* a day, while in the reign of Henry IV., about 1600, they could barely live for twenty. Through all that century the desire, the need for barrenness grew more and more.

Under this growing dread of love's allurements the Sabbath would have become quite dull and wearisome, had not the conductresses cleverly made the most of its comic side, enlivening it with farcical interludes. Thus, the opening scene in which Satan, like the Priapus of olden times, bestowed his coarse endearments on the Witch, was followed by another game, a kind of chilly purification, which the sorceress underwent with much grimacing, and a great show of unpleasant shuddering. Then came another swinish farce, described by Lancre and Boguet, in which some young and pretty wife would take the Witch's place as Queen of the Sabbath, and submit her body to the vilest handling. A farce not less repulsive was the "Black Sacrament," performed with a black radish, which Satan would cut into little pieces and gravely swallow.

The last act of all, according to Lancre, or at least according to the two bold hussies who made him their fool, was an astounding event to happen in such crowded meetings. Since witchcraft had become hereditary in whole families, there was no further need of openly divulging the old incestuous ways of producing witches, by the intercourse of a mother with her son. Some sort of comedy perhaps was made out of the old materials, in the shape of a grotesque Semiramis or an imbecile Ninus. But the more serious game, which doubtless really took place, attests the existence of great profligacy in the upper walks of society: it took the form of a most hateful and barbarous hoax.

Some rash husband would be tempted to the spot, so fuddled with a baleful draught of datura or belladonna, that, like one entranced, he came to lose all power of speech and motion, retaining only his sight. His wife, on the other hand, being so bewitched with erotic drinks as to lose all sense of what she was doing, would appear in a woeful state of nature, letting herself be caressed under the indignant eyes of one who could no longer help himself 'in the least. His manifest despair, his bootless efforts to unshackle his tongue, and set free his powerless limbs, his dumb rage and wildly rolling eyes, inspired beholders with a cruel joy, like that produced by some of Molière's comedies. The poor woman, stung with a real delight, yielded herself up to the most shameful usage, of which on the morrow neither herself nor her husband would have the least remembrance. But those who had seen or shared in the cruel farce, would they, too, fail to remember?

In such heinous outrages an aristocratic element seems traceable. In no way do they remind us of the old brotherhood of serfs, of the original Sabbath, which, though ungodly, and foul enough, was still a free straightforward matter, in which all was done readily and without constraint.

Clearly, Satan, depraved as he was from all time, goes on spoiling more and more. A polite, a crafty Satan is he now become, sweetly insipid, but all the more faithless and unclean. It is a new, a strange thing to see at the Sabbaths, his fellowship with priests. Who is yon parson coming along with his *Benédicté,* his sextoness, he who jobs the things of the Church, saying the White Mass of mornings, the Black at night? "Satan," says Lancre, "persuades him to make love to his daughters in the spirit, to debauch his fair penitents." Innocent magistrate! He pretends to be unaware that for a century back the Devil had been working away at the Church livings, like one who knew his business! He had made himself father-confessor; or, if you would rather have it so, the father-confessor had turned Devil.

The worthy M. de Laucre should have remembered the trials that began in 1491, and helped perchance to bring the Parliament of Paris into a tolerant frame of mind. It gave up burning Satan, for it saw nothing of him but a mask.

A good many nuns were conquered by his new device of borrowing the form of some favourite confessor. Among them was Jane Pothierre, a holy woman of Quesnoy, of the ripe age of forty-five, but still, alas! all too impressible. She owns her passion to her ghostly counsellor, who loth to listen to her, flies to Falempin, some leagues off. The Devil, who never sleeps, saw his advantage, and perceiving her, says the annalist, "goaded by the thorns of Venus, he slily took the shape of the aforesaid 'Father,' and returning every night to the convent, was so successful in befooling her, that she owned to having received him 434 times." [1] Great pity was felt for her on her repenting; and she was speedily saved from all need of blushing, being put into a fine walled-tomb built foe her in the Castle of Selles, where a few days after she died the death of a good Catholic. Is it not a deeply moving tale? But this is nothing to that fine business of Gauffridi, which happened at Marseilles while Lancre was drawing up deeds at Bayonne.

The Parliament of Provence had no need to envy the success attained by that of Bordeaux. The lay authorities caught at the first occasion of a trial for witchcraft to institute a reform in the morals of the clergy. They sent forth a stern glance towards the close-shut convent-world. A rare opportunity was offered by the strange concurrence of many causes, by the fierce jealousies, the revengeful longings which severed priest from priest. But for those mad passions which ere long began to burst forth at every moment, 'we should have gained no insight into the real lot of that great world of women who died in those gloomy dwellings; not one word should we have heard of the things that passed behind those parlour gratings, within those mighty walls which only the confessor could overleap.

The example of the Basque priest, whom Lancre presents to us as worldly, trifling, going with his sword upon him, and his deaconess by his side, to dance all night at the Sabbath, was not one to inspire fear. It was not such as he whom the Inquisition took such pains to screen, or towards whom a body so stern for others, proved itself, for once, indulgent. It is easy to see through all Lancre's reticences the existence of *something else*. And the States-General of 1614, affirming that priests should not be tried by priests, are also thinking of *something else*. This very mystery it is which gets torn in twain by the Parliament of Provence. The director of nuns gaining the mastery over them and disposing of them, body and soul, by means of witchcraft, such is the fact which comes forth from the trial of Gauffridi; at a later date from the dreadful occurrences at Loudun and Louviers; and also in the scenes described by Llorente, Ricci, and several more.

One common method was employed alike for reducing the scandal, for misleading the public, for hiding away the inner fact while it was busied with the outer aspects of it. On the trial of a priestly wizard, all was done to juggle away the priest by bringing out the wizard; to impute everything to the art of the magician, and put out of sight the natural fascination wielded by the master of a troop of women all abandoned to his charge.

But there was no way of hushing up the first affair. It had been noised abroad in all Provence, in a land of light, where the sun pierces without any disguise. The chief scene of it lay not only in Aix and Marseilles, but also in Sainte-Baume, the famous centre of pilgrimage for a crowd of curious people, who thronged from all parts of France to be present at a deadly duel between two bewitched nuns and their demons.

The Dominicans, who attacked the affair as inquisitors, committed themselves by the noise they made about it through their partiality for one of these nuns. For all the care Parliament presently took to hurry the conclusion, these monks were exceedingly anxious to excuse her and justify themselves. Hence the important work of the monk Michaëlis, a mixture of truth and fable; wherein he raises Gauffridi, the priest he had sent to the flames, into the Prince of Magicians, not only in France, but even in Spain, Germany,

England, Turkey, nay, in the whole inhabited earth.

Gauffridi seems to have been a talented, agreeable man. Born in the mountains of Provence, he had travelled much in the Low Countries and the East. He bore the highest character in Marseilles, where he served as priest in the Church of Acoules. His bishop made much of him: the most devout of the ladies preferred him for their confessor. He had a wondrous gift, they say, of endearing himself to all. Nevertheless, he might have preserved his fair reputation had not a noble lady of Provence, whom he had already debauched, carried her blind, doting fondness to the extent of entrusting him, perhaps for her religious training, with the care of a charming child of twelve, Madeline de la Palud, a girl of fair complexion and gentle nature. Thereon, Gauffridi lost his wits, and respected neither the youth nor the holy ignorance, the utter unreserve of his pupil.

As she grew older, however, the young highborn girl discovered her misfortune, in loving thus beneath her, without hope of marriage. To keep his hold on her, Gauffridi vowed he would wed her before the Devil, if he might not wed her before God. He soothed her pride by declaring that he was the Prince of Magicians, and would make her his queen. He put on her finger a silver ring, engraved with magic characters. Did he take her to the Sabbath, or only make her believe she had been there, by confusing her with strange drinks and magnetic witcheries? Certain it is, at least, that torn by two different beliefs, full of uneasiness and fear, the girl thenceforth became mad at certain times, and fell into fits of epilepsy. She was afraid of being carried off alive by the Devil. She durst no longer stay in her father's house, and took shelter in the Ursuline Convent at Marseilles.

[1] Massée, *Chronique du Monde*, 1540; and the Chroniclers of Hainault, &c.

Chapter Six - Gauffridi: 1610

THE order of Ursuline nuns seemed to be the calmest, the least irrational of them all. They were not wholly idle, but found some little employment in the bringing up of young girls. The Catholic reaction which, aiming at a higher flight of ecstasy than was possible at that time even in Spain, had foolishly built a number of convents, Carmelite, Bernardine, and Capuchin, soon found itself at the end of its motive-powers. The girls of whom people got rid by shutting them up so strictly therein, died off immediately, and their swift decease led to frightful statements of the cruelty shown by their families. They perished, indeed, not by their excessive penances, but rather of heart-sickness and despair. After the first heats of zeal were over, the dreadful disease of the cloister, described by Cassieu as dating from the fifteenth century, that crushing, sickening sadness which came on of an afternoon that tender listlessness which plunged them into a state of unutterable exhaustion, speedily wore them away. A few among them would turn as if raging mad, choking, as it were, with the exceeding strength of their blood.

A nun who hoped to die decently, without bequeathing too large a share of remorse to her kindred, was bound to live on about ten years, the mean term of life in the cloister. She needed to be let gently down; and men of sense and experience felt that her days could only be prolonged by giving her something to do, by leaving her not quite alone. St. Francis of Sales [1] founded the Visitandine order, whose duty it was to visit the sick in pairs. Caesar of Bus and Romillion, who had established the Teaching Priests in connection with the Oratorians, [2] afterwards ordained what might be called the Teaching Sisters, the Ursulines, who taught under the direction of the said priests. The whole thing was under the supervision of the bishops, and had very little of the monastic about it: the nuns were not shut up again in cloisters. The Visitandines went out; the Ursulines received, at any rate, their pupils' kinsfolk. Both of them had connection with the world under guardians of good repute. The result was a certain mediocrity. Though the Oratorians and the Doctrinaries numbered among them persons of high merit, the general character of the order was uniformly moderate, commonplace; it took care never to soar too high. Romillion, founder of the Ursulines, was an oldish man, a convert from Protestantism, who had roamed everywhere, and come back again to his starting point. He deemed his young Provencials wise enough already, and counted on keeping his little flock on the slender pasturage of an Oratorian faith, at once monotonous and rational. And being such, it came in time to be utterly wearisome. One fine morning all had disappeared.

Gauffridi, the mountaineer of Provence, the travelled mystic, the man of strong feelings and restless mind, had quite another effect upon them, when he came thither as Madeline's ghostly guide. They felt a certain power, and by those who had already passed out of their wild, amorous youth, were doubtless assured that it was nothing less than a power begotten of the Devil. All were seized with fear, and more than one with love also. Their imaginations soared high; their heads began to turn. Already six or seven may be seen weeping, shrieking, yelling, fancying themselves caught by the Devil. Had the Ursulines lived in cloisters, within high walls, Gauffridi, being their only director, might one way or another have made them all agree. As in the cloisters of Quesnoy, in 1491, so here also it might have happened that the Devil, who gladly takes the form of one beloved, had under that of Gauffridi made himself lover-general to the nuns. Or rather, as in those Spanish cloisters named by Llorente, he would have persuaded them that the priestly office hallowed those to whom the priest made love, that to sin with him, was only to be sanctified. A notion, indeed, ripe through France, and even in Paris, where the mistresses of priests were called "the hallowed ones." [3]

Did Gauffridi, thus master of all, keep to Madeline only? Did not the lover change into the libertine? We know not. The sentence points to a nun who never showed herself during the trial, but reappeared at the end, as having given herself up to the Devil and to him.

The Ursuline convent was open to all visitors. The nuns were under the charge of their Doctrinaries, men of fair character, and jealous withal. The founder himself was there, indignant, desperate. How woeful a mishap for the rising order, just as it was thriving amain and spreading all over France! After all its pretensions to wisdom, calmness, good sense, thus suddenly to go mad! Romillion would have hushed up the matter if he could. He caused one of his priests to exorcise the maidens. But the demons laughed the exerciser to scorn. He who dwelt in the fair damsel, even the noble demon Beelzebub, Spirit of Pride, never deigned to unclose his teeth.

Among the possessed was one sister from twenty to twenty-five years old, who had been specially adopted by Romillion; a girl of good culture, bred up in controversy; a Protestant by birth, but left an orphan, to fall into the hands of the Father, a convert like herself from Protestantism. Her name, Louisa Capeau, sounds plebeian. She showed herself but too clearly a girl of exceeding wit, and of a raging passion. Her strength, moreover, was fearful to see. For three months, in addition to the hellish storm within, she carried on a desperate struggle, which would have killed the strongest man in a week.

She said she had three devils: Verrine, a good Catholic devil, a volatile spirit of the air; Leviathan, a wicked devil, an arguer and a Protestant; lastly, another, acknowledged by her to be the spirit of uncleanness. One other she forgot to name, the demon of jealousy.

She bore a savage hate to the little fair-faced damsel, the favoured rival, the proud young woman of rank. This latter, in one of her fits, had said that she went to the Sabbath, where she was made queen, and received homage, and gave herself up, but only to the prince "What prince?" To Louis Grauffridi, prince of magicians.

Pierced by this revelation as by a dagger, Louisa was too wild to doubt its truth. Mad herself, she believed the mad woman's story in order to ruin her. Her own devil was backed by all the jealous demons. The women all exclaimed that Gauffridi was the very king of wizards. The report spread everywhere, that a great prize had been taken, a priest-king of magicians, even the prince of universal magic. Such was the dreadful diadem of steel and flame which these feminine demons drove into his brow.

Everyone lost his head, even to old Romillion himself. Whether from hatred of Gauffridi, or fear of the Inquisition, he took the matter out of the bishop's hands, and brought his two bewitched ones, Louisa and Madeline, to the Convent of Sainte-Baume, whose prior was the Dominican Michaëlis, papal inquisitor in the Pope's domain of Avignon, and, as he himself pre. tended, over all Provence. The great point was to get them exorcised. But as the two women were obliged to accuse Gauffridi, the business ended in making him fall into the hands of the Inquisition.

Michaëlis had to preach on Advent Sunday at Aix, before the Parliament. He felt how much so striking a drama would exalt him. He grasped at it with all the eagerness of a barrister in a Criminal Court, when a very dramatic murder, or a curious case of adultery comes before him.

The right thing in matters of this sort was, to spin out the play through Advent, Christmas, Lent, and burn no one before the Holy Week, the vigil, as it were, of the great day of Easter. Michaëlis kept himself for the last act, entrusting the bulk of the business to a Flemish Dominican in his service, Doctor Dompt, from Louvain, who had already exorcised, was well-skilled in fooleries of that nature.

The best thing the Fleming could do, was to do nothing. In Louisa, he found a terrible helpmate, with thrice as much zeal in her as the Inquisition itself, unquenchable in her rage, of a burning eloquence, whimsical, and sometimes very odd, but always raising a shudder; a very torch of Hell.

The matter was reduced to a public duel between the two devils, Louisa and Madeline.

Some simple folk who came thither on a pilgrimage to Sainte-Baume, a worthy goldsmith, for instance, and a draper, both from Troyes, in Champagne, were charmed to see Louisa's devil deal such cruel blows at the other demons, and give so sound a thrashing to the magicians. They wept for joy, and went away thanking God.

It is a terrible sight, however, even in the dull wording of the Fleming's official statement, to look upon this unequal strife; to watch the elder woman, the strong and sturdy Provencial, come of a race hard as the flints of its native Crau, as day after day she stones, knocks down, and crushes her young and almost childish victim, who, wasted with love and shame, has already been fearfully punished by her own distemper, her attacks of epilepsy.

The Fleming's volume, which, with the additions made by Michaëlis, reaches to four hundred pages in all, is one condensed epitome of the invectives, threats, and insults spewed forth by this young woman in five months; interspersed with sermons also, for she used to preach on every subject, on the sacraments, on the next coming of Antichrist, on the frailty of women, and so forth. Thence, on the mention of her devils, she fell into the old rage, and renewed twice a-day, the execution of the poor little girl; never taking breath, never for one minute staying the frightful torrent, until at least the other in her wild distraction, "with one foot in hell" - to use her own words - should have fallen into a convulsive fit, and begun beating the flags with her knees, her body, her swooning head.

It must be acknowledged that Louisa herself is a trifle mad: no amount of mere knavishness would have enabled her to maintain so long a wager. But her jealousy points with frightful clearness to every opening by which she may prick or rend the sufferer's heart.

Everything gets turned upside down. This Louisa, possessed of the Devil, takes the sacrament whenever she pleases. She scolds people of the highest authority. The venerable Catherine of France, the oldest of the Ursulines, came to see the wonder, asked her questions, and at the very outset caught her telling a flagrant and stupid falsehood. The impudent woman got out of the mess by saying in the name of her evil spirit, "The Devil is the Father of Lies."

A sensible Minorite who was present, took up the word and said, "Now, thou liest." Turning to the exercisers, he added, "Cannot ye make her hold her tongue? "Then he quoted to them the story of one Martha, a sham demoniac of Paris. By way of answer, she was made to take the communion before him. The Devil communicate, the Devil receive the body of God!

The poor man was bewildered; humbled himself before the Inquisition. They were too many for him, so he said not another word.

One of Louisa's tricks was to frighten the bystanders, by saying she could see wizards among them; which made every one tremble for himself.

Triumphant over Sainte-Baume, she hits out even at Marseilles. Her Flemish exerciser, being reduced to the strange part of secretary and bosom-counsellor to the Devil, writes, under her dictation, five letters: first, to the Capuchins of Marseilles, that they may call upon Gauffridi to recant; second, to the same Capuchins, that they may arrest Gauffridi, bind him fast with a stole, and keep him prisoner in a house of her describing; thirdly, several letters to the moderate party, to Catherine of France, to the Doctrinal Priests, who had declared against her; and then this lewd, outrageous termagant ends with insulting her own prioress: "When I left, you bade me be humble and obedient. Now take back your own advice."

Her devil Verrine, spirit of air and wind, whispered to her some trivial nonsense, words of senseless pride which harmed friends and foes, and the Inquisition itself. One day she took to laughing at Michaëlis, who was shivering at Aix, preaching in a desert while all the world was gone to hear strange things at Sainte-Baume. "Michaëlis, you preach away, indeed, but you get no further forward; while Louisa has reached, has caught hold of the quintessence of all perfection."

This savage joy was mainly caused by her having quite conquered Madeline at last. One word had done more for her than a hundred sermons: "Thou shalt be burnt." Thenceforth in her distraction the young girl said whatever the other pleased, and upheld her statements in the meanest way. Humbling herself before them all, she besought forgiveness of her mother, of her superior Romillion, of the bystanders, of Louisa. According to the latter, the frightened girl took her aside, and begged her to be merciful, not to chasten her too much.

The other woman, tender as a rock and merciful as a hidden reef, felt that Madeline was now hers, to do whatever she might choose. She caught her, folded her round, and bedazed her out of what little spirit she had left. It was a second enchantment; but all unlike that by Gauffridi, a *possession* by means of terror. The poor downtrodden wretch, moving under rod and scourge, was pushed onward in a path of exquisite suffering which led her to accuse and murder the man she loved still.

Had Madeline stood out, Gauffridi would have escaped, for every one was against Louisa. Michaëlis himself at Aix, eclipsed by her as a preacher, treated by her with so much coolness, would have stopped the whole business rather than leave the honour of it in her hands.

Marseilles supported Gauffridi, being fearful of seeing the Inquisition of Avignon pushed into her neighbourhood, and one of her own children carried off from her threshold. The Bishop and Chapter were specially eager to defend their priest, maintaining that the whole affair sprang from nothing but a rivalry between confessors, nothing but the hatred commonly shown by monks towards secular priests.

The Doctrinaries would have quashed the matter. They were sore troubled by the noise it made. Some of them in their annoyance were ready to give up everything and forsake their house.

The ladies were very wroth, especially Madame Libertat, the lady of the Royalist leader who had given Marseilles up to the King.

The Capuchins whom Louisa had so haughtily commanded to seize on Gauffridi, were, like all other of the Franciscan orders, enemies of the Dominicans. They were jealous of the prominence gained for these latter by their demoniac friend. Their wandering life, moreover, by throwing them into continual contact with the women, brought them a good deal of moral business. They had no wish to see too close a scrutiny made into the lives of clergymen; and so they also took the side of Gauffridi, Demoniacs were not so scarce, but that one was easily found and brought forward at the first summons. Her devil, obedient to the rope-girdle of St. Francis, gainsaid everything said by the Dominicans' devil: it averred and the words were straightway written down that "Gauffridi was no magician at all, and could not therefore be arrested."

They were not prepared for this at Sainte-Baume. Louisa seemed confounded. She could only manage to say that apparently the Capuchins had not made their devil swear to tell the truth: a sorry reply, backed up, however, by the trembling Madeline, who, like a beaten hound that fears yet another beating, was ready for anything, ready even to bite and tear. Through her it was that Louisa at such a crisis inflicted an awful bite.

She herself merely said that the Bishop was offending God unawares. She clamoured against "the wizards of Marseilles" without naming any one. But the cruel, the deadly word was spoken at her command by Madeline. A woman who had lost her child two years before, was pointed out by her as having throttled it. Afraid of being tortured, she fled or hid herself. Her husband, her father, went weeping to Sainte-Baume, hoping of course to soften the inquisitors. But Madeline durst not unsay her words; so she renewed the charge.

No one now could feel safe. As soon as the Devil came to be accounted God's avenger, from the moment that people under his dictation began writing the names of those who should pass through the fire, every one had before him, day and night, the hideous nightmare of the stake.

To withstand these bold attempts of the Papal Inquisition, Marseilles ought to have been backed up by the Parliament of Aix. Unluckily she knew herself to be little liked at Aix. That small official town of magistrates and nobles was always jealous of the wealth and splendour of Marseilles, the Queen of the South. On the other hand, the great opponent of Marseilles, the Papal Inquisitor, forestalled Gauffridi's appeal to the Parliament by carrying his own suit thither first. This was a body of utter fanatics, headed by some heavy nobles, whose wealth had been greatly increased in a former century by the massacre of the Vaudois. As lay judges, too, they were charmed to see a Papal Inquisitor set the precedent of acknowledging that, in a matter touching a priest, in a case of witchcraft, the Inquisition could not go beyond the preliminary inquiry. It was just as though the inquisitors had formally laid aside their old pretensions. The people of Aix, like those of Bordeaux before them, were also bitten by the flattering thought, that these lay-folk had been set up by the Church herself as censors and reformers of the priestly morals.

In a business where all would needs be strange and miraculous, not least among those marvels was it to see so raging a demon grow all at once so fair-spoken towards the Parliament, so politic and fine-mannered. Louisa charmed the Royalists by her praises of the late King. Henry IV. - who would have thought it? - was canonized by the Devil. One morning, without any invitation, he broke forth into praises of "that pious and saintly King who had just gone up to heaven."

Such an agreement between two old enemies, the Parliament and the Inquisition, which latter was thenceforth sure of the secular arm, its soldiers, and executioner; this and the sending of a commission to Sainte-Baume to examine the possessed, take down their statements, hear their charges, and impannel a jury, made up a frightful business indeed. Louisa openly pointed out the Capuchins, Gauffridi's champions, and proclaimed "their coming punishment *temporally*" in their bodies, and in their flesh.

The poor Fathers were sorely bruised. Their devil would not whisper one word. They went to find the Bishop, and told him that indeed they might not refuse to bring Gauffridi forward at Sainte-Baume, in obedience to the secular power; but afterwards the Bishop and Chapter could claim him back, and replace him under the shelter of episcopal justice.

Doubtless they had also reckoned on the agitation that would be shown by the two young women at the sight of one they loved; on the extent to which even the terrible Louisa might be shaken by the reproaches of her own heart.

That heart indeed woke up at the guilty one's approach: for one moment the furious woman seemed to grow tender. I know nothing more fiery than her prayer for God to save the man she has driven to death: "Great God, I offer thee all the sacrifices that have been offered since the world began, that will be offered until it ends. All, all, for Lewis. I offer thee all the tears of every saint, all the transports of every angel. All, all, for Lewis. Oh, that there were yet more souls to reckon up, that so the oblation might be all the greater! It should be all for Lewis. O God, the Father of Heaven, have pity on Lewis! God the Son, Redeemer of the world, have pity on Lewis!" &c.

Bootless pity! baneful as well as bootless! Her real desire was that the accused *should not harden his heart,* should plead guilty. In that case by our laws he would most assuredly be burnt.

She herself, in short, was worn out, unable to do anything more. The inquisitor Michaëlis was so humbled by a victory he could not have gained without her, so wroth with the Flemish exerciser who had become her obedient follower, and let her see into all the hidden springs of the tragedy, that he came simply to crush Louisa, and save Madeline by substituting the one for the other, if he could, in this popular drama. This move of his implies some skill, and a knowing eye for scenery. The winter and the Advent season had been wholly taken up with the acting of that awful sibyl, that raging bacchante. In the milder days of a Provencial spring, in the season of Lent, he would bring upon the scene a more moving personage, a demon all womanly, dwelling in a sick child, in a fair-haired frightened girl. The nobles and the Parliament of Provence would feel an interest in a little lady who belonged to an eminent house.

Far from listening to his Flemish agent, Louisa's follower, Michaëlis shut the door upon him when he sought to enter the select council of Parliament-men. A Capuchin who also came, on the first words spoken by Louisa, cried out, "Silence, accursed devil!"

Meanwhile Gauffridi had arrived at Sainte-Baume, where he cut a sorry figure. A man of sense, but weak and blameworthy, he foreboded but too truly how that kind of popular tragedy would end; and in coming to a strait so dreadful, he saw himself forsaken and betrayed by the child he loved. He now entirely forsook himself. When he was confronted with Louisa, she seemed to him like a judge, like one of those cruel and subtle schoolmen who judged the causes of the Church. To all her questions concerning doctrine, he only answered *yes,* assenting even to points most open to dispute; as, for instance, to the assumption "that the Devil in a court of justice might be believed on his word and his oath."

This lasted only a week, from the 1st to the 8th January. The clergy of Marseilles demanded Gauffridi back. His friends, the Capuchins, declared that they had found no signs of magic in his room. Four canons of Marseilles came with authority to take him, and carried him away home.

If Gauffridi had fallen very low, his adversaries had not risen much. Even the two inquisitors, Michaëlis and the Fleming, were in shameful variance with each other. The partiality of the former for Madeline, of the latter for Louisa, went beyond mere words, leading them into opposite lines of action. That chaos of accusations, sermons, revelations, which the Devil had dictated by the mouth of Louisa, the Fleming who wrote it down maintained to be the very word of God, and expressed his fear that somebody might tamper with the same. He owned to a great mistrust of his chief, Michaëlis, who, he was sore afraid, would so amend the papers In behalf of Madeline, as to ensure the ruin of Louisa. To guard them to the best of his power, he shut himself up in his room and underwent a regular siege. Michaëlis, with the Parliament-men on his side, could only get at the manuscript by using the King's name and breaking the door open.

Louisa, afraid of nothing, sought to array the Pope against the King. The Fleming carried an appeal to the legate at Avignon, against his chief, Michaëlis. But the Papal Court had a prudent fear of causing scandal by letting one inquisitor accuse another. Lacking its support, the Fleming had no resource but to submit. To keep him quiet Michaëlis gave him back his papers.

Those of Michaëlis, forming a second report, dull and nowise comparable with the former, are full of nought but Madeline. They played music to try and soothe her: care was taken to note down when she ate, and when she did not eat. Too much time indeed was taken up about her, often in a way but little edifying. Strange questions are put to her touching the Magician, and what parts of his body might bear the mark of the Devil. She herself was examined. This would have to be done at Aix by surgeons and doctors; but meanwhile, in the height of his zeal, Michaëlis examined her at Sainte-Baume, and put down the issue of his researches. No matron was called to see her. The judges, lay and monkish, agreeing in this one matter, and having no fear of each other's overlooking, seem to have quietly passed over this contempt of outward forms.

In Louisa, however, they found a judge. The bold woman branded the indecency as with hot iron. "They who were swallowed up by the Flood never behaved so ill! ... Even of thee, Sodom, the like was never said!"

She also averred that Madeline was given over to uncleanness. This was the saddest thing of all. In her blind joy at being alive, at escaping the flames, or else from some cloudy notion that it was her turn now to act upon her judges, the poor simpleton would sing and dance at times with a shameful freedom, in a coarse, indecent way. The old Doctrinal father, Romillion, blushed for his Ursuline. Shocked to remark the admiration of the men for her long hair, he said that such a vanity must be taken from her, be cut away.

In her better moments she was gentle and obedient.

They would have liked to make her a second Louisa; but her devils were vain and amorous; not, like the other's, eloquent and raging. When they wanted her to preach, she could only utter sorry things. Michaëlis was fain to play out the piece by himself. As chief inquisitor, and bound greatly to outdo his Flemish underling, he avowed that he had already drawn out of this small body a host of six thousand, six hundred, and sixty devils: only a hundred still remained. By way of convincing the public, he made her throw up the charm or spell which by his account she had swallowed, and he drew it from her mouth in some slimy matter. Who could hold out any longer? Assurance itself stood stupefied and convinced.

Madeline was in a fair way to escape: the only hindrance was herself. Every moment she would be saying something rash, something to arouse the misgivings of her judges, and urge them beyond all patience. She declared that everything to her recalled Gauffridi, that everywhere she saw him present. Nor would she hide from them her dreams of love. "Tonight," she said, "I was at the Sabbath. To my statue all covered with gilding the magicians offered their homage. Each of them, in honour thereof, made oblation of some blood drawn from his hands with a lancet. He was also there, on his knees, a rope round his neck, beseeching me to go back and betray him not. I held out. Then said he, 'Is there anyone here who would die for her?' 'I,' said a young man, and he was sacrificed by the magician."

At another time she saw him, and he asked her only for one of her fine fair locks. "And when I refused, he said, 'Only the half of one hair.'"

She swore, however, that she never yielded. But one day, the door happening to be open, behold our convert running off at the top of her speed to rejoin Gauffridi!

They took her again, at least her body. But her soul? Michaëlis knew not how to catch that again. Luckily he caught sight of her magic ring, which, was taken off, cut up, destroyed, and thrown into the fire. Fancying, moreover, that this perverseness on the part of one so gentle was due to unseen wizards who found their way into her room, he set there a very substantial man at arms, with a sword to slash about him everywhere, and cut the invisible imps into pieces.

But the best physic for the conversion of Madeline was the death of Gauffridi. On the 5th February, the inquisitor went to Aix for his Lent preachings, saw the judges, and stirred them up. The Parliament, swiftly yielding to such a pressure, sent off to Marseilles an order to seize the rash man, who, finding himself so well backed by Bishop, Chapter, Capuchins, and all the world, had fancied they would never dare so far.

Madeline from one quarter, Gauffridi from another, arrived at Aix. She was so disturbed that they were forced to bind her. Her disorder was frightful, and all were in great perplexity what to do. They bethought them at least of one bold way of dealing with this sick child; one of those fearful tricks that throw a woman into fits, and sometimes kill her outright. A vicar-general of the archbishopric said that the palace contained a dark narrow charnel-house, such as you may see in the Escurial, and called in Spain a "rotting vat."

There, in olden days, old bones of unknown dead were left to waste away. Into this tomb-like cave the trembling girl was led. They exorcised her by putting those chilly bones to her face. She did not die of fright, but thenceforth gave herself up to their will and pleasure; and so they got what they wanted, the death of the conscience, the destruction of all that remained to her of moral insight and free will.

She became their pliant tool, ready to obey their least desire, to flatter them, to try and guess beforehand what would give them most pleasure. Huguenots were brought before her: she called them names. Confronted with Gauifridi, she told forth by heart her grievances against him, better than the King's own officers could have done. This did not prevent her from squalling violently, when she was brought to the church to excite the people against Gauffridi, by making her devil blaspheme in the magician's name. Beelzebub speaking through her said, "In the name of Gauffridi I abjure God;" and again, at the lifting up of the Host, "Let the blood of the just be upon me, in the name of Gauffridi!"

An awful fellowship indeed! This twofold devil condemns one out of the other's mouth; whatever Madeline says, is ascribed to Gauffridi. And the scared crowd were impatient to behold the burning of the dumb blasphemer, whose ungodliness so loudly declared itself by the voice of the girl.

The exercisers then put to her this cruel question, to which they themselves could have given the best answer:- "Why, Beelzebub, do you speak so ill of your great friend?" Her answer was frightful: "If there be traitors among men, why not among demons also? When I am. with Gauffridi, I am his to do all his will. But when you constrain me, I betray him and turn him to scorn."

However, she could not keep up this hateful mockery. Though the demon of fear and fawning seemed to have gotten fast hold of her, there was room still for despair. She could no longer take the slightest food; and they who for five months had been killing her with exorcisms and pretending to relieve her of six or seven thousand devils, were fain to admit that she longed only to die, and greedily sought after any means of self-destruction. Courage alone was wanting to her. Once she pricked herself with a lancet, but lacked the spirit to persevere. Once she caught up a knife, and when that was taken from her, tried to strangle herself. She dug needles into her body, and then made one last foolish effort to drive a long pin through her ear into her head.

What became of Gauffridi? The inquisitor, who dwells so long on the two women, says almost nothing about him. He walks as it were over the fire. The little he does say is very strange. He relates that having bound Gauffridi's eyes, they pricked him with needles all over the body, to find out the callous places where the Devil had made his mark. On the removal of the bandage, he learned, to his horror and amazement, that the needle had thrice been stuck into him without his feeling it; so he was marked in three places with the sign of Hell. And the inquisitor added, "If we were in Avignon, this man should be burnt tomorrow."

He felt himself a lost man; and defended himself no more. His only thought now was to see if he could save his life through any of the Dominicans' foes. He wished, he said, to confess himself to the Oratorians. But this new order, which might have been called the right mean of Catholicism, was too cold and wary to take up a matter already so hopeless and so far advanced.

Thereon he went back again to the Begging Friars, confessing himself to the Capuchins, and acknowledging all and more than all the truth, that he might purchase life with dishonour. In Spain he would assuredly have been enlarged, barring a term of penance in some convent. But our Parliaments were sterner: they felt bound to prove the greater purity of the lay jurisdiction. The Capuchins, themselves a little shaky in the matter of morals, were not the people to draw the lightning down on their own body. They surrounded Gauffridi, sheltered him, gave him comfort day and night; but only in order that he might own himself a magician, and so, because magic formed the main head of his indictment, the seduction wrought by a confessor to the great discredit of the clergy might be left entirely in the background.

So his friends the Capuchins, by dint of tender caresses and urgent counsel, drew from him the fatal confession which, by their showing, was to save his soul, but which was very certain to hand his body over to the stake.

The man thus lost and done for, they made an end with the girls whom it was not their part to burn. A farcical scene took place. In a large gathering of the clergy and the Parliament, Madeline was made to appear, and, in words addressed to herself, her devil Beelzebub was summoned to quit the place or else offer some opposition. Not caring to do the latter, he went off in disgrace.

Then Louisa, with her demon Verrine, was made to appear. But before they drove away a spirit so friendly to the Church, the monks regaled the Parliamentaries, who were new to such things, with the clever management of this devil, making him perform a curious pantomime. "How do the Seraphim, the Cherubim, the Thrones, behave before God?" "A. hard matter this:" says Louisa, "they have no bodies." But on their repeating the command, she made an effort to obey, imitating the flight of the one class, the fiery longing of the others; and ending with the adoration, when she bowed herself before the judges, falling prostrate with her head downwards. Then was the far-famed Louisa, so proud and so untamable, seen to abase herself, kissing the pavement, and with outstretched arms laying all her length thereon.

It was a strange, frivolous, unseemly exhibition, by which she was made to atone for her terrible success among the people. Once more she won the assembly by dealing a cruel dagger-stroke at Gauffridi, who stood there strongly bound. "Where," said they, "is Beelzebub now, the devil who went out of Madeline?" "I see him plainly at Gauffridi's ear."

Have you had shame and horror enough? "We should like further to know what the poor wretch said, when put to the torture. Both the ordinary and the extraordinary forms were used upon him. His revelations must undoubtedly have thrown light on the curious history of the nunneries. Those tales the Parliament stored up with greediness, as weapons that might prove serviceable to itself; but it retained them "under the seal of the Court."

The inquisitor Michaëlis, who was fiercely assailed in public for an excess of animosity so closely resembling jealousy, was summoned by his order to a meeting at Paris, and never saw the execution of Gauffridi, who was burnt alive four days afterwards, 30th April, 1611, at Aix.

The name of the Dominicans, damaged by this trial, was not much exalted by another case of *possession* got up at Beauvais in such a way as to ensure them all the honours of a war, the account of which they got printed in Paris. Louisa's devil having been reproached for not speaking Latin, the new demoniac, Denise Lacaille, mingled a few words of it in her gibberish. They made a plenty of noise about her, often displayed her in the midst of a procession, and even carried her from Beauvais to Our Lady of Liesse. But the matter kept quite cool. This Picard pilgrimage lacked the horror, the dramatic force of the affair at Sainte-Baume. This Lacaille, for all her Latin, had neither the burning eloquence, nor the mettle, nor the fierce rage, that marked the woman of Provence. The only end of all her proceedings was to amuse the Huguenots.

What became of the two rivals, Madeline and Louisa? The former, or at least her shadow, was kept on Papal ground, for fear of her being led to speak about so mournful a business. She was never shown in public, save in the character of a penitent. She was taken out among the poor women to cut wood, which was afterwards sold for alms; the parents, whom she had brought to shame, having forsworn and forsaken her.

Louisa, for her part, had said during the trial: "I shall make no boast about it. The trial over, I shall soon be dead." But this was not to be. Instead of dying, she went on killing others. The murdering devil within her waxed stormier than ever. She set about revealing to the inquisitors the names, both Christian and surnames, of all whom she fancied to have any dealings with magic; among others a poor girl named Honoria, "blind of both eyes," who was burnt alive.

"God grant," says Father Michaëlis, in conclusion, "that all this may redound to His own glory and to that of His Church!"

[1] St. Francis of Sales, famous for his successful missions among the Protestants, and Bishop of Geneva in his later years, died in 1622. - TRANS.
[2] The Brethren of the Oratory, founded at Rome in 1564. - TRANS.
[3] Lestoile, edit. Michaud, p. 561.

Chapter Seven - The Demoniacs of Loudun Urban Grandier: 1632-1634

IN the *State Memoirs,* written by the famous Father Joseph, and known to us by extracts only - the work itself having, no doubt, been wisely suppressed as too instructive - the good Father explained how, in 1633, he had the luck to discover a heresy, a huge heresy, in which ever so many confessors and directors were concerned. That excellent army of Church-constables, those dogs of the Holy Troop, the Capuchins, had, not only in the wildernesses, but even in the populous parts of France - at Chartres, in Picardy, everywhere - got scent of some dreadful game; the *Alumbrados* namely, or Illuminate, of Spain, who being sorely persecuted there, had fled for shelter into France, where, in the world of women, especially among the convents, they dropped the gentle poison which was afterwards called by the name of Molinos. [1]

The wonder was, that the matter had not been sooner known. Having spread so far, it could not have been wholly hidden. The Capuchins swore that in Picardy alone, where the girls are weak and warmerblooded than in the South, this amorously mystic folly owned some sixty thousand professors. Did all the clergy share in it all the confessors and directors? We must remember, that attached to the official directors were a good many laymen, who glowed with the same zeal for the souls of women. One of them, who afterwards made some noise by his talent and boldness, is the author of *Spiritual Delights,* Desmarets of Saint Sorlin.

Without remembering the new state of things, we should fail to understand the all-powerful attitude of the director towards the nuns, of whom he was now a hundred-fold more the master than he had been in days of yore.

The reforming movement of the Council of Trent, for the better enclosing of monasteries, was not much followed up in the reign of Henry IV., when the nuns received company, gave balls, danced, and so forth. In the reign, however, of Louis XIII., it began afresh with greater earnestness. The Cardinal Rochefoucauld, or rather the Jesuits who drew him on, insisted on a great deal of outward decency. Shall we say, then, that all entrance into the convents was forbidden? One man only went in every day, not only into the house, but also, if he chose, into each of the cells; a fact made evident from several known cases, especially that of David at Louviers. By this reform, this closing system, the door was shut upon the world at large, on all inconvenient rivals, while the director enjoyed the sole command of his nuns, the special right of private interviews with them.

What would come of this? The speculative might treat it as a problem; not so practical men or physicians. The physician Wyer tells some plain stories to show what did come of it from the sixteenth century onwards. In his Fourth Book he quotes a number of nuns who went mad for love. And in Book III. he talks of an estimable Spanish priest who, going by chance into a nunnery, came out mad, declaring that the brides of Jesus were his also, brides of the priest, who was a vicar of Jesus. He had masses said in return for the favour which God had granted him in this speedy marriage with a whole convent.

If this was the result of one passing visit, we may understand the plight of a director of nuns when he was left alone with them, and could take advantage of the new restrictions to spend the day among them, listening hour by hour to the perilous secret of their languishings and their weaknesses.

In the plight of these girls the mere senses are not all in all. Allowance must be made for their listlessness of mind; for the absolute need of some change In their way of life; of some dream or diversion to relieve their life-long monotony. Strange things are happening constantly at this period. Travels, events in the Indies, the discovery of a world, the invention of printing; what romance there is everywhere! While all this goes on without, putting men's minds into a flutter, how, think you, can those within bear up against the oppressive sameness of monastic life the irksomeness of its lengthy services, seasoned by nothing better than a sermon preached through the nose?

The laity themselves, living amidst so many distractions, desire, nay insist, that their confessors shall absolve them for their acts of inconstancy. The priests, on their side, are drawn or forced on, step by step. There grows up a vast literature, at once various and learned, of casuistry, of the art of allowing all things; a progressive literature, in which the indulgence of tonight seems to become the severity of the morrow.

This casuistry was meant for the world; that mysticism for the convent. The annihilation of the person and the death of the will form the great mystic principle. The true moral bearings of that principle are well shown by Desmarets. "The devout," he says, "having offered up and annihilated their own selves, exist no longer but in God. *Thenceforth they can do no wrong.* The better part of them is so divine that it no longer knows what the other is doing." [2]

It might have been thought that the zealous Joseph who had raised so loud a cry of alarm against these corrupt teachers, would have gone yet further; that a grand searching inquiry would have taken place; that the countless host whose number, in one province only, were reckoned at sixty thousand, would be found out and closely examined. But not so: they disappear, and nothing more is known about them. A few, it is said, were imprisoned; but trial there was none: only a deep silence. To all appearance Richelieu cared but little about fathoming the business. In his tenderness for the Capuchins he was not so blind as to follow their lead in a matter which would have thrown the supervision of all confessors into their hands.

As a rule, the monks had a jealous dislike of the secular clergy. Entire masters of the Spanish women, they were too dirty to be relished by those of France; who preferred going to their own priests or to some Jesuit confessor, an amphious creature, half monk, half worldling. If Richelieu had once let loose the pack of Capuchins, Recollects, Carmelites, Dominicans, &c., who among the clergy would have been safe? What director, what priest, however upright, but had used, and used amiss, the gentle language of the Quietists towards their penitents?

Richelieu took care not to trouble the clergy, while he was already bringing about the General Assembly from which he was soon to ask a contribution towards the war. One trial alone was granted the monks, the trial of a vicar, but a vicar who dealt in magic; a trial wherein matters were allowed, as in the case of Gauffridi, to get so entangled, that no confessor, no director, saw his own likeness there, but everyone in full security could say, "This is not I."

Thanks to these strict precautions the Grandier affair is involved in some obscurity.[3] Its historian, the Capuchin Tranquille, proves convincingly that Grandier was a wizard, and, still more, a devil; and on the trial he is called, as Ashtaroth might have been called, *Grandier of the Dominations.* On the other hand, Menage is ready to rank him with great men accused of magic, with the martyrs of free thought.

In order to see a little more clearly, we must not set Grandier by himself; we must keep his place in the devilish trilogy of those times, in which he figured only as a second act; we must explain him by the first act, already shown to us in the dreadful business of Sainte-Baume, and the death of Gauffridi; we must explain him by the third act, by the affair at Louviers, which copied Loudun, as Loudun had copied SairitelSaume, and which in its turn owned a Gauffridi and an Urban Grandier.

The three cases are one and selfsame. In each case there is a libertine priest, in each a jealous monk, and a frantic nun by whose mouth the Devil is made to speak; and in all three the priest gets burnt at last.

And here you may notice one source of light which makes these matters clearer to our eyes than if we saw them through the miry shades of a monastery in Spain or Italy. In those lands of Southern laziness, the nuns were astoundingly passive, enduring the life of the seraglio and even worse. [4] Our French women, on the contrary, gifted with a personality at once strong, lively, and hard to please, were equally dreadful in their jealousy and in their hate; and being devils indeed without metaphor, were accordingly rash, blusterous, and prompt to accuse. Their revelations were very plain, so plain indeed at the last, that everyone felt ashamed; and after thirty years and three special cases, the whole thing, begun as it was through terror, got fairly extinguished in its own dulness beneath hisses of general disgust.

It was not in Loudun, amidst crowds of Poitevins, in the presence of so many scoffing Huguenots, in the very town where they held their great national synods, that one would have looked for an event so discreditable to the Catholics. But these latter, living, as it were, in a conquered country, [5] in the old Protestant towns, with the greatest freedom, and thinking, not without cause, of the people they had often massacred and but lately overcome, were not the persons to say a word about it. Catholic Loudun, composed of magistrates, priests, monks, a few nobles, and some workmen, dwelled aloof from the rest, like a true conquering settlement. This settlement, as one might easily guess, was rent in twain by the rivalry of the priests and the monks.

The monks, being numerous and proud, as men specially sent forth to make converts, kept the pick of the pavement against the Protestants, and were confessing the Catholic ladies, when there arrived from Bordeaux a young vicar, brought up by the Jesuits, a man of letters, of pleasing manners, who wrote well and spoke better. He made a noise in the pulpit, and ere long in the world. By birth a townsman of Mantes, of a wrangling turn, he was Southern by education, with all the readiness of a Bordelais, boastful and frivolous as a Gascon. He soon managed to set the whole town by the ears, drawing the women to his side, while the men were mostly against him. He became lofty, insolent, unbearable, devoid of respect for everything. The Carmelites he overwhelmed with jibes; he would rail away from his pulpit against monks in general. They choked with rage at his sermons. Proud and stately, he went along the streets of Loudun like a Father of the Church; but by night he would steal, with less of bluster, down the byeways and through back-doors.

They all surrendered themselves to his pleasure. The wife of the Crown Counsel was aware of his charms; still more so the daughter of the Public Prosecutor, who had a child by him. This did not satisfy him. Master of the ladies, this conqueror pushed his advantage until he had gained the nuns.

By that time the Ursulines abounded everywhere, sisters devoted to education, feminine missionaries in a Protestant land, who courted and pleased the mothers, while they won over the little girls. The nuns of Loudun formed a small convent of young ladies, poor and well-born. The convent in itself was poor, the nuns for whom it was founded, having been granted nothing but their house, an old Huguenot college. The prioress, a lady of good birth and high connections, burned to exalt her nunnery, to enlarge it, make it wealthier and -wider known. Perhaps she would have chosen Grandier, as being then the fashion, had she not already gotten for her director a priest with very different rootage in the country, a near kinsman of the two chief magistrates. The Canon Mignon, as he was called, held the prioress fast. These two were enraged at learning through the confessional the "Ladies Superior" might confess their nuns that the young nuns dreamed of nothing but this Grandier, of whom there was so much talk.

Thereupon three parties, the threatened director, the cheated husband, the outraged father, joined together by a common jealousy, swore together the destruction of Grandier. To ensure success, they only needed to let him go on. He was ruining himself quite fast enough. An incident that came to light made noise enough almost to bring down the town.

The nuns placed in that old Huguenot mansion, were far from easy in their minds. Their boarders, children of the town, and perhaps also some of the younger nuns, had amused themselves with frightening the rest by playing at ghosts and apparitions. Little enough of order was there among this throng of rich spoilt girls. They would run about the passages at night, until they frightened themselves. Some of them were sick, or else sick at heart. But these fears and fancies mingled with the gossip of the town, of which they heard but too much during the day, until the ghost by night took the form of Grandier himself. Several said they saw him, felt him near them in the night,

123

and yielded unawares to his bold advances. "Was all this fancy, or the fun of novices? Had Grandier bribed the porteress or ventured to climb the walls? This part of the business was never cleared up.

From that time the three felt sure of catching him. And first, among the small folk under their protection, they stirred up two good souls to declare' that they could no longer keep as vicar a profligate, a wizard, a devil, a free-thinker, who bent one knee in church instead of two, who scoffed at rules and granted dispensations contrary to the rights of the Bishop. A shrewd accusation, which turned against him his natural defender, the Bishop of Poitiers, and delivered him over to the fury of the monks.

To say truth, all this was planned with much skill. Besides raising up two poor people as accusers, they thought it advisable to have him cudgelled by a noble. In those days of duelling a man who let himself be cudgelled with impunity lost ground with the public, and sank in the esteem of the women. Grandier deeply felt the blow. Fond of making a noise in all cases, he went to the King, threw himself on his knees, and besought vengeance for the insult to his gown. From so devout a king he might have gained it; but here there chanced to be some persons who told the King that it was all an affair of love, the fury of a betrayed husband wreaking itself on his foe.

At the spiritual court of Poitiers, Grandier was condemned to do penance, to be banished from Loudun, and disgraced as a priest. But the civil court took up the matter and found him innocent. He had still to await the orders of him by whom Poitiers was spiritually overruled, Sourdis, Archbishop of Bordeaux. That warlike prelate, an admiral and brave sailor more than a priest, shrugged his shoulders on hearing of such peccadilloes. He acquitted the vicar, but at the same time wisely recommended him to go and live anywhere out of Loudun.

This the proud man did not care to do. He wanted to enjoy his triumph on the very field of battle, to show off before the ladies. He came back to Loudun in broad day, with mighty noise; the women all looking out of window, as he went by with a laurel-branch in his hand.

Not satisfied with that piece of folly, he began to threaten, to demand reparation. Thus pushed and imperilled in their turn, his enemies called to remembrance the affair of Gauffridi, where the Devil, the Father of Lies, was restored to his honours and accepted in a court of justice as a right truthful witness, worthy of belief on the side of the Church, worthy of belief on the side of His Majesty's servants. In despair they invoked a devil and found one at their command. He showed himself among the Ursulines.

A dangerous thing; but then, how many were nearly concerned in its success! The prioress saw her poor humble convent suddenly attracting the gaze of the Court, of the provinces, of all the world. The monks saw themselves victorious over their rivals the priests. They pictured anew those popular battles waged with the Devil in a former century, and often, as at Soissons, before the church doors; the terror of the people, and their joy at the triumph of the Good Spirit; the confession drawn from the Devil touching God's presence in the Sacrament; and the humiliation of the Huguenots at being refuted by the Demon himself.

In these tragi-comedies the exerciser represented God, or at any rate the Archangel, overthrowing the dragon. He came down from the platform in utter exhaustion, streaming with sweat, but victorious, to be borne away in the arms of the crowd, amidst the blessings of good women who shed tears of joy the while.

Therefore it was that in these trials a dash of witchcraft was always needful. The Devil alone roused the interest of the vulgar. They could not always see him coming out of a body in the shape of a black toad, as at Bordeaux in 1610. But it was easy to make it up to them by a grand display of splendid stage scenery. The affair of Provence owed much of its success to Madeline's desolate wildness and the terror of Sainte-Baume. Loudun was regaled with the uproar and the bacchanal frenzy of a host of exercisers distributed among several churches. Lastly, Louviers, as we shall presently see, put a little new life into this fading fashion by inventing midnight scenes, in which the demons who possessed the nuns began digging by the glimmer of torches, until they drew forth certain charms from the holes wherein they had been concealed.

The Loudun business began with the prioress and a lay sister of hers. They had convulsive fits, and talked infernal gibberish. Other of the nuns began copying them, one bold girl especially taking up Louisa's part at Marseilles, with the same devil Leviathan, the leading demon of trickery and evil speaking.

The little town was all in a tremble. Monks of every hue provided themselves with nuns, shared them all round, and exorcised them by threes and fours. The churches were parcelled out among them; the Capuchins alone taking two for themselves. The crowd go after them, swollen by all the women in the place, and in this frightened audience, throbbing with anxiety, more than one cries out that she, too, is feeling the devils. [6] Six girls of the town are possessed. And the bare recital of these alarming events begets two new cases of possession at Chinon.

Everywhere the thing was talked of, at Paris, at the Court. Our Spanish queen, [7] who is imaginative and devout, sends off her almoner; nay more, sends her faithful follower, the old papist, Lord Montague, who sees, who believes everything, and reports it all to the Tope. It is a miracle proven. He had seen the wounds on a certain nun, and the marks made by the Devil on the Lady Superior's hands.

What said the King of France to this? All his devotion was turned on the Devil, on hell, on thoughts of fear. It is said that Richelieu was glad to keep him thus. I doubt it; the demons were essentially Spanish, taking the Spanish side: if ever they talked politics, they must have spoken against Richelieu.

Perhaps he was afraid of them. At any rate, he did them homage, and sent his niece to prove the interest he took in the matter.

The Court believed, but Loudun itself did not. Its devils, but sorry imitators of the Marseilles demons, rehearsed in the morning what they had learnt the night before from the well-known handbook of Father Michaëlis. They would never have known what to say but for the secret exorcisms, the careful rehearsal of the day's farce, by which night after night they were trained to figure before the people.

One sturdy magistrate, bailiff of the town, made a stir: going himself to detect the knaves, he threatened and denounced them. Such, too, was the tacit opinion of the Archbishop of Bordeaux, to whom Grandier appealed. He despatched a set of rules for the guidance at least of the exercisers, for putting a stop to their arbitrary doings; and, better still, he sent his surgeon, who examined the girls, and found them to be neither bewitched, nor mad, nor even sick. What were they then? Knaves, to be sure. [8]

So through the century keeps on this noble duel between the Physician and the Devil, this battle of light and knowledge with the dark shades of falsehood. We saw its beginning in Agrippa and Wyer. Doctor Duncan carried it bravely on at Loudun, and fearlessly impressed on others the belief that this affair was nothing but a farce.

For all his alleged resistance, the Demon was frightened, held his tongue, quite lost his voice. But people's passions had been too fiercely roused for the matter to end there. The tide flowed again so strongly in favour of Grandier, that the assailed became in their turn assailants. An apothecary of kin to the accusers was sued by a rich young lady of the town for speaking of her as the vicar's mistress. He was condemned to apologise for his slander.

The prioress was a lost woman. It would have been easy to prove, what one witness afterwards saw, that the marks upon her were made with paint renewed daily. But she was kinswoman to one of the King's judges, Laubardemont, and he saved her. He was simply charged to overthrow the strong places of Loudun. He got himself commissioned to try Grandier. The Cardinal was given to understand that the accused was vicar and friend of the Loudun shoemaker, [9] was one of the numerous agents of Mary of Medici, had made himself his parishioner's secretary, and written a disgraceful pamphlet in her name. Richelieu, for his part, would have liked to show a high-minded scorn of the whole business, if he could have done so with safety to himself. The Capuchins and Father Joseph had an eye to that also. Richelieu would have given them a fine handle against him with the King, had he displayed a want of zeal. One Quillet, after much grave reflection, went to see the Minister and give him warning. But the other, afraid to listen, regarded him with so stern a gaze that the giver of advice deemed it prudent to seek shelter in Italy.

Laubardemont arrived at Loudun on the 6th December, 1633, bringing along with him great fear, and unbounded powers; even those of the King himself. The whole strength of the kingdom became, as it were, a dreadful bludgeon to crush one little fly.

The magistrates were wroth; the civic lieutenant warned Grandier that he would have to arrest him on the morrow. The latter paid no heed to him, and was arrested accordingly. In a moment he was carried off, without form of trial, to the dungeons of Angers. Presently he was taken back and thrown, where think you? Into the house, the room of one of his enemies, who had the windows walled up so as well-nigh to choke him. The loathsome scrutiny of the wizard's body, in order to find out the Devil's marks by sticking needles all over it, was carried on by the hands of the accusers themselves, who took their revenge upon him beforehand in the foretaste thus given him of his future punishment.

They led him to the churches, confronted him with the girls, who had got their cue from Laubardemont. These Bacchanals, for such they became under the fuddling effect of some drugs administered by the condemned apothecary above-named, flung out in such frantic rages, that Grandier was nearly perishing one day beneath their nails.

Unable to imitate the eloquence of the Marseilles demoniac, they tried obscenity in its stead. It was a hideous thing to see these girls give full vent in public to their sensual fury, on the plea of scolding their pretended devils. Thus indeed it was that they managed to swell their audiences. People flocked to hear from the lips of these women what no woman would else have dared to utter.

As the matter grew more hateful, so it also grew more laughable. They were sure to repeat all awry what little Latin was ever whispered to them. The public found that the devils had never gone through *their lower classes.* The Capuchins, however, coolly said that if these demons were weak in Latin, they were marvellous speakers of Iroquois and Tupinambi. [10]

A farce so shameful, seen from a distance of sixty leagues, from St. Germain or the Louvre, appeared miraculous, awful, terrifying. The Court admired and trembled. Richelieu to please them did a cowardly thing. He ordered money to be paid to the exorcisers, to the nuns.

The height of favour to which they had risen, drove the plotters altogether mad. Senseless words were followed by shameful deeds. Pleading that the nuns were tired, the exorcisers got them outside the town, took them about by themselves. One of them, at least to all appearance, returned pregnant. In the fifth or sixth month all outward trace of it disappeared, and the devil within her acknowledged how wickedly he had slandered the poor nun by making her look so large. This tale concerning Loudun we learn from the historian of Louviers. [11]

It is stated that Father Joseph, after a secret journey to the spot, saw to what end the matter was coming, and noiselessly backed out of it. The Jesuits also went, tried their exorcisms, did next to nothing, got scent of the general feeling, and stole off in like manner.

But the monks, the Capuchins, were gone so far, that they could only save themselves by frightening others. They laid some treacherous snares for the daring bailiff and his wife, seeking to destroy them, and thereby quench the coming reaction of justice. Lastly, they urged on the commissioners to despatch Grandier. Things could be carried no further: the nuns themselves were slipping out of their hands. After that dreadful orgie of sensual rage and immodest shouting in order to obtain the shedding of human blood, two or three of them swooned away, were seized with disgust and horror; vomited up their very selves. Despite the hideous doom that awaited them if they spoke the truth, despite the certainty of ending their days in a dungeon, they owned in church that they were damned, that they had been playing with the Devil, and Grandier was innocent.

They ruined themselves, but could not stay the issue. A general protest by the town to the King failed to stay it also. On the 18th August, 1634, Grandier was condemned to the stake. So violent were his enemies that, for the second time before burning him, they insisted on having him stuck with needles in order to find out the Devil's marks. One of his judges would have had even his nails torn out of him, had not the surgeon withheld his leave.

They were afraid of the last words their victim might say on the scaffold. Among his papers there had been found a manuscript condemning the celibacy of priests, and those who called him a wizard themselves believed him to be a free-thinker. They remembered the brave words which the martyrs of free thought had thrown out against their judges; they called to mind the last speech of Giordano Bruno, the bold defiance of Vanini. [12] So they agreed with Grandier, that if he were prudent, he should be saved from burning, perhaps be strangled. The weak priest, being a man of flesh, yielded to this demand of the flesh, and promised to say nothing. He spoke not a word on the road, nor yet upon the scaffold. When he was fairly fastened to the post, with everything ready, and the fire so arranged as to enfold him swiftly in smoke and flames, his own confessor, a monk, set the faggots ablaze without waiting for the executioner. The victim, pledged to silence, had only time to say, "So, you have deceived me!" when the flames whirled fiercely upwards, and the furnace of pain began, and nothing was audible save the wretch's screams.

Richelieu in his Memoirs says little, and that with evident shame, concerning this affair. He gives one to believe that he only followed the reports that reached him, the voice of general opinion. Nevertheless, by rewarding the exercisers, by throwing the reins to the Capuchins, and letting them triumph over France, he gave no slight encouragement to that piece of knavery. Gauffridi, thus renewed in Grandier, is about to reappear in yet fouler plight in the Louviers affair.

In this very year, 1634, the demons hunted from Poitou pass over into Normandy, copying again and again the fooleries of Sainte-Baume, without any trace of invention, of talent, or of imagination. The frantic Leviathan of

128

Provence, when counterfeited at Loudun, loses his Southern sting, and only gets out of a scrape by talking fluently to virgins in the language of Sodom. Presently, alas! at Louviers he loses even his old daring, imbibes the sluggish temper of the North, and sinks into a sorry sprite. [13]

[1] Molinos, born at Saragossa in 1627, died a prisoner to the Inquisition in 1696. His followers were called Quietists. - TRANS.
[2] An old doctrine which often turns up again in the Middle Ages. In the seventeenth century it prevails among the convents of France and Spain. A Norman angel, in the Louviers business, teaches a nun to despise the body and disregard the flesh, after the example of Jesus, who bared himself for a scourging before all the people. He enforces an utter surrendering of the soul and the will by the example of the Virgin, "who obeyed the angel Gabriel and conceived, without risk of evil, for impurity could not come of a spirit." At Louviers, David, an old director of some authority, taught "that sin could be killed by sin, as the better way of becoming innocent again."
[3] The *History of the Loudun Devils,* by the Protestant Aubin, is an earnest, solid book, confirmed by the *Reports* of Laubardemont himself. That of the Capuchin Tranquille is a piece of grotesquerie. The *Proceedings* are in the Great Library of Paris. M. Figuier has given a long and excellent account of the whole affair, in his *History of the Marvellous.*
[4] See Del Rio, Llorente Ricci, &c.
[5] The capture of Rochelle, the last of the Huguenot strongholds took place in 1628. - TRANS.
[6] The same hysteric contagion marks the "Revivals" of a later period, down to the last mad outbreak in Ireland. The translator hopes some day to work out the physical question here stated. - TRANS.
[7] Anne of Austria, wife of Louis XIII. - TRANS.
[8] Not of necessity knaves, Mr. Michelet; at least not wilfully so; but silly hysteric patients, of the spirit-rapping, revivalist order, victims of nervous derangement, or undue nervous sensibility. - TRANS.
[9] A woman named Hammon, of low birth, who entered the service, and rose high in the good graces of Mary of Medici. See Dumas' Celebrated Crimes. - TRANS.
[10] Indians of the coast of Brazil. - TRANS.
[11] Esprit de Bosroger, p. 135.
[12] Both Neapolitans, burnt alive, the former at Venice in 1619, the latter at Toulouse in 1619. - TRANS.
[13] Wright and Dumas both differ from M. Michelet in their view of Urban Grandier's character. The latter especially, regards him as an innocent victim to his own fearlessness and the hate of his foes, among whom not the least deadly was Richelieu himself, who bore him a deep personal grudge. - TRANS.

Chapter Eight - The Demoniacs of Louviers, Madeline Bavent: 1633-1647

HAD Richelieu allowed the inquiry demanded by Father Joseph into the doings of the Illuminate Confessors, some strange light would have been thrown into the depth of the cloisters, on the daily life of the nuns. Failing that, we may still learn from the Louviers story, which is far more instructive than those of Aix and Loudun, that, notwithstanding the new means of corruption furnished by Illuminism, the director still resorted to the old trickeries of witchcraft, of apparitions, heavenly or infernal, and so forth. [1]

Of the three directors successively appointed to the Convent of Louviers in the space of thirty years, David, the first, was an Illuminate, who forestalled Molinos; the second, Picart, was a wizard dealing with the Devil; and Boule, the third, was a wizard working in the guise of an angel.

There is an excellent book about this business; it is called *The History of Magdalen Bavent*, a nun of Louviers; with her Examination, &c., 1652: Rouen. [2] The date of this book accounts for the thorough freedom with which it was written. During the wars of the Fronde, a bold Oratorian priest, who discovered the nun in one of the Rouen prisons, took courage from her dictation to write down the story of her life.

Born at Rouen in 1607, Madeline was left an orphan at nine years old. At twelve she was apprenticed to a milliner. The confessor, a Franciscan, held absolute sway in the house of this milliner, who as maker of clothes for the nuns, was dependent on the Church. The monk caused the apprentices, whom he doubtless made drunk with belladonna and other magical drinks, to believe that they had been taken to the Sabbath and there married to the devil Dagon. Three were already possessed by him, and Madeline at fourteen became the fourth.

She was a devout worshipper, especially of St. Francis. A Franciscan monastery had just been founded at Louviers, by a lady of Rouen, widow of lawyer Hennequin, who was hanged for cheating. She hoped by this good deed of hers to help in saving her husband's soul. To that end she sought counsel of a holy man, the old priest David, who became director to the new foundation. Standing at the entrance of the town, with a wood surrounding it, this convent, born of so tragical a source, seemed quite gloomy and poor enough for a place of stern devotion. David was known as author of a *Scourge for Rakes*, an odd and violent book against the abuses that denied the Cloister. [3] All of a sudden this austere person took up some very strange ideas concerning purity. He became an Adamite, preached up the nakedness of Adam in his days of innocence. The docile nuns of Louviers sought to subdue and abase the novices, to break them into obedience, by insisting of course in summertime that these young Eves should return to the plight of their common mother. In this state they were sent out for exercise in some secluded gardens, and were taken into the chapel itself. Madeline, who at sixteen had come to be received as a novice, was too proud, perhaps in those days too pure also, to submit to so strange a way of life. She got an angry scolding for having tried at communion to hide her bosom with the altar-cloth.

Not less unwilling was she to uncover her soul, to confess to the Lady Superior, after the usual monastic custom of which the abbesses were particularly fond. She would rather trust herself with old David, who kept her apart from the rest. He himself confided his own ailments into her ear. Nor did he hide from her his inner teaching, the Illuminism, which governed the convent: "You must kill sin by being made humble and lost to all sense of pride through sin." Madeline was frightened at the depths of depravity reached by the nuns, who quietly carried out the teaching with which they had been imbued. She avoided their company, kept to herself, and succeeded in getting made one of the doorkeepers.

David died when she was eighteen. Old age prevented his going far with the girl. But the vicar Picart, who succeeded him, was furious in his pursuit of her; at the confessional spoke to her only of his love. He made her his eextoness, that he might meet her alone in chapel. She liked him not; but the nuns forbade her to have another confessor, lest she might divulge their little secrets. And thus she was given over to Picart. He beset her when she was sick almost to death; seeking to frighten her by insisting that from David he had received some infernal prescriptions. He sought to win her compassion by feigning illness and begging her to come and see him. Thenceforth he became her master, upset her mind with magic potions, and worked her into believing that she had gone with him to the Sabbath, there to officiate as altar and victim. At length, exceeding even the Sabbath usages and daring the scandal that would follow, he made her to be with child.

The nuns were afraid of one who knew the state of their morals; and their interest also bound them to him. The convent was enriched by his energy, his good repute, the alms and gifts he attracted towards it from every quarter. He was building them a large church. We saw in the Loudun business by what rivalries and ambitions these houses were led away, how jealously they strove each to outdo the others. Through the trust reposed in him by the wealthy, Picart saw himself raised into the lofty part of benefactor and second founder of the convent. "Sweetheart," he said to Madeline, "that noble church is all my building! After my death you will see wonders wrought there. Do you not agree to that?"

This fine gentleman did not put himself out at all regarding Madeline. He paid a dowry for her, and made a nun of her who was already a lay-sister. Thus, being no longer a doorkeeper, she could live in. one of the inner rooms, and there be brought to bed at her convenience. By means of certain drugs, and practices of their own, the convents could do without the help of doctors. Madeline said that she was delivered several times. She never said what became of the newly-born.

Picart being now an old man, feared lest Madeline might in her fickleness fly off some day, and utter words of remorse to another confessor. So he took a detestable way of binding her to himself beyond recall, by forcing her to make a will in which she promised "to die when he died, and to be wherever he was." This was a dreadful thought for the poor soul. Must she be drawn along with him into the bottomless pit? Must she go down with him, even into hell? She deemed herself for ever lost. Become his property, his mere tool, she was used and misused by him for all kinds of purposes. He made her do the most shameful things. He employed her as a magical charm to gain over the rest of the nuns. A holy wafer steeped in Madeline's blood, and buried in the garden, would be sure to disturb their senses and their minds.

This was the very year in which Urban Grandier was burnt. Throughout France, men spoke of nothing but the devils of Loudun. The Penitentiary of Evreux, who had been one of the actors on that stage, carried the dreadful tale back with him to Normandy. Madeline fancied herself bewitched and knocked about by devils; followed about by a lewd cat with eyes of fire. By degrees, other nuns caught the disorder, which showed itself in odd supernatural jerks and writhings. Madeline had besought aid of a Capuchin, afterwards of the Bishop of Evrenx. The prioress was not sorry for a step of which she must have been aware, for she saw what wealth and fame a like business had brought to the Convent of Loudun. But for six years the bishop turned a deaf ear to the prayer, doubtless through fear of Richelieu, who was then at work on a reform of the cloisters.

Richelieu wanted to bring these scandals to an end. It was not till his own death, and that of Louis XIII., during the break-up which followed on the rule of the Queen and Mazarin, that the priests again betook themselves to working wonders, and waging war with the Devil. Picart being dead, they were less shy of a matter in which so dangerous a man might have accused others in his turn. They met the visions of Madeline, by looking out a visionary for themselves. They got admission into the convent for a certain Sister Anne of the Nativity, a girl of sanguine, hysteric temperament, frantic at need and half-mad, so far at least as to believe in her own lies. A kind of dogfight was got up between the two. They besmeared each other with false charges. Anne saw the Devil quite naked, by Madeline's side. Madeline swore to seeing Anne at the Sabbath, along with the Lady Superior, the Mother-Assistant, and the Mother of the Novices. Besides this, there was nothing new; merely a hashing up of the two great trials at Aix and Loudun. They read and followed the printed narratives only. No wit, no invention, was shown by either.

Anne, the accuser, and her devil Leviathan, were backed by the Penitentiary of Evreux, one of the chief actors in the Loudun affair. By his advice, the Bishop of Evreux gave orders to disinter the body of Picart, so that the devils might leave the convent when Picart himself was taken away from the neighbourhood. Madeline was condemned, without a hearing, to be disgraced, to have her body examined for the marks of the Devil. They tore off her veil and gown, and made her the wretched sport of a vile curiosity, that would have pierced her till she bled again, in order to win the right of sending her to the stake. Leaving to no one else the care of a scrutiny which was in itself a torture, these virgins acting as matrons, ascertained if she was with child or no, shaved all her body, and dug their needles into her quivering flesh, to find out the insensible spots that betrayed the mark of the Devil. At every dig they discovered signs of pain: if they had not the luck to prove her a Witch, at any rate, they could revel in her tears and cries.

But Sister Anne was not satisfied, until, on the mere word of her own devil, Madeline, though acquitted by the results of this examination, was condemned for the rest of her life to an *In pace*. It was said that the convent would be quieted by her departure; but such was not the case. The Devil was more violent than ever j some twenty nuns began to cry out, to prophesy, to beat themselves.

Such a sight drew thither a curious crowd from Rouen, and even from Paris. Yvelin, a young Parisian surgeon, who had already seen the farce at Loudun, came to see that of Louviers. He brought with him a very clear-headed magistrate, the Commissioner of Taxes at Rouen. They devoted unwearying attention to the matter, settled themselves at Louviers, and carried on their researches for seventeen days.

From the first day they saw into the plot. A conversation they had had with the Penitentiary of Evreux on their entrance into the town, was repeated back to them by Sister Anne's demon, as if it had been a revelation. The scenic arrangements were very bewitching. The shades of night, the torches, the nickering and smoking lights, produced effects which had not been seen at Loudun. The rest of the process was simple enough. One of the bewitched said that in a certain part of the garden they would find a charm. They dug for it, and it was found. Unluckily, Yvelin's friend, the sceptical magistrate, never budged from the side of the leading actress, Sister Anne. At the very edge of a hole they had just opened he grasped her hand, and on opening it, found the charm, a bit of black thread, which she was about to throw into the ground.

The exercisers, the penitentiary, priests, and Capuchins, about the spot, were overwhelmed with confusion. The dauntless Yvelin, on his own authority, began a scrutiny, and saw to the uttermost depth of the affair.

Among the fifty-two nuns, said he, there were six *possessed*, but deserving of chastisement. Seventeen more were victims under a spell, a pack of girls upset by the disease of the cloisters. He describes it with great precision: the girls are regular but hysterical, blown out with certain inward storms, lunatics mainly, and disordered in mind. A nervous contagion has ruined them; and the first thing to do is to keep them apart.

He then, with the liveliness of Voltaire, examines the tokens by which the priests were wont to recognize the supernatural character of the bewitched. They foretel, he allows, but only what never happens. They translate, indeed, but without understanding; as when, for instance, they render *"ex parte virginis"* by "the departure of the Virgin." They know Greek before the people of Louviers, but cannot speak it before the doctors of Paris. They cut capers, take leaps of the easiest kind, climb up the trunk of a tree which a child three years old might climb. In short, the only thing they do that is really dreadful and unnatural, is to use dirtier language than men would ever do.

133

In tearing off the mask from these people, the surgeon rendered a great service to humanity. For the matter was being pushed further; other victims were about to be made. Besides the charms were found some papers, ascribed to David or Picart, in which this and that person were called witches, and marked out for death. Each one shuddered lest his name should be found there. Little by little the fear of the priesthood made its way among the people.

The rotten age of Mazarin, the first days of the weak Anne of Austria, were already come. Order and government were no more. "But one phrase was left in the language: *The Queen is so good.*" Her goodness gave the clergy a chance of getting the upper hand. The power of the laity entombed with Richelieu, bishops, priests, and monks, were about to reign. The bold impiety of the magistrate and his friend Yvelin imperilled so sweet a hope. Groans and wailings went forth to the Good Queen, not from the victims, but from the knaves thus caught in the midst of their offences. Up to the Court they went, weeping for the outrage to their religion.

Yvelin was not prepared for this stroke: he deemed himself firm at Court, having for ten years borne the title of Surgeon to the Queen. Before he returned from Louviers to Paris, the weakness of Anne of Austria had been tempted into granting another commission named by his opponents, consisting of an old fool in his dotage, one Diafoirus of Rouen, and his nephew, both attached to the priesthood. These did not fail to discover that the Louviers affair was supernatural, transcending all art of man.

Any other than Yvelin would have been discouraged. The Rouen physicians treated with utter scorn this surgeon, this barber fellow, this mere sawbones. The Court gave him no encouragement. Still, he held on his way in a treatise which will live yet. He accepts this battle of science against priestcraft, declaring, as Wyer did in the sixteenth century, that "in all such matters the right judge is not the priest but the man of science." With great difficulty he found some one bold enough to print, but no one willing to sell his little work. So in broad daylight the heroic young man set about distributing it with his own hands. Placing himself on the Pont Neuf, the most frequented spot in Paris, at the foot of Henry the Fourth's statue, he gave 'out copies of his memoir to the passers by. At the end of it they found a formal statement of the shameful fraud, how in the hand of the female demons the magistrate had caught the unanswerable evidence of their dishonour.

Return we to the wretched Madeline. Her enemy, the Penitentiary of Evreux, by whose influence she had been searched with needles, carried her off as his prey to the heart of the episcopal dungeons in that town. Below an underground passage dipped a cave, below the cave a cell, where the poor human creature lay buried in damps and darkness. Reckoning upon her speedy death, her dread companions had not even the kindness to give her a piece of linen for the dressing of her ulcer. There, as she lay in her own filth, she suffered alike from pain and want of cleanliness. The whole night long she was disturbed by the running to and fro of ravenous rats, those terrors of every prison, who were wont to nibble men's ears and noses.

But all these horrors fell short of those which her tyrant, the Penitentiary, dealt out to her himself. Day after day he would come into the upper vault and speak to her through the mouth of her pit, threatening her, commanding her, and making her, whether she would or no, confess to this or that crime as having been wrought by others. At length she ceased to eat. Fearing that she might die at once, he drew her for a while out of her *In Pace*, and laid her in the upper vault. Then, in his rage against Yvelin's memoir, he cast her back into her sewer below.

That glimpse of light, that short renewal and sudden death of hope, gave the crowning impulse to her despair. Her wound was closing, so that her strength was greater. She was seized with a deep and violent thirst for death. She swallowed spiders, but instead of dying, only brought them up again. Pounded glass she swallowed, but in vain. Finding an old bit of sharp iron, she tried to cut her throat, but could not. Then, as an easier way, she dug the iron into her belly. For four hours she worked and bled, but without success. Even this wound shortly began to close. To crown, all, the life she hated so returned to her stronger than before. Her heart's death was of no avail.

She became once more a woman; still, alas! an object of desire, of temptation for her jailers, those brutish varlets of the bishopric, who, notwithstanding the horror of the place, and the unhappy creature's own sad and filthy plight, would come to make sport of her, believing that they might do all their pleasure against a Witch. But an angel succoured her, so she said. From men and rats alike she defended herself. But against herself, herself she could not protect. Her prison corrupted her mind. She dreamed of the Devil, he sought him to come and see her, to restore to her the shameful pleasures in which she had wallowed at Louviers. He never deigned to come back. Once more amidst this corruption of her senses, she fell back on her old desire for death. One of the jailers had given her a drug to kill the rats. She was just going to swallow it herself, when an angel - an angel, was it, or a devil? - stayed her hand, reserving her for other crimes.

Thenceforward - sunk into the lowest depths of vileness, become an unspeakable cipher of cowardice and servility - she signed endless lists of crimes which she had never committed. Was she worth the trouble of burning? Many had given up that idea, but the ruthless Penitentiary clung to it still. He offered money to a Wizard of Evreux, then in prison, if he would bear such witness as might bring about the death of Madeline.

For the future, however, they could use her for other purposes - to bear false witness, to become a tool for any slander. Whenever they sought the ruin of any man, they had only to drag down to Louviers or to Evreux this accursed ghost of a dead woman, living only to make others die. In this way she was brought out to kill with her words a poor man named Duval. What the Penitentiary dictated to her, she repeated readily: when he told her by what marks she should know Duval, whom she had never seen, she pointed him out and said she had seen him at the Sabbath. Through her it fell out that he was burnt!

She owned her dreadful crime, and shuddered to think what answer she could make before God. She was fallen into such contempt that no one now deigned to look after her. The doors stood wide open: sometimes she had the keys herself. But where now should she go, object as she was of so much dread? Thenceforth the world repelled her - cast her out: the only world she had left was her dungeon.

During the anarchy of Mazarin and his Good Lady the chief authority remained with the Parliaments. That of Rouen, hitherto the friendliest to the clergy, grew wroth at last at their arrogant way of examining, ordering, and burning people. A mere decree of the Bishop had caused Picart's body to be disinterred and thrown into the common sewer. And now they were passing on to the trial of Boullé, the curate, and supposed abettor of Picart. Listening to the plaint of Picart's family, the Parliament sentenced the Bishop of Evreux to replace him at his own expense in his tomb at Louviers. They called up Boullé, undertook his trial themselves, and at the same time sent for the wretched Madeline from Evreux to Rouen.

People were afraid that Yvelin and the magistrate who had caught the nuns in the very act of cheating, would be made to appear. Hiding away to Paris, they found the knave Mazarin ready to protect their knavish selves. The whole matter was appealed to the King's Council an indulgent court, without eyes or ears whose care it was to bury, hush up, bedarken everything connected with justice.

Meanwhile, some honey-tongued priests had comforted Madeline in her Rouen dungeon; they heard her confessions, and enjoined her, by way of penance, to ask forgiveness of her persecutors, the nuns of Louviers. Thenceforth, happen what might, Madeline could never more be brought in evidence against those who had thus bound her fast. It was a triumph indeed for the clergy, and the victory was sung by a knave of an exerciser, the Capuchin Esprit de Bosroger, in his *Piety Afflicted*, a farcical monument of stupidity, in which he accuses, unawares, the very people he fancies himself defending.

The Fronde, as I said before, was a revolution for honest ends. Fools saw only its outer form its laughable aspects; but at bottom it was a serious business, a moral reaction. In August, 1647, with the first breath of freedom, Parliament stepped forward and cut the knot. It ordered, in the first place, the destruction of the Louviers Sodom; the girls were to be dispersed and sent back to their kinsfolk. In the next, it decreed that thenceforth the bishops of the province should, four times a-year, send special confessors to the nunneries, to ascertain that such foul abuses were not renewed.

One comfort, however, the clergy were to receive. They were allowed to burn the bones of Picart and the living body of Boullé, who, after making

136

public confession in the cathedral, was drawn on a hurdle to the Fish Market, and there, on the 21st August, 1647, devoured by the flames. Madeline, or rather her corpse, remained in the prisons of Rouen.

[1] It was very easy to cheat those who wished to be cheated. By this time celibacy was harder to practise than in the Middle Ages, the number of fasts and bloodlettings being greatly reduced. Many died from the nervous plethora of a life so cruelly sluggish. They made no secret of their torments, owning them to their sisters, to their confessor, to the Virgin herself. A pitiful thing, a thing to sorrow for, not to ridicule. In Italy, a nun besought the Virgin for pity's sake to grant her a lover.
[2] I know of no book more important, more dreadful, or worthier of being reprinted. It is the most powerful narrative of its class. *Piety Afflicted,* by the Capuchin Esprit de Bosroger, is a work immortal in the annals of tomfoolery. The two excellent pamphlets by the doughty surgeon, Yvelin, the *Inquiry* and the *Apology,* are in the Library of Ste. Geneviève.
[3] See Floquet; *Parliament of Normandy*, vol. v. p. 636.

Chapter Nine - The Devil Triumphs in The Seventeenth Century

THE Fronde was a kind of Voltaire. The spirit of Voltaire, old as France herself, but long restrained, burst forth in the political, and anon in the religious, world. In vain did the Great King seek to establish a solemn gravity. Beneath it laughter went on.

Was there nought else, then, but laughter and jesting? Nay, it was the Advent of Reason. By means of Kepler, of Galileo, Descartes, Newton, there was now triumphantly enthroned the reasonable dogma of faith in the unchangeable laws of nature. Miracle dared no longer show itself, or, when it did dare, was hissed down. In other and better words, the fantastic miracles of mere whim had vanished, and in their stead was seen the mighty miracle of the universe - more regular, and therefore more divine.

The great rebellion decidedly won the day. You may see it working in the bold forms of those earlier outbursts; in the irony of Galileo; in the absolute doubt wherewith Descartes leads off his system. The Middle Ages would have said, "'Tis the spirit of the Evil One."

The victory, however, is not a negative one, but very affirmative and surely based. The spirit of nature and the natural sciences, those outlaws of an elder day, return in might irresistible. All idle shadows are hunted out by the real, the substantial.

They had said in their folly, "Great Pan is dead." Anon, observing that he was yet alive, they had made him a god of evil: amid such a chaos they might well be deceived. But, lo! he lives, and lives harmonious, in the grand stability of laws that govern alike the star and the deep-hidden mystery of life.

Of this period two things, by no means contradictory, may be averred: the spirit of Satan conquers, while the reign of witchcraft is at an end.

All marvel-mongering, hellish or holy, is fallen very sick at last. Wizards and theologians are powerless alike. They are become, as it were, empirics, who pray in vain for some supernatural change, some whim of Providence, to work the wonders which science asks of nature and reason only.

For all their zeal, the Jansenists of this century succeed only in bringing forth a miracle very small and very ridiculous. Still less lucky are the rich and powerful Jesuits, who cannot get a miracle done at. any price; who have to be satisfied with the visions of a hysteric girl, Sister Mary Alacoque, of an exceedingly sanguine habit, with eyes for nothing but blood. In view of so much impotence, magic and witchcraft may find some solace for themselves.

While the old faith in the supernatural was thus declining, priests and witches shared a common fate. In the fears, the fancies of the Middle Ages, these two. were bound up together. Together they were still to face the general laughter and disdain. "When Molière made fun of the Devil and his "seething cauldrons," the clergy were deeply stirred, deeming that the belief in Paradise had fallen equally low.

A government of laymen only, that of the great Colbert, who was long the virtual King of France, could not conceal its scorn for such old questions. It emptied the prisons of the wizards whom the Rouen Parliament still crowded into them, and, in 1672, forbade the law courts from entertaining any prosecutions for witchcraft. The Parliament protested, and gave people to understand that by this denial of sorcery many other things were put in peril. Any doubting of these lower mysteries would cause many minds to waver from their belief in mysteries of a higher sort.

The Sabbath disappears, but why? Because it exists everywhere. It enters into the people's habits, becomes the practice of their daily life. The Devil, the Witches, had long been reproached with loving death more than life, with hating and hindering the generative powers of nature. And now in the pious seventeenth century, when the Witch is fast dying out, a love of barrenness, and a fear of being fruitful, are found to be, in very truth, the one prevalent disease.

If Satan ever read, he would have good cause for laughter as he read the casuists who took him up where he left off. For there was one difference at least between them. In times of terror Satan made provision for the famished, took pity on the poor. But these fellows have compassion only for the rich. With his vices, his luxury, his court life, the rich man is still a needy miserable beggar. He comes to confession with a humbly threatening air, in order to wrest from his doctor permission to sin with a good conscience. Some day will be told, by him who may -have the courage to tell it, an astounding tale of the cowardly things done, and the shameful tricks so basely ventured by the casuist who wished to keep his penitent. From Navarro to Escobar the strangest bargains were continually made at the wife's expense, and some little wrangling went on after that. But all this would not do. The casuist was conquered, was altogether a coward. From Zoccoli to Liguori 1670 to 1770 - he gave up banning Nature.

The Devil, so it was said, showed two countenances at the Sabbath: the one in front seemed threatening, the other behind was farcical. Now that he has nothing to do with it, he has generously given the latter to the casuist,

It must have amused him to see his trusty friends settled among honest folk, in the serious households swayed by the Church. The worldling who bettered himself by that great resource of the day, lucrative adultery, laughed at prudence, and boldly followed his natural bent. Pious families, on the other hand, followed nothing but their Jesuits. ID order to preserve, to concentrate their property, to leave each one wealthy heir, they entered on the crooked ways of the new spiritualism. Buried in a mysterious gloom, losing at the faldstool all heed and knowledge of themselves, the proudest of them followed the lesson taught by Molinos: "In this world we live to suffer. But in time that suffering is soothed and lulled to sleep by a habit of pious indifference. We thus attain to a negation. Death do you say? Not altogether. Without mingling in the world, or heeding its voices, we get thereof an echo dim and soft. It is like a windfall of Divine Grace, so mild and searching; never more so than in moments of self-abasement, when the will is wholly obscured."

Exquisite depths of feeling! Alas, poor Satan! how art thou left behind! Bend low, acknowledge, and admire thy children!

The physicians who, having sprung from the popular empiricism which men called witchcraft, were far more truly his lawful children, were too forgetful of him. who had left them his highest patrimony, as being his favoured heirs. They were ungrateful to the Witch, who laid the way for themselves. Nay, they went further than that. On this fallen king, their father and creator, they dealt some hard strokes with the whip. *"Thou, too, my son?"* They gave the jesters cruel weapons against him.

Even in the sixteenth century there were some to scoff at the spirit who through all time, from the days of the Sibyl to those of tne "Witch, had filled and troubled the woman. They maintained that he was neither God nor Devil, but only "the Prince of the Air," as the Middle Ages called him. Satan was nothing but a disease!

Possession to them was only a result of the prisonlike, sedentary, dry, unyielding life of the cloister. As for the 6500 devils in Gauffridi's little Madeline, and the hosts that fought in the bodies of maddened nuns at Loudun and Louviers, these doctors called them physical storms. "If Aeolus can shake the earth," said Yvelin, "why not also the body of a girl?" La Cadière's surgeon, of whom more anon, had the coolness to say, "it was nothing more than a choking of the womb."

Wonderful descent! Routed by the simplest remedies, by exorcisms after Molière, the terror of the Middle Ages would flee away and vanish utterly!

This is too sweeping a reduction of the question. Satan was more than that. The doctors saw neither the height nor the depth of him; neither his grand revolt in the form of science, nor that strange mixture of impurity and pious intrigue, that union of Tartuffe and Priapus, which he brought to pass about the year 1700.

People fancy they know something about the eighteenth century, and yet have never seen one of its most essential features. The greater its outward civilization, the clearer and fuller the light that bathed its uppermost layers, so much the more hermetically sealed lay all those widespread lower realms, of priests and monks, and women credulous, sickly, prone to believe whatever they heard or saw. In the years before Cagliostro, Mesmer, and the magnetisers, who appeared towards the close of the century, a good many priests still worked away at the old dead witchcraft. They talked of nothing but enchantments, spread the fear of them abroad, and undertook to hunt out the devils with their shameful exorcisms. Many set up for wizards, well knowing how little risk they ran, now that people were no longer burnt. They knew they were sheltered by the milder spirit of their age, by the tolerant teachings of their foes the philosophers, by the levity of the great jesters, who thought that anything could be extinguished with a laugh. Now it was just because people laughed, that these gloomy plot-spinners went their way without much fear. The new spirit, that of the Regent namely, was sceptical and easy-natured. It shone forth in the *Persian Letters,* it shone forth everywhere in the all-powerful journalist who filled that century, Voltaire. At any shedding of human blood his whole heart rises indignant. All other matters only make him laugh. Little by little, the maxim of the worldly public seems to be, "Punish nothing, and laugh at all."

This tolerant spirit suffered Cardinal Tencin to appear in public as his sister's husband. This, too, it was that ensured to the masters of convents the peaceful possession of their nuns, who were even allowed to make declarations of pregnancy, to register the births of their children. [1] This tolerant temper made excuses for Father Apollinaire, when he was caught in a shameful piece of exorcism. That worthy Jesuit, Cauvrigny, idol of the provincial convents, paid for his adventures only by a recall to Paris, in other words by fresh preferment.

Such also was the punishment awarded the famous Jesuit, Girard, who was loaded with honours when he should have got the rope. He died in the sweetest savour of holiness. His was the most curious affair of that century. It enables us to probe the peculiar methods of that day, to realize the coarse jumble of jarring machinery which was then at work. As a thing of course, it was preluded by the dangerous suavities of the Song of Songs. It was carried on by Mary Alacoque, with a marriage of Bleeding Hearts spiced with the morbid blandishments of Molinos. To these Girard added the whisperings of

Satan and the terrors of enchantment. He was at once the Devil and the Devil's exerciser. At last, horrible to say, instead of getting justice done to her, the unhappy girl whom he sacrificed with so much cruelty, was persecuted to death. She disappeared, shut up perhaps by a *lettre de cachet*, and buried alive in her tomb.

[1] The noble Chapter of Canons of Pignan were sixteen in number. In one year the provost received from the nuns sixteen declarations of pregnancy. (See MS. History of Besse, by M. Renoux.) One good fruit of this publicity was the decrease of infanticide among the religious orders. At the price of a little shame, the nuns let their children live, and doubtless became good mothers. Those of Pignan put their babes out to nurse with the neighbouring peasants, who brought them up as their own.

Chapter Ten - Father Girard and La Cadière: 1730

THE Jesuits were unlucky. Powerful at Versailles, where they ruled the Court, they had not the slightest credit with Heaven. Not one tiny miracle could they do. The Jansenists overflowed, at any rate, with touching stories of miracles done. Untold numbers of sick, infirm, halt, and paralytic obtained a momentary cure at the tomb of the Deacon Paris. Crushed by a terrible succession of plagues, from the time of the Great King to the Regency, when so many were reduced to beggary, these unfortunate people went to entreat a poor, good fellow, a virtuous imbecile, a saint in spite of his absurdities, to make them whole. And what need, after all, of laughter? His life is far more touching than ridiculous. We are not to be surprised if these good folk, in the emotion of seeing their benefactor's tomb, suddenly forgot their own sufferings. The cure did not last, but what matter? A miracle indeed had taken place, a miracle of devotion, of lovingkindness, of gratitude. Latterly, with all this some knavery began to mingle, but at that time, in 1728, these wonderful popular scenes were very pure.

The Jesuits would have given anything for the least of the miracles they denied. For well-nigh fifty years they worked away, embellishing with fables and anecdotes their Legend of the Sacred Heart, the story of Mary Alacoque. For twenty-five or thirty years they had been trying to convince the world that their helpmate, James II. of England, not content with healing the king's evil (in his character of King of France), amused himself after his death in making the dumb to speak, the lame to walk straight, and the squint-eyed to see properly. They who were cured squinted worse than ever. As for the dumb, it so chanced that she who played this part was a manifest rogue, caught in the very act of stealing. She roamed the provinces: at every chapel of any renowned saint she was healed by a miracle and received alms, and then began her work again elsewhere.

For getting wonders wrought the South was a better country. There might be found a plenty of nervous women, easy to excite, the very ones to make into somnambulists, subjects of miracle, bearers of mystic marks, and so forth.

At Marseilles the Jesuits had on their side a bishop, Belzunce, a bold, hearty sort of man, renowned in the memorable plague, [1] but credulous and narrow-minded withal; under whose countenance many a bold venture might be made. Beside him they had placed a Jesuit of Franche-Comté, not wanting in mind, whose austere outside did not prevent his preaching pleasantly, in an ornate and rather worldly style, such as the ladies loved. A true Jesuit, he made his way by two different methods, now by feminine intrigue, anon by his holy utterances. Girard had on his side neither years nor figure; he was a man of forty-seven, tall, withered, weak-looking, of dirty aspect, and given to spitting without end. [2] He had long been a tutor, even till he was thirty-seven; and he preserved some of his college tastes. For the last ten years, namely, ever since the great plague, he had been confessor to the nuns. With them he had fared well, winning over them a high degree of power by enforcing a method seemingly quite at variance with the Provencial temperament, by teaching the doctrine and the discipline of a mystic death, of absolute passiveness, of entire forgetfulness of self. The dreadful crisis through which they had just passed had deadened their spirits, and weakened hearts already unmanned by a kind of morbid languor. Under Girard's leading, the Carmelites of Marseilles carried their mysticism to great lengths; and first among them was Sister Remusat, who passed for a saint.

In spite, or perhaps by reason, of this success, the Jesuits took Girard away from Marseilles: they wanted to employ him in raising anew their house at Toulon. Colbert's splendid institution, the Seminary for Naval Chaplains, had been entrusted to the Jesuits, with the view of cleansing the young chaplains from the influence of the Lazarists, who ruled them almost everywhere. But the two Jesuits placed in charge were men of small capacity. One was a fool; the other, Sabatier, remarkable, in spite of his age, for heat of temper. With all the insolence of our old navy he never kept himself under the least control. In Toulon he was reproached, not for having a mistress, nor yet a married woman, but for intriguing in a way so insolent and outrageous as to drive the husband wild. He sought to keep the husband specially alive to his own shame, to make him wince with every kind of pang. Matters were pushed so far that at last the husband died outright.

Still greater was the scandal caused by the Jesuits' rivals, the Observantines, who, having spiritual charge of a sisterhood at Ollioules, made mistresses openly of the nuns, and, not content with this, dared even to seduce the little boarders. One Aubany, the Father Guardian, violated a girl of thirteen; when her parents pursued him, he found shelter at Marseilles.

As Director of the Seminary for Chaplains, Girard began, through his seeming sternness and his real dexterity, to win for the Jesuits an ascendant over monks thus compromised, and over parish -priests of very vulgar manners and scanty learning.

In those Southern regions, where the men are abrupt, not seldom uncouth of speech and appearance, the women have a lively relish for the gentle gravity of the men of the North: they feel thankful to them for speaking a language at once aristocratic, official, and French.

"When Girard reached Toulon, he must already have gained full knowledge of the ground before him. Already had he won over a certain Guiol, who sometimes came to Marseilles, where she had a daughter, a Carmelite nun. This Guiol, wife of a small carpenter, threw herself entirely into his hands, even more so than he wanted. She was of ripe age, extremely vehement for a woman of forty-seven, depraved and ready for anything, ready to do him service of whatever kind, no matter what he might do or be, whether he were a sinner or a saint.

This Guiol, besides her Carmelite daughter at Marseilles, had another, a lay-sister to the Ursulines of Toulon. The Ursulines, an order of teaching nuns, formed everywhere a kind of centre; their parlour, the resort of mothers, being a half-way stage between the cloister and the world. At their house, and doubtless through their means, Girard saw the ladies of the town, among them one of forty years, a spinster, Mdlle. Gravier, daughter of an old contractor for the royal works at the Arsenal. This lady had a shadow who never left her, her cousin La Reboul, daughter of a skipper and sole heiress to herself; a woman, too, who really meant to succeed her, though very nearly her own age, being five-and-thirty. Around these gradually grew a small roomful of Girard's admirers, who became his regular penitents. Among them were sometimes introduced a few young girls, such as La Cadière, a tradesman's daughter and herself a seamstress, La Laugier, and La Batarelle, the daughter of a waterman. They had godly readings together, and now and then small suppers. But they were specially interested in certain letters which recounted the miracles and ecstasies of Sister Remusat, who was still alive; her death occurring in February, 1730. What a glorious thing for Father Girard, who had led her to a pitch so lofty! They read, they wept, they shouted with admiration. If they were not ecstatic yet, they were not far from being so. Already, to please her kinswoman, would La Reboul throw herself at times into a strange plight by holding her breath and pinching her nose.

Among these girls and women the least frivolous certainly was Catherine Cadière, a delicate, sickly girl of seventeen, taken up wholly with devotion and charity, of a mournful countenance, which seemed to say that, young as she was, she had felt more keenly than anyone else the great misfortunes of the time, those, namely, of Provence and Toulon. This is easily explained. She was born during the frightful famine of 1709; and just as the child was growing into a maiden, she witnessed the fearful scenes of the great plague. Those two events seemed to have left their mark upon her, to have taken her out of the present into a life beyond.

This sad flower belonged wholly to Toulon, to the Toulon of that day. To understand her better we must remember what that town is and what it was.

Toulon is a thoroughfare, a landing-place, the entrance of an immense harbour and a huge arsenal. The sense of this carries the traveller away, and prevents his seeing Toulon itself. There is a town however there, indeed an ancient city. It contains two different sets of people, the stranger functionaries, and the genuine Toulonnese, who are far from friendly to the former, regarding them with envy, and often roused to rebellion by the swaggering of the naval officers. All these differences were concentred in the gloomy streets of a town in those days choked up within its narrow girdle of fortifications. The most peculiar feature about this small dark town is, that it lies exactly between two broad seas of light, between the marvellous mirror of its roadstead and its glorious amphitheatre of mountains, baldheaded, of a dazzling grey, that blinds you in the noonday sun. All the gloomier look the streets themselves. Such as do not lead straight to the harbour and draw some light therefrom, are plunged at all hours in deep gloom. Filthy byeways, and small tradesmen with shops ill-furnished, invisible to anyone coming for the day, such is the general aspect of the place. The interior forms a maze of passages in which you may find plenty of churches, and old convents now turned into barracks. Copious kennels, laden and foul with sewage water, run down in torrents. The air is almost stagnant, and in so dry a climate you are surprised at seeing so much moisture.

In front of the new theatre a passage called La Rue de l'Hôpital leads from the narrow Rue Royale into the narrow Rue des Cannoniers. It might almost be called a blind alley. The sun, however, just looks down upon it at noon, but, finding the place so dismal, passes on forthwith, and leaves the passage to its wonted darkness.

Among these gloomy dwellings the smallest was that of the Sister Cadière, a retail dealer, or huckster. There was no entrance but by the shop, and only one room on each floor. The Cadières were honest pious folk, and Madame Cadière the mirror of excellence itself. These good people were not altogether poor. Besides their small dwelling in the town, they too, like most of their fellowtownsmen, had a countryhouse of their own. This latter is, commonly, a mere hut, a little stony plot of ground yielding a little wine. In the days of its naval greatness, under Colbert and his son, the wondrous bustle in the harbour brought some profit to the town. French money flowed in. The many great lords who passed that way brought their households along with them, an army of wasteful domestics, who left a good many things behind them. All this came to a sudden end. The artificial movement stopped short: even the workmen at the arsenal could no longer get their wages; shattered vessels were left unrepaired; and at last the timbers themselves were sold.

Toulon was keenly sensible of the rebound. At the siege of 1707 it seemed as if dead. What, then, was it in the dreadful year 1709, the 71st of Louis XIV., when every plague at once, a hard, winter, a famine, and an epidemic, seemed bent on utterly destroying France? The very trees of Provence were not spared. All traffic came to an end. The roads were covered with starving beggars. Begirt with bandits who stopped up every outlet, Toulon quaked for fear.

To crown all, Madame Cadière, in this year of sorrow, was with child. Three boys she had borne already. The eldest stayed in the shop to help his father. The second was with the Friar Preachers, and destined to become a Dominican, or a Jacobin as they were then called. The third was studying in the Jesuit seminary as a priest to be. The wedded couple wanted a daughter; Madame prayed to Heaven for a saint. She spent her nine months in prayer, fasting, or eating nought but rye bread. She had a daughter, namely Catherine. The babe was very delicate and like her brothers, unhealthy. The dampness of an ill-aired dwelling, and the poor nourishment gained from a mother so thrifty and more than temperate, had something to do with this. The brothers had scrofulous glands, and in her earlier years the little thing suffered from the same cause. Without being altogether ill, she had all the suffering sweetness of a sickly child. She grew up without growing stronger. At an age when other children have all the strength and gladness of upswelling life in them, she was already saying, "I have not long to live."

She took the small-pox, which left her rather marked. I know not if she was handsome, but it is clear that she was very winning, with all the charming contrasts, the twofold nature of the maidens of Provence. Lively and pensive, gay and sad, by turns, she was a good little worshipper, but given to harmless pranks withal. Between the long church services, if she went into the country with girls of her own age, she made no fuss about doing as they did, but would sing and dance away and flourish her tambourine. But such days were few. Most times her chief delight was to climb up to the top of the house, to bring herself nearer heaven, to obtain a glimpse of daylight, to look out, perhaps, on some small strip of sea, or some pointed peak in the vast wilderness of hills. Thenceforth to her eyes they were serious still, but less unkindly than before, less bald and leafless, in a garment thinly strewn with arbutus and larch.

This dead town of Toulon numbered 26,000 inhabitants when the plague began. It was a huge throng cooped up in one spot. But from this centre let us take away a girdle of great convents with their backs upon the ramparts, convents of Minorites, Ursulines, Visitandines, Bernardines, Oratorians, Jesuits, Capuchins, Recollects; those of the Refuge, the Good Shepherd, and, midmost of all, the enormous convent of Dominicans. Add to these the parish churches, parsonages, bishop's palace, and it seems that the clergy filled up the place, while the people had no room at all, to speak of. [3]

On a centre so closely thronged, we may guess how savagely the plague would fasten. Toulon's kind heart was also to prove her bane. She received with generous warmth some fugitives from Marseilles. These are just as likely to have brought the plague with them, as certain bales of wool to which was traced the first appearance of that scourge. The chief men of the place were about to fly, to scatter themselves over the country. But the First Con-

145

sul, M. d'Antrechaus, a man of heroic soul, withheld them, saying, with a stern air, "And what will the people do, sirs, in this impoverished town, if the rich folk carry their purses away?" So he held them back, and compelled all persons to stay where they were. Now the horrors of Marseilles had been ascribed to the mutual intercourse of its inhabitants. D'Antrechaus, however, tried a system entirely the reverse, tried to isolate the people of Toulon, by shutting them up in their houses. Two huge hospitals were established, in the roadstead and in the hills. All who did not come to these, had to keep at home on pain of death. For seven long months D'Antrechaus carried out a wager, which would have been held impossible, the keeping, namely, and feeding in their own houses, of a people numbering 26,000 souls. All that time Toulon was one vast tomb. No one stirred save in the morning, to deal out bread from door to door, and then to carry off the dead. Most of the doctors perished, and the magistrates all but D'Antrechaus. The gravediggers also perished, and their places were filled by condemned deserters, who went to work with brutal and headlong violence. Bodies were thrown into the tumbril, head downwards, from the fourth storey. One mother, having just lost her little girl, shrunk from seeing her poor wee body thus hurled below, and by dint of bribing, managed to get it lowered the proper way. As they were bearing it off, the child came to; it lived still. They took her up again, and she survived, to become the grandmother of the learned M. Brun, who wrote an excellent history of the port.

Poor little Cadière was exactly the same age as this girl who died and lived again, being twelve years old, an age for her sex so full of danger. In the general closing of the churches, in the putting down of all holidays, and chiefly of Christmas, wont to be so merry a season at Toulon, the child's fancy saw the end of all things. It seems as though she never quite shook off that fancy. Toulon never raised her head again. She retained her desert-like air. Everything was in ruins, everyone in mourning; widowers, orphans, desperate beings were everywhere seen. In the midst, a mighty shadow, moved D'Antrechaus himself; he had seen all about him perish, his sons, his brothers, and his colleagues; and was now so gloriously ruined, that he was fain to look to his neighbours for his daily meals. The poor quarelled among themselves for the honour of feeding him.

The young girl told her mother that she would never more wear any of her smarter clothes, and she must, therefore, sell them. She would do nothing but wait upon the sick, and she was always dragging her to the hospital at the end of the street. A little neighbour-girl of fourteen, Laugier by name, who had lost her father, was living with her mother in great wretchedness. Catherine was continually going to them with food and clothes, and anything she could get for them. She begged her parents to defray the cost of apprenticing Laugier to a dressmaker; and such was her sway over them that they could not refuse to incur so heavy an outlay. Her piety, her many little charms of soul, rendered her all-powerful. She was impassioned in her charity, giving not alms only, but love as well. She longed to make Laugier perfect, rejoiced to have her by her side, and often gave her half her bed. The pair had been admitted among the *Daughters of Saint Theresa,* the third order established by the Carmelites. Mdlle. Cadière was their model nun, and seemed at thirteen a Carmelite complete. Already she devoured some books of mysticism borrowed from a Visitandine. In marked contrast with herself seemed Laugier, now a girl of fifteen, who would do nothing but eat and look handsome. So indeed she was, and on that account had been made sextoness to the chapel of Saint Theresa. This led her into great familiarities with the priests', and so, when her conduct called for her expulsion from the congregation, another authority, the vicar-general, flew into such a rage as to declare that, if she were expelled, the chapel itself would be interdicted.

Both these girls had the temperament of their country, suffering from great excitement of the nerves, and from what was called flatulence of the womb. But in each the result was entirely different; being very carnal in the case of Laugier, who was gluttonous, lazy, passionate; but wholly cerebral with regard to the pure and gentle Catherine, who owing to her ailments or to a lively imagination that took everything up into itself, had no ideas concerning sex. "At twenty she was like a child of seven." For nothing cared she but praying and giving of alms; she had no wish at all to marry. At the very word "marriage," she would fall a-weeping, as if she had been asked to abandon God.

They had lent her the life of her patroness, Catherine of Genoa, and she had bought for herself *The Castle of the Soul,* by St. Theresa. Tew confessors could follow her in these mystic flights. They who spoke clumsily of such things gave her pain. She could not keep either her mother's confessor, the cathedral-priest, or another, a Carmelite, or even the old Jesuit Sabatier. At sixteen she found a priest of Saint Louis, a highly spiritual person. She spent days in church, to such a degree that her mother, by this time a widow and often in want of her, had to punish her, for all her own piety, on her return home. It was not the girl's fault, however: during her ecstasies she quite forgot herself. So great a saint was she accounted by the girls of her own age, that sometimes at mass they seemed to see the Host drawn on by the moving power of her love, until it flew up and placed itself of its own accord in her mouth.

Her two young brothers differed from each other in their feelings towards Girard. The elder, who lived with the Friar Preachers, shared the natural dislike of all Dominicans for the Jesuit. The other, who was studying with the Jesuits in order to become a priest, regarded Girard as a great man, a very saint, a man to honour as a hero. Of this younger brother, sickly like herself, Catherine was very fond. His ceaseless talking about Girard was sure to do its work upon her. One day she met the father in the street. He looked so grave, but so good and mild withal, that a voice within her said, "Behold the man to whose guidance thou art given!" The next Saturday, when she came to confess to him, he said that he had been expecting her. In her amazed emotion she never dreamed that her brother might have given him warning, but fancied that the mysterious voice had spoken to him also, and that they two were sharing the heavenly communion of warnings from the world above.

Six months of summer passed away, and yet Girard, who confessed her every Saturday, had taken no step towards her. The scandal about old Sabatier had set him on his guard. His own prudence would have held him to an attachment of a darker kind for such a one as the Guiol, who was certainly very mature, but also ardent and a devil incarnate.

It was Cadière who made the first advances towards him, innocent as they were. Her brother, the giddy Jacobin, had taken it into his head to lend a lady and circulate through the town a satire called *The Morality of the Jesuits*. The latter were soon apprised of this. Sabatier swore that he would write to the Court for a sealed order (lettre-de-cachet) to shut up the Jacobin. In her trouble and alarm, his sister, with tears in her eyes, went to beseech Father Girard for pity's sake to interfere. On her coming again to him a little later, he said, "Make yourself easy; your brother has nothing to fear; I have settled the matter for him." She was quite overcome. Girard saw his advantage. A man of his influence, a friend of the King, a friend of Heaven as well, after such proof of goodness as he had just been giving, would surely have the very strongest sway over so young a heart! He made the venture, and in her own uncertain language said to her, "Put yourself in my hands; yield yourself up to me altogether." Without a blush she answered, in the fulness of her angelic purity, "Yes;" meaning nought else than to have him for her sole director.

What were his plans concerning her? Would he make her a mistress or the tool of his charlatanry? Girard doubtless swayed to and fro, but he leant, I think, most towards the latter idea. He had to make his choice, might manage to seek out pleasures free from risk. But Mdlle. Cadière was under a pious mother. She lived with her family, a married brother and the two churchmen, in a very confined house, whose only entrance lay through the shop of the elder brother. She went no whither except to church. With all her simplicity she knew instinctively what things were impure, what houses dangerous. The Jesuit penitents were fond of meeting together at the top of a house, to eat, and play the fool, and cry out, in their Provencial tongue, "Vivent les *Jesuitons!*" A neighbour, disturbed by their noise, went and found them lying on their faces, singing and eating fritters, all paid for, it was said, out of the alms-money. Cadière was also invited, but taking a disgust to the thing she never went a second time.

She was assailable only through her soul. And it was only her soul that Girard seemed to desire. That she should accept those lessons of passive faith which he had taught at Marseilles, this apparently was all his aim. Hoping that example would do more for him than precept, he charged his tool Guiol to escort the young saint to Marseilles, where lived the friend of Cadière's childhood, a Carmelite nun, a daughter of Guiol's. The artful woman sought to win her trust by pretending that she, too, was sometimes ecstatic. She crammed her with absurd stories. She told her, for instance, that on finding a cask of wine spoilt in her cellar, she began to pray, and immediately the wine became good. Another time she felt herself pierced by a crown of thorns, but the angels had comforted her by serving up a good dinner, of which she partook with Father Girard.

Cadière gained her mother's leave to go with this worthy Guiol to Marseilles, and Madame Cadière paid her expenses. It was now the most scorching month that of August, 1729 in a scorching climate, when the country was all dried up, and the eye could see nothing but a rugged mirror of rocks and flintstone. The weak, parched brain of a sick girl suffering from the fatigues of travel, was all the more easily impressed by the dismal air of a nunnery of the dead. The true type of this class was the Sister Remusat, already a corpse to outward seeming, and soon to be really dead. Cadière was moved to admire so lofty a piece of perfection. Her treacherous companion allured her with the proud conceit of being such another and filling her place anon.

During this short trip of hers, Girard, who remained amid the stifling heats of Toulon, had met with a dismal fall. He would often go to the girl Laugier, who believed herself to be ecstatic, and "comfort" her to such good purpose that he got her presently with child. When Mdlle. Cadière came back in the highest ecstasy, as if like to soar away, he for his part was become so carnal, so given up to pleasure, that he "let fall on her ears a whisper of love." Thereat she took fire, but all, as anyone may see, in her own pure, saintly, generous way; as eager to keep him from falling, as devoting herself even to die for his sake.

One of her saintly gifts was her power of seeing into the depths of men's hearts. She had sometimes chanced to learn the secret life and morals of her confessors, to tell them of their faults; and this, in their fear and amazement, many of them had borne with great humility. One day this summer, on seeing Guiol come into her room, she suddenly said, "Wicked woman! what have you been doing?"

"And she was right," said Guiol herself, at a later period; "for I had just been doing an evil deed." Perhaps she had just been rendering Laugier the same midwife's service which next year she wished to render Batarelle.

Very likely, indeed, Laugier had entrusted to Catherine, at whose house she often slept, the secret of her good fortune, the love, the fatherly caresses of her saint. It was a hard and stormy trial for Catherine's spirits. On the one side, she had learnt by heart Girard's maxim, that whatever a saint may do is holy. But on the other hand, her native honesty and the whole course of her education compelled her to believe that over-fondness for the creature was ever a mortal sin. This woeful tossing between two different doctrines quite finished the poor girl, brought on within her dreadful storms, until at last she fancied herself possessed with a devil.

And here her goodness of heart was made manifest. Without humbling Girard, she told him she had a vision of a soul tormented with impure thoughts and deadly sin; that she felt the need of rescuing that soul, by offering the Devil victim for victim, by agreeing to yield herself into his keeping in Girard' s stead. He never forbade her, but gave her leave to be possessed for one year only.

Like the rest of the town, she had heard of the scandalous loves of Father Sabatier: an insolent passionate man, with none of Girard's prudence. The scorn which the Jesuits to her mind, such pillars of the Church were sure to incur, had not escaped her notice. She said one day to Girard, "I had a vision of a gloomy sea, with a vessel full of souls tossed by a storm of unclean thoughts. On this vessel were two Jesuits. Said I to the Redeemer, whom I saw in heaven, 'Lord, save them, and let me drown! The whole of their shipwreck do I take upon myself.' And God, in His mercy, granted my prayer."

All through the trial, and when Girard, become her foe, was aiming at her death, she never once recurred to this subject. These two parables, so clear in meaning, she never explained. She was too high-minded to say a word about them. She had doomed herself to very damnation. Some will say that in her pride she deemed herself so deadened and impassive as to defy the impurity with which the Demon troubled a man of God. But it is quite clear that she had no accurate knowledge of sensual things, foreseeing nought in such a mystery save pains and torments of the Devil. Girard was very cold, and quite unworthy of all this sacrifice. Instead of being moved to compassion, he sported with her credulity through a vile deceit. Into her casket he slipped a paper, in which God declared that, for her sake, He would indeed save the vessel. But he took care not to leave so absurd a document there: she would have read it again and again until she came to perceive how spurious it was. The angel who brought the paper carried it off the next day.

With the same coarseness of feeling Girard lightly allowed her, all unsettled and incapable of praying as she plainly was, to communicate as much as she pleased in different churches every day. This only made her worse. Filled already with the Demon, she harboured the two foes in one place. With equal power they fought within her against each other. She thought she would burst asunder. She would fall into a dead faint, and so remain for several hours. By December she could not move even from her bed.

Girard had now but too good a plea for seeing her. He was prudent enough to let himself be led by the younger brother at least as far as her door. The sick girl's room was at the top of the house. Her mother stayed discreetly in the shop. He was left alone as long as he pleased, and if he chose could turn the key. At this time she was very ill. He handled her as a child, drawing her forward a little to the front of the bed, holding her head, and kissing her in a fatherly way.

She was very pure, but very sensitive. A slight touch, that no one else would have remarked, deprived her of her senses: this Girard found out for himself, and the knowledge of it possessed him with evil thoughts. He threw her at will into this trance, [4] and she, in her thorough trust in him, never thought of trying to prevent it, feeling only somewhat troubled and ashamed at causing such a man to waste upon her so much of his precious time. His visits were very long. It was easy to foresee what would happen at last. Ill as she was, the poor girl inspired Girard with a passion none the less wild and uncontrollable. One freedom led to another, and her plaintive remonstrances were met with scornful replies. "I am your master your god. You must bear all for obedience sake."

At length, about Christmas-time, the last barrier of reserve was broken down; and the poor girl awoke from her trance to utter a wail which moved even him to pity.

An issue which she but dimly realized, Girard, as better enlightened, viewed with growing alarm. Signs of what was coming began to show themselves in her bodily health. To crown the entanglement, Laugier also found herself with child. Those religious meetings, those suppers watered with the light wine of the country, led to a natural raising of the spirits of a race so excitable, and the trance that followed spread from one to another. With the more artful all this was mere sham; but with the sanguine, vehement Laugier the trance was genuine enough. In her own little room she had real fits of raving and swooning, especially when Girard came in. A little later than Cadière she, too became fruitful.

The danger was great. The girls were neither in a desert nor in the heart of a convent, but rather, as one might say, in the open street: Laugier in the midst of prying neighbours, Cadière in her own family. The latter's brother, the Jacobin, began to take Girard's long visits amiss. One day when Girard came, he ventured to stay beside her as though to watch over her safety. Girard boldly turned him out of the room, and the mother angrily drove her son from the house.

This was very like to bring on an explosion. Of course, the young man, swelling with rage at this hard usage, at this expulsion from his home, would cry aloud to the Preaching Friars, who in their turn would seize so fair an opening, to go about repeating the story and stirring up the whole town against the Jesuit. The latter, however, resolved to meet them with a strangely daring move, to save himself by a crime. The libertine became a scoundrel.

He knew his victim, had seen the scrofulous traces of her childhood, traces healed up but still looking different from common scars. Some of these were on her feet, others a little below her bosom. He formed a devilish plan of renewing the wounds and passing them off as "stigmata" like those procured from heaven by St. Francis and other saints, who sought after the closest conformity with their pattern, the crucified Redeemer, even to bearing on themselves the marks of the nails and the spear-wound in the side. The Jesuits were distressed at having nought to show against the miracles of the Jansenists. Girard felt sure of pleasing them by an unlooked-for miracle. He could not but receive the support of his own order, of their house at Toulon. One of them, old Sabatier, was ready to believe anything: he had of yore been Cadière's confessor, and this affair would bring him into credit. Another of these was Father Grignet, a pious old dotard, who would see whatever they pleased. If the Carmelites or any others were minded to have their doubts, they might be taught, by warnings from a high quarter, to consult their safety by keeping silence. Even the Jacobin Cadière, hitherto a stern and jealous foe, might find his account in turning round and believing in a tale which made his family illustrious and himself the brother of a saint.

"But," some will say, "did not the thing come naturally? We have instances numberless, and well-attested, of persons really marked with the sacred wounds."

The reverse is more likely. When she was aware of the new wounds, she felt ashamed and distressed with the fear of displeasing Girard by this return of her childish ailments; for such she deemed the sores which he had opened afresh while she lay unconscious in the trance. So she sped away to a neighbour, one Madame True, who dabbled in physic, and of her she bought, as if for her youngest brother, an ointment to burn away the sores.

She would have thought herself guilty of a great sin, if she had not told everything to Girard. So, however fearful she might be of displeasing and disgusting him, she spoke of this matter also. Looking at the wounds, he began playing his comedy, rebuked her attempt to heal them, and thus set herself against God. They were the marks, he said, of Heaven. Falling on his knees, he kissed the wounds on her feet. She crossed herself in self-abasement, struggled long-time against such a belief. Girard presses and scolds, makes her show him her side, and looks admiringly at the wound. "I, too," he said, "have a wound; but mine is within."

And now she is fain to believe in herself as a living miracle. Her acceptance of a thing so startling was greatly quickened by the fact, that Sister Remusat was just then dead. She had seen her in glory, her heart borne upward by the angels. Who was to take her place on earth? Who should inherit her high gifts, the heavenly favours wherewith she had been crowned? Girard offered her the succession, corrupting her through her pride.

From that time she was changed. In her vanity she set down every natural movement within her as holy. The loathings, the sudden starts of a woman great with child, of all which she knew nothing, were accounted for as inward struggles of the Spirit. As she sat at table with her family on the first day of Lent, she suddenly beheld the Saviour, who said, "I will lead thee into the desert, where thou shalt share with Me all the love and all the suffering of the holy Forty Days." She shuddered for dread of the suffering she must undergo. But still she would offer up her single self for a whole world of sinners. Her visions were all of blood; she had nothing but blood before her eyes. She beheld Jesus like a sieve running blood. She herself began to spit blood, and lose it in other ways. At the same time her nature seemed quite changed. The more she suffered, the more amorous she grew. On the twentieth day of Lent she saw her name coupled with that of Girard. Her pride, raised and quickened by these new sensations, enabled her to comprehend the *special sway* enjoyed by Mary, the "Woman, with respect to God. She felt *how much lower angels* are than the least of saints, male or female. She saw the Palace of Glory, and mistook herself for the Lauib. To crown these illusions she felt herself lifted off the ground, several feet into the air. She could hardly believe it, until Mdlle. Gravier, a respectable person, assured her of the fact. Everyone came, admired, worshipped. Girard brought his colleague Grignet, who knelt before her and wept with joy.

Not daring to goto her every day, Girard often made her come to the Jesuits' Church. There, before the altar, before the cross, he surrendered himself to a passion all the fiercer for such a sacrilege. Had she no scruples? did she still deceive herself? It seems as if, in the midst of an elation still unfeigned and earnest, her conscience was already dazed and darkened. Under cover of her bleeding wounds, those cruel favours of her heavenly Spouse, she began to feel some curious compensations...

In her reveries there are two points especially touching. One is the pure ideal she had formed of a faithful union, when she fancied that she saw her name and that of Girard joined together for ever in the Book of Life. The other is her kindliness of heart, the charmingly childlike nature which shines out through all her extravagances. On Palm Sunday, looking at the joyous party around their family table, she wept three hours together, for thinking that "on that very day no one had asked Jesus to dinner."

Through all that Lent, she could hardly eat anything: the little she took was thrown up again. The last fifteen days she fasted altogether, until she reached the last stage of weakness. ,Who would have believed that against this dying girl, to whom nothing remained but the mere breath, Girard could practise new barbarities? He had kept her sores from closing. A new one was now formed on her right side. And at last, on Good Friday, he gave the finishing touch to his cruel comedy, by making her wear a crown of iron-wire, which pierced her forehead, until drops of blood rolled down her face. All this was done without much secrecy. He began by cutting off her long hair and carrying it away. He ordered the crown of one Bitard, a cagemaker in the town. She did not show herself to her visitors with the crown on: they saw the result only, the drops of blood and the bleeding visage. Impressions of the latter, like so many *Veronicas,* [5] were taken off on napkins, and doubtless given away by Girard to people of great piety.

The mother, in her own despite, became an abettor in all this juggling. In truth, she was afraid of Girard; she began to find him capable of anything, and somebody, perhaps the Guiol, had told her, in the deepest confidence, that, if she said a word against him, her daughter would not be alive twenty-four hours.

153

Cadière, for her part, never lied about the matter. In the narrative taken down from her own lips of what happened this Lent, she expressly tells of a crown, with sharp points, which stuck in her head, and made it bleed. Nor did she then make any secret of the source whence came the little crosses she gave her visitors. From a model supplied by Girard, they were made to her order by one of her kinsfolk, a carpenter in the Arsenal.

On Good Friday, she remained twenty-four hours in a swoon, which they called a trance; remained in special charge of Girard, whose attentions weakened her, and did her deadly harm. She was now three months gone with child. The saintly martyr, the transfigured marvel, was already beginning to fill out. Desiring, yet dreading the more violent issues of a miscarriage, he plied her daily with reddish powders and dangerous drinks.

Much rather would he have had her die, and so have rid himself of the whole business. At any rate, he would have liked to get her away from her mother, to bury her safe in a convent. Well acquainted with houses of that sort, he knew, as Picard had done in the Louviers affair, how cleverly and discreetly such cases as Cadière's could be hidden away. He talked of it this very Good Friday. But she seemed too weak to be taken safely from her bed. At last, however, four days after Easter, a miscarriage took place.

The girl Laugier had also been having strange convulsive fits, and absurd beginnings of stigmata: one of them being an old wound, caused by her scissors when she was working as a seamstress, the other an eruptive sore in her side. Her transports suddenly turned to impious despair. She spat upon the crucifix: she cried out against Girard, "that devil of a priest, who had brought a poor girl of two-and-twenty into such a plight, only to forsake her afterwards!" Girard dared not go and face her passionate outbreaks. But the women about her, being all in his interest, found some way of bringing this matter to a quiet issue.

Was Girard a wizard, as people afterwards maintained.? They might well think so, who saw how easily, being neither young nor handsome, he had charmed so many women. Stranger still it was, that after getting thus compromised, he swayed opinion to such a degree. For a while, he seemed to have enchanted the whole town.

The truth was, that everyone knew the strength of the Jesuits. Nobody cared to quarrel with them. It was hardly reckoned safe to speak ill of them, even in a whisper. The bulk of the priesthood consisted of monklings of the Mendicant orders, who had no powerful friends or high connections. The Carmelites themselves, jealous and hurt as they were at losing Cadière, kept silence. Her brother, the young Jacobin, was lectured by his trembling mother into resuming his old circumspect ways. Becoming reconciled to Girard, he came at length to serve him as devotedly as did his younger brother, even lending himself to a curious trick by which people were led to believe that Girard had the gift of prophecy.

Such weak opposition as he might have to fear, would come only from the very person whom he seemed to have most thoroughly mastered. Submissive hitherto, Cadière now gave some slight tokens of a coming in dependence which could not help showing itself. On the 30th of April, at a country party got up by the polite Girard, and to which he sent his troop of young devotees in company with Guiol, Cadière fell into deep thought. The fair spring-time, in that climate so very charming, lifted her heart up to God. She exclaimed with a feeling of true piety, "Thee, Thee only, do I seek, Lord! Thine angels are not enough for me." Then one of the party, a blithesome girl, having, in the Provencial fashion, hung a tambourine round her neck, Cadière skipped and danced about like the rest; with a rug thrown across her shoulders, she danced the Bohemian measure, and made herself giddy with a hundred mad capers.

She was very unsettled. In May she got leave from her mother to make a trip to Sainte-Baume, to the Church of St. Mary Magdalen, the chief saint of girls on penance. Girard would only let her go under charge of two faithful overlookers, Guiol and Reboul. But though she had still some trances on the way, she showed herself weary of being a passive tool to the violent spirit, whether divine or devilish, that annoyed her. The end of her year's possession was not far off. Had she not won her freedom? Once issued forth from the gloom and witcheries of Toulon, into the open air, in the midst of nature, beneath the full sunshine, the prisoner regained her soul, withstood the stranger spirit, dared to be herself, to use her own will. Girard's two spies were far from edified thereat. On their return from this short journey, from the 17th to the 22nd May, they warned him of the change. He was convinced of it from his own experience. She fought against the trance, seeming no longer wishful to obey aught save reason.

He had thought to hold her both by his power of charming and through the holiness of his high office, and, lastly, by right of possession and carnal usage. But he had no hold upon her at all. The youthful soul, which, after all, had not been so much conquered as treacherously surprised, resumed its own nature. This hurt him. Besides his business of pedant, his tyranny over the children he chastised at will, over nuns not less at his disposal, there remained within a hard bottom of domineering jealousy. He determined to snatch Cadière back by punishing this first little revolt, if such a name could.be given to the timid fluttering of a soul rising again from its long compression. On the 22nd May she confessed to him after her wont; but he refused to absolve her, declaring her to be so guilty that on the morrow he would have to lay upon her a very great penance indeed.

What would that be? A fast? But she was weakened and wasted already. Long prayers, again, were; not in fashion with Quietist directors, - were in fact forbidden. There remained the *discipline*, or bodily chastisement. This punishment, then everywhere habitual, was enforced as prodigally in convents as in colleges. It was a simple and summary means of swift execution, sometimes, in a rude and simple age, carried out in the churches themselves. The *Fabliaux* show us an artless picture of manners, where, after confessing husband and wife, the priest gave them the discipline without any ceremony, just as they were behind the confessional. Scholars, monks, nuns, were all punished in the same way. [6]

Girard knew that a girl like Cadière, all unused to shame, and very modest for what she had hitherto suffered took place unknown to herself in her sleep would feel so cruelly tortured, so fatally crushed by this unseemly chastisement, as utterly to lose what little buoyancy she had. She was pretty sure too, if we must speak out, to be yet more cruelly mortified than other women, in respect of the pang endured by. her woman's vanity. With so much suffering, and so many fasts, followed by her late miscarriage, her body, always delicate, seemed worn away to a shadow. All the more surely would she shrink from any exposure of a form so lean, so wasted, so full of aches. Her swollen legs and such-like small infirmities would serve to enhance her humiliation.

We lack the courage to relate what followed. It may all be read in those three depositions, so artless, so manifestly unfeigned, in which, without being sworn, she made it her duty to avow what self-interest bade her conceal, owning even to things which were afterwards turned to the cruellest account against her.

Her first deposition was made on the spur of the moment, before the spiritual judge who was sent to take her by surprise. In this we seem to be ever hearing the utterances of a young heart that speaks as though in God's own presence. The second was taken before the King I should rather say before the magistrate who represented him, the Lieutenant Civil and Criminal of Toulon. The last was heard before the great assembly of the Parliament of Aix.

Observe that all three, agreeing as they do wonderfully together, were printed at Aix under the eye of her enemies, in a volume where, as I shall presently prove, an attempt was made to extenuate the guilt of Girard, and fasten the reader's gaze on every point likely to tell against Cadière. And yet the editor could not help inserting depositions like these, which bear with crushing weight on the man he sought to uphold.

It was a monstrous piece of inconsistency on Girard's part. He first frightened the poor girl, and then suddenly took a base, a cruel advantage of her fears.

In this case no plea of love can be offered in extenuation. The truth is far otherwise: he loved her no more. And this forms the most dreadful part of the story. We have seen how cruelly he drugged her; we have now to see her utterly forsaken. He owed her a grudge for being of greater worth than those other degraded women. He owed her a grudge for having unwittingly tempted him and brought him into danger. Above all, he could not forgive her for keeping her soul in safety. He sought only to tame her down, but caught hopefully at her oft-renewed assurance, "I feel that I shall not live." Villainous profligate that he was, bestowing his shameful kisses on that poor shattered body whose death he longed to see!

How did he account to her for this shocking antagonism of cruelty and caresses? Was it meant to try her patience and obedience, or did lie boldly pass on to the true depths of Molinos' teaching, that "only by dint of sinning can sin be quelled "? Did she take it all in full earnest, never perceiving that all this show of justice, penitence, expiation, was downright profligacy and nothing else?

She did not care to understand him in the strange moral crash that befell her after that 23rd May, under the influence of a mild warm June. She submitted to her master, of whom she was rather afraid, and with a singularly servile passion carried on the farce of undergoing small penances day by day. So little regard did Girard show for her feelings that he never hid from her his relations with other women. All he wanted was to get her into a convent. Meanwhile she was his plaything: she saw him, let him have his way. Weak, and yet further weakened by the shame that unnerved her, growing sadder and more sad at heart, she had now but little hold on life, and would keep on saying, in words that brought no sorrow to Girard's soul, "I feel that I shall soon be dead."

[1] The great plague of 1720, which carried off 60,000 people about Marseilles. Belzunce is the "Marseilles' good bishop" of Pope's line. - TRANS.

[2] See "The Proceedings in the Affair of Father Girard and La Cadière," Aix, 1733.

[3] See the work by M. d'Antrechaus, and the excellent treatise by M. Gustave Lambert.

[4] A case of mesmerism applied to a very susceptible patient. – TRANS.

[5] After the saint of that name, whose handkerchief received the impress of Christ's countenance. - TRANS.

[6] The Dauphin was cruelly flogged. A boy of fifteen, according to St. Simon, died from the pain of a like infliction. The prioress of the Abbey-in-the-Wood, pleaded before the King; against the "afflictive chastisement" threatened by her superior. For the credit of the convent, she was spared the public shame; but the superior, to whom she was consigned, doubtless punished her in a quiet way. The immoral tendency of such a practice became more and more manifest. Fear and shame led to woeful entreaties and unworthy bargains.

Chapter Eleven - Cadière in the Convent: 1730

THE Abbess of the Ollioules Convent was young for an abbess, being only thirty-eight years old. She was not wanting in mind. She was lively, swift alike in love and in hatred, hurried away by her heart and her senses also, endowed with very little of the tact and the moderation needed for the governing of such a body.

This nunnery drew its livelihood from two sources. On the one side, there came to it from Toulon two or three nuns of consular families, who brought good dowers with them, and therefore did what they pleased. They lived with the Observantine monks who had the ghostly direction of the convent. On the other hand, these monks, whose order had spread to Marseilles and many other places, picked up some little boarders and novices who paid for their keep: a contact full of danger and unpleasantness for the children, as one may see by the Aubany affair.

There was no real confinement, nor much internal order. In the scorching summer nights of that African climate, peculiarly oppressive and wearying in the airless passes of Ollioules, nuns and novices went to and fro with the greatest freedom. The very same things were going on at Ollioules in I 730 which we saw in 1630 at Loudun. The bulk of nuns, well-nigh a dozen out of the fifteen who made up the house, being rather forsaken by the monks, who preferred ladies of loftier position, were poor creatures, sick at heart, and disinherited, with nothing to console them but tattling, child's play, and other school-girls' tricks.

The abbess was afraid that Cadière would soon see through all this. She made some demur about taking her in. Anon, with some abruptness, she entirely changed her cue. In a charming letter, all the more flattering as sent so unexpectedly from such a lady to so young a girl, she expressed a hope of her leaving the ghostly guidance of Father Girard. The girl was not, of course, to be transferred to her Observantines, who were far from capable of the charge. The abbess had formed the bold, enlivening idea of taking her into her own hands and becoming her sole director.

She was very vain. Deeming herself more agreeable than an old Jesuit confessor, she reckoned on making this prodigy her own, on conquering her without trouble. She would have worked the young saint for the benefit of her house.

She paid her the marked compliment of receiving her on the threshold, at the street-door. She kissed her, caught her up, led her into the abbess's own fine room, and bade her share it with herself. She was charmed with her modesty, with her invalid grace, with a certain strangeness at once mysterious and melting. In that short journey the girl had suffered a great deal. The abbess wanted to lay her down in her own bed, saying she loved her so that she would have them sleep together like sisters in one bed.

For her purpose this was probably more than was needful. It would have been quite enough to have the saint under her own roof. She would now have too much the look of a little favourite. The lady, however, was surprised at the young girl's hesitation, which doubtless sprang from her modesty or her humility; in part, perhaps, from a comparison of her own ill-health with the young health and blooming beauty of the other. But the abbess tenderly urged her request.

Under the influence of a fondling so close and so continual, she deemed that Girard would be forgotten. With all abbesses it had become the ruling fancy, the pet ambition, to confess their own nuns, according to the practice allowed by St. Theresa. By this pleasant scheme of hers the same result would come out of itself, the young woman telling her confessors only of small things, but keeping the depths of her heart for one particular person. Caressed continually by one curious woman, at eventide, in the night, when her head was on the pillow, she would have let out many a secret, whether her own or another's.

From this living entanglement she could not free herself at the first. She slept with the abbess. The latter thought she held her fast by a twofold tie, by the opposite means employed on the saint and on the woman; that is, on the nervous, sensitive, and, through her weakness, perhaps sensual girl. Her story, her sayings, whatever fell from her lips, were all written down. From other sources she picked up the meanest details of her physical life, and forwarded the report thereof to Toulon. She would have made her an idol, a pretty little pet doll. On a slope so slippery the work of allurement doubtless moved apace. But the girl had scruples and a kind of fear. She made one great effort, of which her weak health would have made her seem incapable. She humbly asked leave to quit that dove's-nest, that couch too soft and delicate, to go and live in common with the novices or the boarders.

Great was the abbess's surprise; great her mortification. She fancied herself scorned. She took a spite against the thankless girl, and never forgave her.

From the others Cadière met with a very pleasant welcome. The mistress of the novices, Madame de Lescot,. a nun from Paris, refined and good, was a worthier woman than the abbess. She seemed to understand the other to see in her a poor prey of fate, a young heart full of God, but cruelly branded by some eccentric spell which seemed like to hurry her onward to disgrace, to some unhappy end. She busied herself entirely with looking after the girl, saving her from her own rashness, interpreting her to others, excusing those things which might in her be least excusable.

Saving the two or three noble ladies who lived with the monks and had small relish for the higher mysticism, they were all fond of her, and took her for an angel from heaven. Their tender feelings having little else to engage them, became concentred in her and her alone. They found her not only pious and wonderfully devout, but a good child withal, kind-hearted, winning, and entertaining. They were no longer listless and sick at heart. She engaged and edified them with her dreams, with stories true, or rather, perhaps, unfeigned, mingled ever with touches of purest tenderness. She would say, "At night I go everywhere, even to America. Everywhere I leave letters bidding people repent. To-night I shall go and seek you out, even when you have locked yourselves in. We will all go together into the Sacred Heart."

The miracle was wrought. Each of them at midnight, so she said, received the delightful visit. They all fancied they felt Cadière embracing them, and making them enter the heart of Jesus. They were very frightened and very happy. Tenderest, most credulous of all, was Sister Raimbaud, a woman of

Marseilles, who tasted this happiness fifteen times in three months, or nearly once in every six days.

It was purely the effect of imagination. The proof is, that Cadière visited all of them at one same moment. The abbess meanwhile was hurt, being roused at the first to jealousy by the thought that she only had been left out, and afterwards feeling assured that, lost as the girl might be in her own dreams, she would get through so many intimate friends but too clear an inkling into the scandals of the house.

These were scarcely hidden from her at all. But as nothing came to Cadière save by the way of spiritual insight, she fancied they had been told her in a revelation. Here her kindliness shone out. She felt a large compassion for the God who was thus outraged. And once again she imagined herself bound to atone for the rest, to save the sinners from the punishment they deserved, by draining herself the worst cruelties which the rage of devils would have power to wreak.

All this burst upon her on the 25th June, the Feast of St. John. She was spending the evening with the sisters in the novices' rooms. With a loud cry she fell backward in contortions, and lost all consciousness.

When she came to, the novices surrounded her, waiting eager to hear what she was going to say. But the governess, Madame Lescot, guessed what she would say, felt that she was about to ruin herself. So she lifted her up, and led her straight to her room, where she found herself quite flayed, and her linen covered with blood.

Why did Girard fail her amidst these struggles inward and from without? She could not make him out. She had much need of support, and yet he never came, except for one moment at rare intervals, to the parlour.

She wrote to him on the 28th June, by her brothers; for though she could read, she was scarcely able to write. She called to him in the most stirring, the most urgent tones, and he answers by putting her off. He has to preach at Hyerès, he has a sore throat, and so on.

Wonderful to tell, it is the abbess herself who brings him thither. No doubt she was uneasy at Cadière's discovering so much of the inner life of the convent. Making sure that the girl would talk of it to Girard, she wished to forestall her. In a very nattering and tender note of the 3rd July, she besought the Jesuit to come and see herself first, for she longed, between themselves, to be his pupil, his disciple, as humble Nicodemus had been of Christ. "Under your guidance, by the blessing of that holy freedom which my post ensures me, I should move forward swiftly and noiselessly in the path of virtue. The state of our young candidate here will serve me as a fair and useful pretext."

A startling, ill-considered step, betraying some unsoundness in the lady's mind. Having failed to supplant Girard with Cadière, she now essayed to supplant Cadière with Girard. Abruptly, without the least preface, she stepped forward. She made her decision, like a great lady, who was still agreeable and quite sure of being taken at her word, who would go so far as even to talk of the *freedom* she enjoyed!

In taking so false a step she started from a true belief that Girard had ceased to care much for Cadière. But she might have guessed that he had other things to perplex him in Toulon. He was disturbed by an affair no longer turning upon a young girl, but on a lady of ripe age, easy circumstances, and good standing; on his wisest penitent, Mdlle. Gravier. Her forty years failed to protect her. He would have no self-governed sheep in his fold. One day, to her surprise and mortification, she found herself pregnant, and loud was her wail thereat.

Taken up with this new adventure, Girard looked but coldly on the abbess's unforeseen advances. He mistrusted them as a trap laid for him by the Observantines. He resolved to be cautious, saw the abbess, who was already embarrassed by her rash step, and then saw Cadière, but only in the chapel where he confessed her.

The latter was hurt by his want of warmth. In truth his conduct showed strange inconsistencies. He unsettled her with his light, agreeable letters, full of little sportive threats which might have been called lover-like. And yet he never deigned to see her save in public.

In a note written the same evening she revenged herself in a very delicate way. She said that when he granted her absolution, she felt wonderfully dissevered both from herself and from *every other creature.*

It was just what Girard would have wanted. His plots had fallen into a sad tangle, and Cadière was in the way. Her letter enchanted him: far from being annoyed with her, he enjoined her to keep dissevered. At the same time, he hinted at the need he had for caution. He had received a letter, he said, warning him sharply of her faults. However, as he would set off on the 6th July for Marseilles, he would see her on the road.

She awaited him, but no Girard came. Her agitation was very great. It brought on a sharp fit of her old bodily distemper. She spoke of it to her dear Sister Raimbaud, who would not leave her, who slept with her, against the rules. This was on the night of the 6th July, when the heat in that close oven of Ollioules was most oppressive and condensed. At four or five o'clock, seeing her writhe in sharp suffering, the other "thought she had the colic, and went to fetch some fire from the kitchen." While she was gone, Cadière tried by one last effort to bring Girard to her side forthwith. Whether with her nails she had re-opened the wounds in her head, or whether she had stuck upon it the sharp iron crown, she somehow made herself all bloody. The pain transfigured her, until her eyes sparkled again.

This lasted not less than two hours. The nuns flocked to see her in this state, and gazed admiringly. They would even have brought their Observantines thither, had Cadière not prevented them.

The abbess would have taken good care to tell Girard nothing, lest he should see her in a plight so touching, so very pitiful. But good Madame Lescot comforted the girl by sending the news to the father. He came, but like a true juggler, instead of going up to her room at once, had himself an ecstatic fit in the chapel, staying there a whole hour on his knees, prostrate before the Holy Sacrament. Going at length upstairs, he found Cadière surrounded by all the nuns. They tell him how for a moment she looked as if she was at mass, how she seemed to open her lips to receive the Host. "Who should know that better than myself?" said the knave. "An angel had told me. I repeated the mass, and gave her the sacrament from Toulon." They were so upset by the miracle, that one of them was two days ill. Girard then addressed Cadière with unseemly gaiety: "So, so, little glutton! would you rob me of half my share?"

They withdraw respectfully, leaving these two alone. Behold him face to face with his bleeding victim, so pale, so weak, but agitated all the more! Anyone would have been greatly moved. The avowal expressed by her blood, her wounds, rather than spoken words, was likely to reach his heart. It was a humbling sight; but who would not have pitied her? This innocent girl could for one moment yield to nature! In her short unhappy life, a stranger as she was to the charms of sense, the poor young saint could still show one hour of weakness! All he had hitherto enjoyed of her without her knowledge, became mere nought. With her soul, her will, he would now be master of everything.

In her deposition Cadi ere briefly and bashfully said that she lost all knowledge of what happened next. In a confession made to one of her friends she uttered no complaints, but let her understand the truth.

And what did Girard do in return for so charmingly bold a flight of that impatient heart? He scolded her. He was only chilled by a warmth which would have set any other heart on fire. His tyrannous soul wanted nothing but the dead, the merest plaything of his will. And this girl, by the boldness of her first move, had forced him to come. The scholar had drawn the master along. The peevish pedant treated the matter as he would have treated a rebellion at school. His lewd severities, his coolly selfish pursuit of a cruel pleasure, blighted the unhappy girl, who now had nothing left her but remorse.

It was no less shocking a fact, that the blood poured out for his sake had no other effect than to tempt him to make the most of it for his own purposes. In this, perhaps his last, interview he sought to make so far sure of the poor thing's discretion, that, however forsaken by him, she herself might still believe in him. He asked if he was to be less favoured than the nuns who had seen the miracle. She let herself bleed before him. The water with which he washed away the blood he drank himself, [1] and made her drink also, and by this hateful communion he thought to bind fast her soul.

This lasted two or three hours, and it was now near noon. The abbess was scandalized. She resolved to go with the dinner herself, and make them open the door. Girard took some tea: it being Friday, he pretended to be fasting; though he had doubtless armed himself well at Toulon. Cadière asked for coffee. The lay sister who managed the kitchen was surprised at this on such a day. But without that strengthening draught she would have fainted away. It set her up a little, and she kept hold of Girard still. He stayed with her, no longer indeed locked in, till four o'clock, seeking to efface the gloomy impression caused by his conduct in the morning. By dint of lying about friendship and fatherhood, he somewhat reassured the susceptible creature, and calmed her troubled spirits. She showed him the way out, and, walking after him, took, child-like, two or three skips for joy. He said, drily, "Little fool!"

She paid heavily for her weakness. At nine of that same night she had a dreadful vision, and was heard crying out, "God! keep off from me! get back!" On the morning of the 8th, at mass she did not stay for the communion, deeming herself, no doubt, unworthy, but made her escape to her own room. Thereon arose much scandal. Yet so greatly was she beloved, that one of the nuns ran after her, and, telling a compassionate falsehood, swore she had beheld Jesus giving her the sacrament with His own hand.

Madame Lescot delicately and cleverly wrote a legend out of the mystic ejaculations, the holy sighs, the devout tears, and whatever else burst forth from this shattered heart. Strange to say, these women tenderly conspired to shield a woman. Nothing tells more than this in behalf of poor Cadière and her delightful gifts. Already in one month's time she had become the child of all. They defended her in everything she did. Innocent though she might be, they saw in her only the victim of the Devil's attacks. One kind sturdy woman of the people, Matherone, daughter of the Ollioules locksmith, and porteress herself to the convent, on seeing some of Girard's indecent liberties, said, in spite of them, "No matter: she is a saint." And when he once talked of taking her from the convent, she cried out, "Take away our Mademoiselle Cadière! I will have an iron door made to keep her from going."

Alarmed at the state of things, and at the use to which it might be turned by the abbess and her monks, Cadière's brethren who came to her every day, took courage to be beforehand; and in a formal letter written in her name to Girard, reminded him of the revelation given to her on the 25th June regarding the morals of the Observantines. It was time, they said, "to carry out God's purposes in this matter," namely, of course, to demand an inquiry, to accuse the accusers.

Their excess of boldness was very rash. Cadière, now all but dying, had no such thoughts in her head. Her women-friends imagined that he who had caused the disturbance would, perhaps, bring back the calm. They besought Girard to come and confess her. A dreadful scene took place. At the confessional she uttered cries and wailings audible thirty paces off. The curious among them found some amusement listening to her. and were not disappointed. Girard was inflicting chastisement. Again and again he said, "Be calm, mademoiselle!" In vain did he try to absolve her. She would not be absolved. On the 12th, she had so sharp a pang below her heart, that she felt as though her sides were bursting. On the 14th, she seemed fast dying, and her mother was sent for. She received the viaticum; and on the morrow made a

163

public confession, "the most touching, the most expressive that had ever been heard. We were drowned in tears." On the 20th, she was in a state of heartrending agony. After that she had a sudden and saving change for the better, marked by a very soothing vision. She beheld the sinful Magdalen pardoned, caught up into glory, filling in heaven the place which Lucifer had lost.

Girard, however, could only ensure her discretion by corrupting her yet further, by choking her remorse. Sometimes he would come to the parlour and greet her with bold embraces. But oftener he sent his faithful followers, Guiol and others, who sought to initiate her into their own disgraceful secrets, while seeming to sympathise tenderly with the sufferings of their outspoken friend. Girard not only winked at this, but himself spoke freely to Cadière of such matters as the pregnancy of Mdlle. Gravier. He wanted her to ask him to Ollioules, to calm his irritation, to persuade him that such a circumstance might be a delusion of the Devil's causing, which could perchance be dispelled.

These impure teachings made no way with Cadière. They were sure to anger her brethren, to whom they were not unknown. The letters they wrote in her name are very curious. Enraged at heart and sorely wounded, accounting Girard a villain, but obliged to make their sister speak of him with respectful tenderness, they still, by snatches, let their wrath become visible.

As for Girard's letters, they are pieces of laboured writing, manifestly meant for the trial which might take place. Let us talk of the only one which he did not get into his hands to tamper with. It is dated the 22nd July. It is at once sour and sweet, agreeable, trifling, the letter of a careless man. The meaning of it is thus:

"The bishop reached Toulon this morning, and will go to see Cadière... They will settle together what to do and say. If the Grand Vicar and Father Sabatier wish to see her, and ask to see her wounds, she will tell them that she has been forbidden to do or say aught.

"I am hungering to see you again, to see the whole of you. You know that I only demand *my right.* It is so long since I have seen more than half of you (he means to say, at the parlour grating). Shall I tire you? Well, do you not also tire me?" And so on.

A strange letter in every way. He distrusts alike the bishop and the Jesuit, his own colleague, old Sabatier. It is at bottom the letter of a restless culprit. He knows that in her hands she holds his letters, his papers, the means, in short, of ruining him. The two young men write back in their sister's name a spirited answer the only one that has a truthful sound. They answer him line for line, without insult, but with a roughness often ironical, and betraying the wrath pent-up within them. The sister promises to obey him, to say nothing either to the bishop or the Jesuit. She congratulates him on having "boldness enough to exhort others to suffer." She takes up and returns him his shocking gallantry, but in a shocking way; and here we trace a man's hand, the hand of those two giddy heads.

Two days after, they went and told her to decide on leaving the convent forthwith. Girard was dismayed. He thought his papers would disappear with her.

The greatness of his terror took away his senses. He had the weakness to go and weep at the Ollioules parlour, to fall on his knees before her, and ask her if she had the heart to leave him. Touched by his words, the poor girl said "No," went forward, and let him embrace her. And yet this Judas wanted only to deceive her, to gain a few days' time for securing help from a higher quarter.

On the 29th there is an utter change. Cadière stays at Ollioules, begs him to excuse her, vows submission. It is but too clear that he has set some mighty influences at work; that from the 29th threats come in, perhaps from Aix, and presently from Paris. The Jesuit bigwigs have been writing, and their courtly patrons from Versailles.

In such a struggle, what were the brethren to do? No doubt they took counsel with their chiefs, who would certainly warn them against setting too hard on Girard as *a libertine confessor*, for thereby offence would be given to all the clergy, who deemed confession their dearest prize. It was needful, on the contrary-, to sever him from the priests by proving the strangeness of his teaching, by bringing him forward as a *Quietist.* With that one word they might lead him a long way. In 1698, a vicar in the neighbourhood of Dijon had been burnt for Quietism. They conceived the idea of drawing up a memoir, dictated apparently by their sister, to whom the plan was really unknown, in which the high and splendid Quietism of Girard should be affirmed, and therefore in effect denounced. This memoir recounted the visions she had seen in Lent. In it the name of Girard was already in heaven. She saw it joined with her own in the Book of Life.

They durst not take this memoir to the bishop. But they got their friend, little Camerle, his youthful chaplain, to steal it from them. The bishop read it, and circulated some copies about the town. On the 21st August, Girard being at the palace, the bishop laughingly said to him, "Well, father, so your name is in the Book of Life!"

He was overcome, fancied himself lost, wrote to Cadière in terms of bitter reproach. Once more with tears he asked for his papers. Cadière in great surprise vowed that her memoir had never gone out of her brother's hands. But when she found out her mistake, her despair was unbounded. The sharpest pangs of body and soul beset her. Once she thought herself on the point of death. She became like one mad. "I long so much to suffer. Twice I caught up the rod of penance, and wielded it so savagely as to draw a great deal of blood." In the midst of this dreadful outbreak, which proved at once the weakness of her head and the boundless tenderness of her conscience, Guiol finished her by describing Girard as nearly dead. This raised her compassion to the highest pitch.

She was going to give up the papers. And yet it was but too clear that these were her only safeguard and support, the only proofs of her innocence, and the tricks of which she had been made the victim. To give them up was to risk a change of characters, to risk the imputation of having herself seduced a saint, the chance, in short, of seeing all the blame transferred to her own side.

But, if she must either be ruined herself or else ruin Girard, she would far sooner accept the former result. A demon, Guiol of course, tempted her in this very way, with the wondrous sublimity of such a sacrifice. God, she wrote, asked of her a bloody offering. She could tell her of saints who, being accused, did not justify, but rather accused themselves, and died like lambs. This example Cadière followed. When Girard was accused before her, she defended him, saying, "He is right, and I told a falsehood."

She might have yielded up the letters of Girard only; but in so great an out-flowing of heart she would have no haggling, and so gave him even copies of her own.

Thus at the same time he held these drafts written by the Jacobin, and the copies made and sent him by the other brother. Thenceforth he had nothing to fear: no further check could be given him. He might make away with them or put them back again; might destroy, blot out, and falsify at pleasure. He was perfectly free to carry on his forger's work, and he worked away to some purpose. Out of twenty-four letters, sixteen remain; and these still read like elaborately forged afterthoughts.

With everything in his own hands, Girard could laugh at his foes. It was now their turn to be afraid. The bishop, a man of the upper world, was too well acquainted with Versailles and the name won by the Jesuits not to treat them with proper tenderness. He even thought it safest to make Girard some small amends for his unkind reproach about The Book of Life; and so he graciously informed him that he would like to stand godfather to the child of one of his kinsmen.

The Bishops of Toulon had always been high lords. The list of them shows all the first names of Provence, and some famous names from Italy. From 1712 to 1737, under the Regency and Fleury, the bishop was one of the La Tours of Pin. He was very rich, having also the Abbeys of Aniane and St. William of the Desert, in Languedoc. He behaved well, it was said, during the plague of 1721. However, he stayed but seldom at Toulon, lived quite as a man of the world, never said mass, and passed for something more than a lady's man.

In July he went to Toulon, and though Girard would have turned him aside from Ollioules and Cadière, he was curious to see her nevertheless. He saw her in one of her best moments. She took his fancy, seemed to him a pretty little saint; and so far did he believe in her enlightenment from above, as to speak to her thoughtlessly of all his affairs, his interests, his future doings, consulting her as he would have consulted a teller of fortunes.

In spite, however, of the brethren's prayers he hesitated to take her away from Ollioules and from Girard. A means was found of resolving him. A report was spread about Toulon, that the girl had shown a desire to flee into the wilderness, as her model saint, Theresa, had essayed to do at twelve years old. Girard, they said, had put this fancy into her head, that he might one day carry her off beyond the diocese whose pride she was, and box-up his treasure in some far convent, where the Jesuits, enjoying the whole monopoly, might turn to the most account her visions, her miracles, her winsome ways as a young saint of the people. The bishop felt much hurt. He instructed the abbess to give Mdlle. Cadière up to no one save her mother, who was certain to come very shortly and take her away from the convent to a country-house belonging to the family.

In order not to offend Girard, they got Cadière to write and say that, if such a change incommoded him, he could find a colleague and give her a second confessor. He saw their meaning, and preferred disarming jealousy by abandoning Cadière. He gave her up on the 15th September, in a note most carefully worded and piteously humble, by which he strove to leave her friendly and tender towards himself. "If I have sometimes done wrong as concerning you, you will never at least forget how wishful I have been to help you. ... I am, and ever will be, all yours in the Secret Heart of Jesus."

The bishop, however, was not reassured. He fancied that the three Jesuits, Girard, Sabatier, and Grignet, wanted to beguile him, and some day, with some order from Paris, rob him of his little woman. On the 17th September, he decided once for all to send his carriage, a light fashionable *phaeton*, as it was called, and have her taken off at once to her mother's country-house.

By way of soothing and shielding her, of putting her in good trim, he looked out for a confessor, and applied first to a Carmelite who had confessed her before Girard came. But he, being an old man, declined. Some others also probably hung back. The bishop had to take a stranger, but three months come from the County (Avignon), one Father Nicholas, prior of the Barefooted Carmelites. He was a man of forty, endowed with brains and boldness, very firm and even stubborn. He showed himself worthy of such a trust by rejecting it. It was not the Jesuits he feared, but the girl herself. He foreboded no good therefrom, thought that the angel might be an angel of darkness, and feared that the Evil One under the shape of a gentle girl would deal his blows with all the more baleful effect.

But he could not see her without feeling somewhat reassured. She seemed so very simple, so pleased at length to have a safe, steady person, on whom she might lean. The continual wavering in which she had been kept by Girard, had caused her the greatest suffering. On the first day she spoke more than she had done for a month past, told him of her life, her sufferings, her devotions, and her visions. Night itself, a hot night in mid-September, did not stop her. In her room everything was open, the windows, and the three doors. She went on even to daybreak, while her brethren lay near her asleep. On the morrow she resumed her tale under the vine-bower. The Carmelite was amazed, and asked himself if the Devil could ever be so earnest in praise of God.

Her innocence was clear. She seemed a nice obedient girl, gentle as a lamb, frolicsome as a puppy. She wanted to play at bowls, a common game in those country-places, nor did he for his part refuse to join her.

If there was a spirit in her, it could not at any rate be called the spirit of lying. On looking at her closely for a long time, you could not doubt that her wounds now and then did really bleed. He took care to make no such immodest scrutiny of them as Girard had done, contenting himself with a look at the wound upon her foot. Of her trances he saw quite enough. On a sudden, a burning heat would diffuse itself everywhere from her heart. Losing her consciousness, she went into convulsions and talked wildly.

The Carmelite clearly perceived that in her were two persons, the young woman and the Demon. The former was honest, nay, very fresh of heart; ignorant, for all that had been done to her; little able to understand the very things that had brought her into such sore trouble. When, before confession, she spoke of Girard's kisses, the Carmelite roughly said, "But those are very great sins."

"God!" she answered, weeping, "I am lost indeed, for he has done much more than that to me!"

The bishop came to see. For him the country house was only the length of a walk. She answered his questions artlessly, told him at least how things began. The bishop was angry, mortified, very wroth. No doubt he guessed the remainder. There was nought to keep him from raising a great outcry against Girard. Not caring for the danger of a struggle with the Jesuits, he entered thoroughly into the Carmelite's views, allowed that she was bewitched, and added that *Girard himself was the wizard.* He wanted to lay him that very moment under a solemn ban, to bring him to disgrace and ruin. Cadière prayed for him who had done her so much wrong; vengeance she would not have. Falling on her knees before the bishop, she implored him to spare Girard, to speak no more of things so sorrowful. With touching humility, she said, "It is enough for me to be enlightened at last, to know that I was living in sin." Her Jacobin brother took her part, foreseeing the perils of such a war, and doubtful whether the bishop would stand fast.

Her attacks of disorder were now fewer. The season had changed. The burning summer was over. Nature at length showed mercy. It was the pleasant month of October. The bishop had the keen delight of feeling that she had been saved by him. No longer under Girard's influence in the stifling air of Ollioules, but well cared for by her family, by the brave and honest monk, protected, too, by the bishop, who never grudged his visits, and who shielded her with his steady countenance, the young girl became altogether calm.

For seven weeks or so she seemed quite well-behaved. The bishop's happiness was so great that he wanted the Carmelite, with Cadière's help, to look after Girard's other penitents, and bring them also back to their senses. They should go to the country house; how unwillingly, and with how ill a grace we can easily guess. In truth, it was strangely ill-judged to bring those women before the bishop's ward, a girl so young still, and but just delivered from her own ecstatic ravings.

The state of things became ridiculous and sorely embittered. Two parties faced each other, Girard's women and those of the bishop. On the side of the latter were a German lady and her daughter, dear friends of Cadière's. On the other side were the rebels, headed by the Guiol. With her the bishop treated, in hopes of getting her to enter into relations with the Carmelite, and bring her friends over to him. He sent her his own clerk, and then a solicitor, an old lover of Guiol's. All this failing of any effect, the bishop came to his last resource, determined to summon them all to his palace. Here they mostly denied those trances and mystic marks of which they had made such boast. One of them, Guiol, of course, astonished him yet more by her shamelessly treacherous offer to prove to him, on the spot, that they had no marks whatever about their bodies. They had deemed him wanton enough to fall into such a snare. But he kept clear of it very well, declining the offer with thanks to those who, at the cost of their own modesty, would have had him copy Girard, and provoke the laughter of all the town.

The bishop was not lucky. On the one hand, these bold wenches made fun of him. On the other, his success with Cadière was now being undone. She had hardly entered her own narrow lane in gloomy Toulon, when she began to fall off. She was just in those dangerous and baleful centres where her illness began, on the very field of the battle waged by the two hostile parties. The Jesuits, whose rearguard everyone saw in the Court, had on their side the crafty, the prudent, the knowing. The Carmelite had none but the bishop with him, was not even backed by his own brethren, nor yet by the clergy. He had one weapon, however, in reserve. On the 8th November, he got out of Cadière a written power to reveal her confession in case of need.

It was a daring, dauntless step, which made Girard shudder. He was not very brave, and would have been undone had his cause not been that of the Jesuits also. He cowered down in the depths of their college. But his colleague Sabatier, an old, sanguine, passionate fellow, went straight to the bishop's palace. He entered into the prelate's presence, like another Popilius, bearing peace or war in his gown. He pushed him to the wall, made him understand that a suit with the Jesuits would lead to his own undoing; that he would remain for ever Bishop of Toulon; would never rise to an archbishopric. Yet further, with the freedom of an apostle strong at Versailles, he assured him that if this affair exposed the morals of a Jesuit, it would shed no less light on the morals of a bishop. In a letter, clearly planned by Girard, it was pretended that the Jesuits held themselves ready in the background, to hurl dreadful recriminations against the prelate, declaring his way of life not only unepiscopal, but *abominable* withal. The sly, faithless Girard and the hot-headed Sabatier, swollen with rage and spitefulness, would have pressed the calumnious charge. They would not have failed to say that all this matter was about a girl; that if Girard had taken care of her when ill, the bishop had gotten her when she was well. What a commotion would be caused by such a scandal in the well-regulated life of the great worldly lord! It were too laughable a piece of chivalry to make war in revenge for the maidenhood of a weak little fool, to embroil oneself for her sake with all honest people! The Cardinal of Bonzi died indeed of grief at Toulouse, but that was on account of a fair lady, the Marchioness of Ganges. The bishop, on his part, risked his ruin, risked the chance of being overwhelmed with shame and ridicule, for the child of a retail-dealer in the Rue de l'Hôpital!

Sabatier's threatenings made all the greater impression, because the bishop himself clung less firmly to Cadière. He did not thank her for falling ill again; for giving the lie to his former success; for doing him a wrong by her relapse. He bore her a grudge for having failed to cure her. He said to himself that Sabatier was in the right; that he had better come to a compromise. The change was sudden a kind of warning from above. All at once, like Paul on the way to Damascus, he beheld the light, and became a convert to the Jesuits.

Sabatier would not let him go. He put paper before him, and made him write and sign a decree forbidding the Carmelite, his agent with Cadière, and another forbidding her brother, the Jacobin.

[1] This communion of blood prevailed among the Northern Reiters. See my *Origines.*

Chapter Twelve - The Trial of Cadière: 1730-1731

WE can guess how this alarming blow was taken by the Cadière family. The sick girl's attacks became frequent and fearful. By a cruel chance they brought on a kind of epidemic among her intimate friends. Her neighbour, the German lady, who had trances also, which she had hitherto deemed divine, now fell into utter fright, and fancied they came from hell. This worthy dame of fifty years remembered that she, too, had often had unclean thoughts: she believed herself given over to the Devil; saw nothing but devils about her; and escaping from her own house in spite of her daughter's watchfulness, entreated shelter from the Cadières. From that time the house became unbearable; business could not be carried on. The elder Cadière inveighed furiously against Girard, crying, "He shall be served like Gauffridi: he, too, shall be burnt!" And the Jacobin added, "Rather would we waste the whole of our family estate!"

On the night of the 17th November, Cadière screamed, and was like one choking. They thought she was going to die. The eldest Cadière, the tradesman, lost his wits, and called out to his neighbours from the window, "Help! the Devil is throttling my sister!" They came running up almost in their shirts. The doctors and surgeons wanted to apply the cupping-glasses to a case of what they called "suffocation of the womb." While some were gone to fetch these, they succeeded in unlocking her teeth and making her swallow a drop of brandy, which brought her to herself. Meanwhile there also came to the girl some doctors of the soul; first an old priest confessor to Cadière's mother, and then some parsons of Toulon. All this noise and shouting, the arrival of the priests in full dress, the preparations for exorcising, had brought everyone out into the street. The newcomers kept asking what was the matter. "Cadière has been bewitched by Girard," was the continual reply. We may imagine the pity and the wrath of the people.

Greatly alarmed, but anxious to cast the fear back on others, the Jesuits did a very barbarous thing. They returned to the bishop, ordered and insisted that Cadière should be brought to trial; that the attack should be made that very day; that justice should make an unforeseen descent on this poor girl, as she lay rattling in the throat after the last dreadful seizure.

Sabatier never left the bishop until the latter had called his judge, his officer, the Vicar-general Larmedieu, and his prosecutor or episcopal advocate, Esprit Reybaud, and commanded them to go to work forthwith.

By the Canon Law this was impossible, illegal. A *preliminary inquiry was needed* into the facts, before the judicial business could begin. There was another difficulty: the spiritual judge had no right to make such an arrest save for *a rejection of the Sacrament.* The two church-lawyers must have made these objections. But Sabatier would hear of no excuses. If matters were allowed to drag in this cold legal way, he would miss his stroke of terror.

Larmedieu was a compliant judge, a friend of the clergy. He was not one of your rude magistrates who go straight before them, like blind boars, on the high-road of the law, without seeing or respecting anyone. He had shown great regard for Aubany, the patron of Ollioules, during his trial; helping him to escape by the slowness of his own procedure. Afterwards, when he knew him to be at Marseilles, as if that was far from France, in the *ultima thule* or *terra incognita* of ancient geographers, he would not budge any further. This, however, was a very different case: the judge who was so paralytic against Aubany, had wings, and wings of lightning, for Cadière. It was nine in the morning when the dwellers in the lane saw with much curiosity a grand procession arrive at the Cadières' door, with Master Larmedieu and the episcopal advocate at the head, honoured by an escort of two clergymen, doctors of theology. The house was invaded: the sick girl was summoned before them. They made her swear to tell the truth against herself; swear to defame herself by speaking out in the ears of justice matters that touched her conscience and the confessional only.

She might have dispensed with an answer, for none of the usual forms had been observed: but she would not raise the question. She took the oath that was meant to disarm and betray her. For, being once bound thereby, she told everything, even to those shameful and ridiculous details which it must be very painful for any girl to acknowledge.

Larmedieu's official statement and his first examination point to a clearly settled agreement between him and the Jesuits. Girard was to be brought forward as the dupe and prey of Cadière's knavery. Fancy a man of sixty, a doctor, professor, director of nuns, being therewithal so innocent and credulous, that a young girl, a mere child, was enough to draw him into the snare! The cunning, shameless wanton had beguiled him with her visions, but failed to draw him into her own excesses. Enraged thereat, she endowed him with every baseness that the fancy of a Messalina could suggest to her!

So far from giving grounds for any such idea, the examination brings out the victim's gentleness in a very touching way. Evidently she accuses others only through constraint, under the pressure of her oath just taken. She is gentle towards her enemies, even to the faithless Guiol who, in her brother's words, had betrayed her; had done her worst to corrupt her; had ruined her, last of all, by making her give up the papers which would have insured her safety.

The Cadière brothers were frightened at their sister's artlessness. In her regard for her oath she gave herself up without reserve to be vilified, alas! for ever; to have ballads sung about her; to be mocked by the very foes of Jesuits and silly scoffing libertines.

The mischief done, they wanted at least to have it defined, to have the official report of the priests checked by some more serious measure. Seeming, though she did to be the party accused, they made her the accuser, and prevailed on Marteli Chantard, the King's Lieutenant Civil and Criminal, to come and take her deposition. In this document, short and clear, the fact of her seduction is clearly established; likewise the reproaches she uttered against Girard for his lewd endearments, reproaches at which he only laughed; likewise the advice he gave her, to let herself be possessed by the Demon; likewise the means he used for keeping her wounds open, and so on.

The King's officer, the Lieutenant, was bound to carry the matter before his own court. For the spiritual judge in his hurry had failed to go through the forms of ecclesiastic law, and so made his proceedings null. But the lay magistrate lacked the courage for this. He let himself be harnessed to the clerical inquiry, accepted Larmedieu for his colleague, went himself to sit and hear the evidence in the bishop's court. The clerk of the bishopric wrote it down, and not the clerk of the King's Lieutenant. Did he write it down faithfully? We have reason to doubt that, when we find him threatening the witnesses, and going every night to show their statements to the Jesuits.

The two curates of Cadière's parish, who were heard first, deposed drily, net in her favour, yet by no means against her, certainly not in favour of the Jesuits. These latter saw that everything was going amiss for them. Lost to all shame, at the risk of angering the people, they determined to break all down.

They got from the bishop an order to imprison Cadière and the chief witnesses she wanted to be heard. These were the German lady and Batarelle. The girl herself was placed in the Refuge, a convent-prison; the ladies in a bridewell, the *Good-Shepherd*, where mad women and foul streetwalkers needing punishment were thrown. On the 26th November, Cadière was dragged from her bed and given over to the Ursulines, penitents of Girard's, who laid her duly on some rotten straw.

A fear of them thus established, the witnesses might now be heard. They began with two, choice and respectable. One was the Guiol, notorious for being Girard's pander, a woman of keen and clever tongue, who was commissioned to hurl the first dart and open the wound of slander. The other was Laugier, the little seamstress, whom Cadière had supported and for whose apprenticeship she had paid. While she lay with child by Girard, this Laugier had cried out against him; now she washed away her fault by sneering at Cadière and defiling her benefactress, but in a very clumsy way, like the shameless wanton she was; ascribing to her impudent speeches quite contrary to her known habits. Then came Mdlle. Gravier and her cousin Reboul - all the *Girardites*, in short, as they were called in Toulon.

But, do as they would, the light would burst forth now and then. The wife of a purveyor in the house where these Girardites met together, said, with cruel plainness, that she could not abide them, that they disturbed the whole house; she spoke of their noisy bursts of laughter, of their suppers paid for out of the money collected for the poor, and so forth.

They were sore afraid lest the nuns should speak out for Cadière. The bishop's clerk told them, as if from the bishop himself, that those who spoke evil should be chastised. As a yet stronger measure, they ordered back from Marseilles the gay Father Aubany, who had some ascendant over the nuns. His affair with the girl he had violated was 'got settled for him. Her parents were made to understand that justice could do nothing in their case. The child's good name was valued at eight hundred livres, which were paid on Aubany's account. So, full of zeal, he returned, a thorough Jesuit, to his troop at Ollioules. The poor troop trembled indeed, when this worthy father told them of his commission to warn them that, if they did not behave themselves, "they should be put to the torture."

For all that, they could not get as much as they wanted from these fifteen nuns. Two or three at most were on Girard's side, but all stated facts, especially about the 7th July, which bore directly against him.

In despair the Jesuits came to an heroic decision, in order to make sure of their witnesses. They stationed themselves in an outer hall which led into the court. There they stopped those going in, tampered with them, threatened them, and, if they were against Girard, coolly debarred their entrance by thrusting them out of doors.

Thus the clerical judge and the King's officer were only as puppets in the Jesuits' hands. The whole town saw this and trembled. During December,

January, and February, the Cadière family drew up and diffused a complaint touching the way in which justice was denied them and witnesses suborned. The Jesuits themselves felt that the place would no longer hold them. They evoked help from a higher quarter. This seemed best available in the shape of a decree of the Great Council, which would have brought the matter before itself and hushed up everything, as Mazarin had done in the Louviers affair. But the Chancellor was D'Aguesseau; and the Jesuits had no wish to let the matter go up to Paris. They kept it still in Provence. On the 16th January, 1731, they got the King to determine that the Parliament of Provence, where they had plenty of friends, should pass sentence on the inquiry which two of its councillors were conducting at Toulon.

M. Faucon, a layman, and M. de Charleval, a councillor of the Church, came in fact and straightway marched down among the Jesuits. These eager commissioners made so little secret of their loud and bitter partiality, as to toss out an order for Cadière's remand, just as they might have done to an accused prisoner; whilst Girard was most politely called up .and allowed to go free, to keep on saying mass and hearing confessions. And so the plaintiff was kept under lock and key, in her enemies' hands, exposed to all manner of cruelty from Girard's devotees.

From these honest Ursulines she met with just such a reception as if they had been charged to bring about her death. The room they gave her was the cell of a mad nun who made everything filthy. In the nun's old straw, in the midst of a frightful stench, she lay. Her kinsmen on the morrow had much ado to get in a coverlet and mattress for her use. For her nurse and keeper she was allowed a poor tool of Girard's, a lay-sister, daughter to that very Guiol who had betrayed her; a girl right worthy of her mother, capable of any wickedness, a source of danger to her modesty, perhaps even to her life. They submitted her to a course of penance in her case specially painful, refusing her the right of confessing herself or taking the sacrament. She relapsed into her illness from the time she was debarred the latter privilege. Her fierce foe, the Jesuit Sabatier, came into her cell, and formed a new and startling scheme to win her by a bribe of the holy wafer. The bargaining began. They offered her terms: she should communicate if she would only acknowledge herself a slanderer, unworthy of communicating. In her excessive humbleness she might have done so. But, while ruining herself, she would also have ruined the Carmelite and her own brethren.

Reduced to Pharisaical tricks, they took to expounding her speeches. Whatever she uttered in a mystic sense they feigned to accept in its material hardness. To free herself from such snares she displayed, what they had least expected, very great presence of mind.

A yet more treacherous plan for robbing her of the public sympathy and setting the laughers against her, was to find her a lover. They pretended that she had proposed to a young blackguard that they should set off together and roam the world.

The great lords of that day, being fond of having children and little pages to wait on them, readily took in the better-mannered of their peasant's sons. In this way had the bishop dealt with the boy of one of his tenants. He washed his face, as it were; made him tidy. Presently, when the favourite grew up, he gave him the tonsure, dressed him up like an abbe, and dubbed him his chaplain at the age of twenty. This person was the Abbé Camerle. Brought up with the footmen and made to do everything, he was, like many a half-scrubbed country youth, a sly, but simple lout. He saw that the prelate since his arrival at Toulon had been curious about Cadière and far from friendly to Girard. He thought to please and amuse his master by turning himself, at Ollioules, into a spy on their suspected intercourse. But after the bishop changed through fear of the Jesuits, Camerle became equally zealous in helping Girard with active service against Cadière.

He came one day, like another Joseph, to say that Mdlle. Cadière had, like Potiphar's wife, been tempting him, and trying to shake his virtue. Had this been true, it was all the more cowardly of him thus to punish her for a moment's weakness, to take so mean an advantage of some light word. But his education as page and seminarist was not such as to bring him either honour or the love of women.

She extricated herself with spirit and success, covering him with shame. The two angry commissioners saw her making so triumphant an answer, that they cut the investigation short, and cut down the number of her witnesses. Out of the sixty-eight she summoned, they allowed but thirty-eight to appear. Regardless alike of the delays and the forms of justice, they hurried forward the confronting of witnesses. Yet nothing was gained, thereby. On the 25th and again on the 26th February, she renewed her crushing declarations.

Such was their rage thereat, that they declared their regret at the want of torments and executioners in Toulon, "who might have made her sing out a little." These things formed their *ultima ratio.* They were employed, by the Parliaments through all that century. I have before me a warm defence of torture, [1] written in 1780, by a learned member of Parliament, who also became a member of the Great Council; it was dedicated to the King, Louis XVI., and crowned with the flattering approval of His Holiness Pius VI.

But, in default of the torture that would have made her sing, she was made to speak by a still better process. On the 27th February, Guiol's daughter, the lay-sister who acted as her jailer, came to her at an early hour with a glass of wine. She was astonished: she was not at all thirsty: she never drank wine, especially pure wine, of a morning. The lay-sister, a rough, strong menial, such as they keep in convents to manage crazy or refractory women, and to punish children, overwhelmed the feeble sufferer with remonstrances that looked like threats. Unwilling as she was, she drank. And she was forced to drink it all, to the very dregs, which she found unpleasantly salt.

175

What was this repulsive draught? We have already seen how clever these old confessors of nuns were at remedies of various kinds. In this case the wine alone would have done for so weakly a patient. It had been quite enough to make her drunk, to draw from her at once some stammering speeches, which the clerk might have moulded into a downright falsehood. But a drug of some kind, perhaps some wizard's simple, which would act for several days, was added to the wine, in order to prolong its effects and leave her no way of disproving anything laid to her charge.

In her declaration of the 27th February, how sudden and entire a change! It is nothing but a defence of Girard! Strange to say, the commissioners make no remark on so abrupt a change. The strange, shameful sight of a young girl drunk causes no astonishment, fails to put them on their guard. She is made to own that all which had passed between herself and Girard was merely the offspring of her own diseased fancy; that all she had spoken of as real, at the bidding of her brethren and the Carmelite, was nothing more than a dream. Not content with whitening Girard, she must blacken her own friends, must crush them, and put the halter round their necks.

Especially wonderful is the clearness of her deposition, the neat way in which it is worded. The hand of the skilful clerk peeps out therefrom. It is very strange, however, that now they are in so fair a way, they do not follow it up. From the 27th to the 6th of March there is no further questioning.

On the 28th, the poison having doubtless done its work, and plunged her into a perfect stupor, or else a kind of Sabbatic frenzy, it was impossible to bring her forth. After that, while her head was still disordered, they could easily give her other potions of which she would know and remember nothing. What happened during those six days seems to have been so shocking, so sad for poor Cadière, that neither she nor her brother had the heart to speak of it twice. Nor would they have spoken at all, had not the brethren themselves incurred a prosecution aiming at their own lives.

Having won his cause through Cadière's falsehood, Girard dared to come and see her in her prison, where she lay stupefied or in despair, forsaken alike of earth and heaven, and if any clear thoughts were left her, possessed with the dreadful consciousness of having by her last deposition murdered her own near kin. Her own ruin was complete already. But another trial, that of her brothers and the bold Carmelite, would now begin. She may in her remorse have been tempted to soften Girard, to keep him from proceeding against them, above all to save herself from being put to the torture. Girard, at any rate, took advantage of her utter weakness, and behaved like the determined scoundrel he really was.

Alas! her wandering spirit came but slowly back to her. It was on the 6th March that she had to face her accusers, to renew her former admissions, to ruin her brethren beyond repair. She could not speak; she was choking. The commissioners had the kindness to tell her that the torture was there, at her side; to describe to her the wooden horse, the points of iron, the wedges for jamming fast her bones. Her courage failed her, so weak she was now of body. She submitted to be set before her cruel master, who might laugh triumphant now that he had debased not only her body, but yet more her conscience, by making her the murderess of her own friends.

No time was lost in profiting by her weakness. They prevailed forthwith on the Parliament of Aix to let the Carmelite and the two brothers be imprisoned, that they might undergo a separate trial for their lives, as soon as Cadière should have been condemned.

On the 10th March, she was dragged from the Ursulines of Toulon to Sainte-Claire of Ollioules. Girard, however, was not sure of her yet. He got leave to have her conducted, like some dreaded highway robber, between some soldiers of the mounted police. He demanded that she should be carefully locked up at Sainte-Claire. The ladies were moved to tears at the sight of a poor sufferer who could not drag herself forward, approaching between those drawn swords. Everyone pitied her. Two brave men, M. Aubin, a solicitor, and M. Claret, a notary, drew up for her the deeds in which she withdrew her late confession, fearful documents that record the threats of the commissioners and of the Ursuline prioress, and above all, the fact of the drugged wine she had been forced to drink.

At the same time these daring men drew up for the Chancellor's court at Paris a plea of error, as it is called, exposing the irregular and blameable proceedings, the wilful breaches of the law, effected in the coolest way, first by the bishop's officer and the King's Lieutenant, secondly by the two commissioners. The Chancellor D'Aguesseau showed himself very slack and feeble. He let these foul proceedings stand; left the business in charge of the Parliament of Aix, sullied as it already seemed to be by the disgrace with which two of its members had just been covering themselves

So once more they laid hands on their victim, and had her dragged, in charge as before of the mounted police, from Ollioules to Aix. In those days people slept at a publichouse midway. Here the corporal explained that, by virtue of his orders, he would sleep in the young girl's room. They pretended to believe that an invalid unable to walk, might flee away by jumping out of window. Truly, it was a most villainous device, to commit such a one to the chaste keeping of the heroes of the *dragonnades*. [2] Happily, her mother had come to see her start, had followed her in spite of everything, and they did not dare to beat her away with their butt-ends. She stayed in the room, kept watch neither of them, indeed, lying down and shielded her child from all harm.

Cadière was forwarded to the Ursulines of Aix, who had the King's command to take her in charge. But the prioress pretended that the order had not yet come. We may see here how savage a woman who was once impassioned will grow, until she has lost all her woman's nature. She kept the other four hours at her street-door, as if she were a public show. There was time to fetch a mob of Jesuits' followers, of honest Church artizans, to hoot and hiss, while children might help by throwing stones. For these four hours she was in the pillory. Some, however, of the more dispassionate passers-by asked if the Ursulines had gotten orders to let them kill the girl. We may guess what tender jailers their sick prisoner would find in these good sisters!

The ground was prepared with admirable effect. By a spirited concert between Jesuit magistrates and plotting ladies, a system of deterring had been set on foot. No pleader would ruin himself by defending a girl thus heavily aspersed. No one would digest the poisonous things stored up by her jailers, for him who should daily show his face in their parlour to await an interview with Cadière. The defence in that case would devolve on M. Chaudon, syndic of the Aix bar. He did not decline so hard a duty. And yet he was so uneasy as to desire a settlement, which the Jesuits refused. Thereupon he showed what he really was, a man of unswerving honesty, of amazing courage. He exposed, with the learning of a lawyer, the monstrous character of the whole proceeding. So doing, he would for ever embroil himself with the Parliament no less than the Jesuits. He brought into sharp outline the spiritual incest of the confessor, though he modestly refrained from specifying how far he had carried his profligacy. He also withheld himself from speaking of Girard' s girls, the loose-lived devotees, as a matter well-known, but to which no one would have liked to bear witness. In short, he gave Girard the best case he could by assailing him *as a wizard*. People laughed, made fun of the advocate. He undertook to prove the existence of demons by a series of sacred texts, beginning with the Gospels. This made them laugh the louder.

The case had been cleverly disfigured by the turning of an honest Carmelite into Cadière's lover, and the weaver of a whole chain of libels against Girard and the Jesuits. Thenceforth the crowd of idlers, of giddy worldlings, scoffers and philosophers alike, made merry with either side, being thoroughly impartial as between Carmelite and Jesuit, and exceedingly rejoiced to see this battle of monk with monk. Those who were presently to be called *Voltairites*, were even better inclined towards the polished Jesuits, those men of the world, than towards any of the old mendicant orders.

So the matter became more and more tangled. Jokes kept raining down, but raining mostly on the victim. They called it a love-intrigue. They saw in it nothing but food for fun. There was not a scholar nor a clerk who did not turn a ditty on Girard and his pupil, who did not hash up anew the old provincial jokes about Madeline in the Gauffridi affair, her six thousand imps, their dread of a flogging, and the wonderful chastening-process whereby Cadière's devils were put to flight.

On this latter point the friends of Girard had no difficulty in proving him clean. He had acted by his right as director, in accordance with the common wont. The rod is the symbol of fatherhood. He had treated his penitent with a view to the healing of her soul. They used to thrash demoniacs, to thrash the insane and sufferers in other ways. This was the favourite mode of hunting out the enemy, whether in the shape of devil or disease. With the people it was a very common idea. One brave workman of Toulon, who had witnessed Cadière's sad plight, declared that a bull's sinew was the poor sufferer's only cure.

Thus strongly supported, Girard had only to act reasonably. He would not take the trouble. His defence is charmingly flippant. He never deigns even to agree with his own depositions. He gives the lie to his own witnesses. He seems to be jesting, and says, with the coolness of a great lord of the Regency, that if, as they charge him, he was ever shut up with her, "it could only have happened nine times."

"And why did the good father do so," would his friends say, "save to watch, to consider, to search out the truth concerning her? 'Tis the confessor's duty in all such cases. Read the life of the most holy Catherine of Genoa. One evening her confessor hid himself in her room, waiting to see the wonders she would work, and to catch her in the act miraculous. But here, unhappily, the Devil, who never sleeps, had laid a snare for this lamb of God, had belched forth this devouring monster of a she-dragon, this mixture of maniac and demoniac, to swallow him up, to overwhelm him in a cataract of slander."

It was an old and excellent custom to smother monsters in the cradle. Then why not later also? Girard's ladies charitably advised the instant using against her of fire and sword. "Let her perish!" cried the devotees. Many of the great ladies also wished to have her punished, deeming it rather too bad that such a creature should have dared to enter such a plea, to bring into court the man who had done her but too great an honour.

Some determined Jansenists there were in the Parliament, but these were more inimical to the Jesuits' than friendly to the girl. And they might well be downcast and discouraged, seeing they had against them at once the terrible Society of Jesus, the Court of Versailles, the Cardinal Minister (Fleury), and, lastly, the drawing-rooms of Aix. Should they be bolder than the head of the law, the Chancellor D'Aguesseau, who had proved so very slack? The Attorney-General did not waver at all: being charged with the indictment of Girard, he avowed himself his friend, advised him how to meet the charges against him.

There was, indeed, but one question at issue, to ascertain by what kind of reparation, of solemn atonement, of exemplary chastening, the plaintiff thus changed into the accused might satisfy Girard and the Company of Jesus. The Jesuits, with all their good-nature, affirmed the need of an example, in the interests of religion, by way of some slight warning both to the Jansenist Convulsionaries and the scribbling philosophers who were beginning to swarm.

There were two points by which Cadière might be hooked, might receive the stroke of the harpoon.

Firstly, she had borne false witness. But, then, by no law could slander be punished with death. To gain that end you must go a little further, and say, "The old Roman text, *De famosis libellis*, pronounces death on those who have uttered libels hurtful to the Emperor or to *the religion of the Empire.* The Jesuits represent that religion. Therefore, a memorial against a Jesuit deserves the last penalty."

A still better handle, however, was their second. At the opening of the trial the episcopal judge, the prudent Larmedieu, had asked her if she had never divined the secrets of many people, and she had answered yes. Therefore they might charge her with the practice named in the list of forms employed in trials for witchcraft, as *Divination and imposture.* This alone in ecclesiastic law deserved the stake. They might, indeed, without much effort, call her a *Witch*, after the confession made by the Ollioules ladies, that at one same hour of the night she used to be in several cells together. Their infatuation, the surprising tenderness that suddenly came over them, had all the air of an enchantment.

What was there to prevent her being burnt? They were still burning everywhere in the eighteenth century. In one reign only, that of Philip V., sixteen hundred people were burnt in Spain: one Witch was burnt as late as 1782. In Germany one was burnt in 1751; in Switzerland one also in 1781. Rome was always burning her victims, on the sly indeed, in the dark holes and cells of the Inquisition. [3]

"But France, at least, is surely more humane?" She is very inconsistent. In 1718, a Wizard is burnt at Bordeaux. [4] In 1724 and 1726, the faggots were lighted in Grève for offences which passed as schoolboy jokes at Versailles. The guardians of the Royal child, the Duke and Fleury, who are so indulgent to the Court, are terrible to the town. A donkey-driver and a noble, one M. des Chauffeurs, are burnt alive. The advent of the Cardinal Minister could not be celebrated more worthily than by a moral reformation, by making a severe example of those who corrupted the people. Nothing more timely than to pass some terrible and solemn sentence on this infernal girl, who made so heinous an assault on the innocent Girard!

Observe what was needed to wash that father clean. It was needful to show that, even if he had done wrong and imitated Des Chauffeurs, he had been the sport of some enchantment. The documents were but too plain. By the wording of the Canon Law, and after these late decrees, somebody ought to be burnt. Of the five magistrates on the bench, two only would have burnt Girard. Three were against Cadière. They came to terms. The three who formed the majority would not insist on burning her, would forego the long, dreadful scene at the stake, would content themselves with a simple awara of death.

In the name of these five, it was settled, pending the final assent of Parliament, "That Cadière, having first been put to the torture in both kinds, should afterwards be removed to Toulon^ and suffer death by hanging on the Place des Prêeheurs."

This was a dreadful blow. An immense revulsion of feeling at once took place. The worldlings, the jesters ceased to laugh: they shuddered. Their love of trifling did not lead them to slur over a result so horrible. That a girl should be seduced., ill-used, dishonoured, treated as a mere toy, that she should die of grief, or of frenzy, they had regarded as right and good; with all that they had no concern. But when it was a case of punishment, when in fancy they saw before them the woeful victim, with rope round her neck, by the gallows where she was about to hang, their hearts rose in revolt. From all sides went forth the cry, "Never, since the world began, was there seen so villainous a reversal of things; the law of rape administered the wrong way, the girl condemned for having been made a tool, the victim hanged by her seducer!"

In this town of Aix, made up of judges, priests, and the world of fashion, a thing unforeseen occurred r a whole people suddenly rose, a violent popular movement was astir. A crowd of persons of every class marched in one close well-ordered body straight towards the Ursulines. Cadière and her mother were bidden to show themselves. "Make yourself easy, mademoiselle," they shouted: "we stand by you: fear nothing!"

The grand eighteenth century, justly called by Hegel the "reign of mind," was still grander as the "reign of humanity." Ladies of distinction, such as the granddaughter of Mde. de Sévigné, the charming Madame de Simiane, took possession of the young girl and sheltered her in their bosoms.

A thing yet prettier and more touching was it, to see the Jansenist ladies, elsewhile so sternly pure, so hard towards each other, in their austerities so severe, now in this great conjuncture offer up Law on the altar of Mercy, by flinging their arms round the poor threatened child, purifying her with kisses on the forehead, baptizing her anew in tears.

If Provence be naturally wild, she is all the more wonderful in these wild moments of generosity and real greatness. Something of this was later seen in the earliest triumphs of Mirabeau, when he had a million of men gathered round him at Marseilles. But here already was a great revolutionary scene, a vast uprising against the stupid Government of the day, and Fleury's pets the Jesuits: a unanimous uprising in behalf of humanity, of compassion, in defence of a woman, a very child, thus barbarously offered up. The Jesuits fancied that among their own rabble, among their clients and their beggars, they might array a kind of popular force, armed with handbells and staves to beat back the party of Cadière. This latter, however, included almost everyone. Marseilles rose up as one man to bear in triumph the son of the Advocate Chaudon. Toulon went so far for the sake of her poor townswoman, as to think of burning the Jesuit college.

The most touching of all these tokens in Cadière's favour, reached her from Ollioules. A simple boarder, Mdlle. Agnes, for all her youthful shyness, followed the impulse of her own heart, threw herself into the press of pamphlets, and published a defence of Cadière.

So widespread and deep a movement had its effect on the Parliament itself. The foes of the Jesuits raised their heads, took courage to defy the threats of those above, the influence of the Jesuits, and the bolts that Fleury might hurl upon them from Versailles. [5]

The very friends of Girard, seeing their numbers fall off, their phalanx grow thin, were eager for the sentence. It was pronounced on the 11th October, 1731.

In sight of the popular feeling, no one dared to follow up the savage sentence of the bench, by getting Cadière hanged. Twelve councillors sacrificed their honour, by declaring Girard innocent. Of the twelve others, some Jansenists condemned him to the flames as a wizard; and three or four, with better reason, condemned him to death as a scoundrel. Twelve being against twelve, the President Lebret had to give the casting vote. He found for Girard. Acquitted of the capital crime of witchcraft, the latter was then made over, as priest and confessor, to the Toulon magistrate, his intimate friend Larmedieu, for trial in the bishop's court.

The great folk and the indifferent ones were satisfied. And so little heed was given to this award, that even in these days it has been said that "both were *acquitted.*" The statement is not correct. Cadière was treated as a slanderer, was condemned to see her memorials and other papers burnt by the hand of the executioner.

There was still a dreadful something in the background. Cadière being so marked, so branded for the use of calumny, the Jesuits were sure to keep pushing underhand their success with Cardinal Fleury, and to urge her being punished in some secret, arbitrary way. Such was the notion imbibed by the town of Aix. It felt that, instead of sending her home, Parliament would rather *yield her up.* This caused so fearful a rage, such angry menaces, against President Lebret, that he asked to have the regiment of Flanders sent thither.

Girard was fleeing away in a close carriage, when they found him out and would have killed him, had he not escaped into the Jesuits' Church. There the rascal betook himself to saying mass. After his escape thence he returned to Dole, to reap honour and glory from the Society. Here, in 1733, he died, *in the perfume of holiness.* The courtier Lebret died in 1735.

Cardinal Fleury did whatever the Jesuits pleased. At Aix, Toulon, Marseilles, many were banished, or cast into prison. Toulon was specially guilty, as having borne Girard's effigy to the doors of his *Girardites,* and carried about the thrice holy standard of the Jesuits.

According to the terms of the award, Cadière should have been free to return home, to live again with her mother. But I venture to say that she was never allowed to re-enter her native town, that naming theatre wherein so many voices had been raised in her behalf.

If only to feel an interest in her was a crime deserving imprisonment, we cannot doubt but that she herself was presently thrown into prison; that the Jesuits easily obtained a special warrant from Versailles to lock up the poor girl, to hush up, to bury with her an affair so dismal for themselves. They would wait, of course, until the public attention was drawn off to something else. Thereon the fatal clutch would have caught her anew; she would have been buried out of sight in some unknown convent, snuffed out in some dark *In pace.*

She was but one-and-twenty at the time of the award, and she had always hoped to die soon. May God have granted her that mercy! [6]

[1] Muyart de Vouglans, in the sequel to his Loix Criminelles, 1780.
[2] Alluding to the cruelties dealt on the Huguenots by the French dragoons, at the close of Louis the Fourteenth's reign. - TRANS.
[3] This fact comes to us from an adviser to the Holy Office, still living.
[4] I am not speaking of executions done by the people of their own accord. A hundred years ago, in a village of Provence, an old woman on being refused alms by a landowner, said in her fury, "You will be dead to-morrow." He was smitten and died. The whole village, high and low, seized the old woman, and set her on a bundle of vine-twigs. She was burnt alive. The Parliament made a feint of inquiring, but punished nobody. - [In 1751 an old couple of Tring, in Hertfordshire, according to Wright, were tortured, kicked, and beaten to death, on the plea of witchcraft, by a maddened country mob. - TRANS.]
[5] There is a laughable tale which expresses the state of Parliament with singular nicety. The Recorder was reading his comments on the trial, on the share the Devil might have had therein, when a loud noise was heard. A black man fell down the chimney. In their fright they all ran away, save the Recorder only, who, being entangled in his robe, could not move. The man made some excuse. It was simply a chimney sweep who had mistaken his chimney.
[6] Touching this matter, Voltaire is very flippant: he scoffs at both parties, especially the Jansenists. The historians of our own day, MM. Cabasse, Fabre, Méry, not having read the *Trial,* believe themselves impartial, while they are bearing down the victim.

Epilogue

A WOMAN of genius, in a burst of noble tenderness, has figured to herself the two spirits whose strife moulded the Middle Ages, as coming at last to recognise each other, to draw together, to renew their olden friendship. Looking closer at each other, they discern, though somewhat late, the marks of a common parentage. How if they were indeed brethren, and this long battle nought but a mistake? Their hearts speak, and they are softened. The haughty outlaw and the gentle persecutor have forgotten everything: they dart forward and throw themselves into each other's arms. - *(Consuelo.)*

A. charming, womanly idea. Others, too, have dreamed the same dream. The sweet Montanelli turned it into a beautiful poem. Ay, who would not welcome the delightful hope of seeing the battle here hushed down and finished by an embrace so moving?

What does the wise Merlin think of it? In the mirror of his lake, whose depths are known to himself only, what did he behold? What said he in the colossal epic produced by him in 1860? Why, that Satan will not disarm, if disarm he ever do, until the Day of Judgment. Then, side by side, at peace with each other, the two will fall asleep in a common death.

It is not so hard, indeed, to bend them into a kind of compromise. The weakening, relaxing effects of so long a battle allow of their mingling in a certain way. In the last chapter we saw two shadows agreeing to form an alliance in deceit; the Devil appearing as the friend of Loyola, devotees and demoniacs marching abreast, Hell touched to softness in the Sacred Heart.

It is a quiet time now, and people hate each other less than formerly. They hate few indeed but their own friends. I have seen Methodists admiring Jesuits. Those lawyers and physicians whom the Church in the Middle Ages called the children of Satan, I have seen making shrewd covenant with the old conquered Spirit.

But get we away from these pretences. They who gravely propose that Satan should make peace and settle down, have they thought much about the matter?

There is no hindrance as regards ill-will. The dead are dead. The millions of former victims sleep in peace, be they Albigenses, Vaudois, or Protestants, Moors, Jews, or American Indians. The Witch, universal martyr of the Middle Ages, has nought to say. Her ashes have been scattered to the winds.

Know you, then, what it is that raises a protest, that keeps these two spirits steadily apart, preventing them from coming nearer? It is a huge reality, born five hundred years ago; a gigantic creation accursed by the Church, even that mighty fabric of science and modern institutions, which she excommunicated stone by stone, but which with every anathema has grown a storey higher. You cannot name one science which has not been itself a rebellion.

There is but one way of reconciling the two spirits, of joining into one the two churches. Demolish the younger, that one which from its first beginning was pronounced guilty and doomed as such. Let us, if we can, destroy the natural sciences, the observatory, the museum, the botanical garden, the schools of medicine, and all the modern libraries. Let us burn our laws, our bodies of statutes, and return to the Canon Law.

All these novelties came of Satan. Each step forward has been a crime of his doing.

He was the wicked logician who, despising the clerical law, preserved and renewed that of jurists and philosophers, grounded on an impious faith, on the freedom of the will.

He was that dangerous magician who, while men were discussing the sex of angels and other questions of like sublimity, threw himself fiercely on realities, and created chemistry, physics, mathematics ay, even mathematics. He sought to revive them, and that was rebellion. People were burnt for saying that three made three.

Medicine especially was a Satanic thing, a rebellion against disease, the scourge so justly dealt by God. It was clearly sinful to check the soul on its way towards heaven, to plunge it afresh into life!

What atonement shall we make for all this? How are we to put down, to overthrow, this pile of insurrections, whereof at this moment all modern life is made up? Will Satan destroy his work, that he may tread once more the way of angels? That work rests on three everlasting rocks, Reason, Right, and Nature.

So great is the triumph of the new spirit, that he forgets his battles, hardly at this moment deigns to remember that he has won.

It were not amiss to remind him of his wretched beginnings, how coarsely mean, how rude and painfully comic were the shapes he wore in the season of persecution, when through a woman, even the unhappy Witch, he made his first homely flights in science. Bolder than the heretic, the half-Christian reasoner, the scholar who kept one foot within the sacred circle, this woman eagerly escaped therefrom, and under the open sunlight tried to make herself an altar of rough moorland stones.

She has perished, as she was certain to perish. By what means? Chiefly by the progress of those very sciences which began with her, through the physician, the naturalist, for whom she had once toiled.

The Witch has perished for ever, but not the Fay. She will re-appear in the form that never dies.

Busied in these latter days with the affairs of men, Woman has in return given up her rightful part, that of the physician, the comforter, the healing

Fairy. Herein lies her proper priesthood a priesthood that does belong to her, whatever the Church may say.

Her delicate organs, her fondness for the least detail, her tender consciousness of life, all invite her to become Life's shrewd interpreter in every science of observation. With her tenderly pitiful heart, her power of divining goodness, she goes of her own accord to the work of doctoring. There is but small difference between children and sick people. For both of them we need the Woman.

She will return into the paths of science, whither, as a smile of nature^ gentleness and humanity will enter by her side.

The Anti-natural is growing dim, nor is the day far off when its eclipse will bring back daylight to the earth.

The gods may vanish, but God is still there. Nay, but the less we see of them, the more manifest is He. He is like a lighthouse eclipsed at moments, but always shining again more clearly than before.

It is a remarkable thing to see Him discussed so fully, even in the journals themselves. People begin to feel that all questions of education, government, childhood, and womanhood, turn on that one ruling and underlying question. As God is, so must the world be.

From this we gather that the times are ripe.

So near, indeed, is that religious dayspring that I seemed momently to see it breaking over the desert where I brought this book to an end.

How full of light, how rough and beautiful looked this desert of mine! I had made my nest on a rock in the mighty roadstead of Toulon, in a lowly villa surrounded with aloe and cypress, with the prickly pear and the wild rose. Before me was a spreading basin of sparkling sea; behind me the bare-topt amphitheatre, where, at their ease, might sit the Parliament of the world.

This spot, so very African, bedazzles you in the daytime with flashings as of steel. But of a winter morning, especially in December, it seemed full of a divine mystery. I was wont to rise exactly at six o'clock, when the signal for work was boomed from the Arsenal gun. From six to seven I enjoyed a delicious time of it. The quick - may I call it piercing? - twinkle of the stars made the moon ashamed, and fought against the daybreak. Before its coming, and during the struggle between two lights, the wonderful clearness of the air would let things be seen and heard at incredible distances. Two leagues away I could make everything out. The smallest detail about the distant mountains, a tree, a cliff, a house, a bend in the ground, was thrown out with the most delicate sharpness. New senses seemed to be given me. I found myself another being, released from bondage, free to soar away on my new wings. It was an hour of utter purity, all hard and clear. I said to myself, "How is this? Am I still a man?"

An unspeakable bluish hue, respected, left untouched by the rosy dawn, hung round me like a sacred ether, a spirit that made all things spiritual.

One felt, however, a forward movement, through changes soft and slow. The great marvel was drawing nearer, to shine forth and eclipse all other things. It came on in its own calm way: you felt no wish to hurry it. The coming transfiguration, the expected witcheries of the light, took not a whit away from the deep enjoyment of being still under the divinity of night, still, as it were, half-hidden, and slow to emerge from so wonderful a spell...Come forth, O Sun! We worship thee while yet unseen, but will reap all of good we yet may from these last moments of our dream!

He is about to break forth. In hope let us await his welcome.

List of Leading Authorities

Graesse, *Bibliotheca Magiae,* Leipsic, 1843.

Magie Antique - as edited by Soldan, A. Maury, &c.

Calcagnini, *Miscell., Magia Amatoria Antiqua,* 1544.

J. Grimm, *German Mythology.*

Acta Sanctorum. - Acta SS. Ordinis S. Benedicti.

Michael Psellus, *Energie des Démons,* 1050.

Caesar of Heisterbach, *Illustria Miranda,* 1220.

Registers of the Inquisition, 1307-1326, in Limburch; and the extracts given by Magi, Llorente, Lamothe-Langon, &c.

Directorium. Eymerici, 1358.

Llorente, *The Spanish Inquisition.*

Lamothe-Langon, *Inquisition de France.*

Handbooks of the Monk-Inquisitors of the Fifteenth and Sixteenth Centuries: Nider's *Formicarius*; Sprenger's *Malleus.*

C. Bernardus's *Lucerna;* Spina, Grillandus, &c.

H. Corn. Agrippae *Opera,* Lyons.

Paracelsi *Opera.*

Wyer, *De Prestigiis Daemonum,* 1569.

Bodin, *Démonomanie,* 1580.

Remigius, *Demonolatria,* 1596.

Del Rio, *Disquisitiones Magicae,* 1599.

Boguet, *Discours des Sorciers,* Lyons, 1605.

Leloyer, *Histoire des Spectres,* Paris, 1605.

Lancre, *Inconstance,* 1612: *Incredulité,* 1622.

Michaëlis, *Histoire d'une Pénitente,* &c., 1613.

Tranquille, *Relation de Loudun,* 1634.

Histoire des Diables de Loudun (by Aubin), 1716.

Histoire de Madeleine Bavent, de Louviers, 1652.

Examen de Louviers. Apologie de l'Examen (by Yvelin), 1643.

Procès du P. Girardet de la Cadière; Aix, 1833.

Pièces relatives à ce Procès; 5 vols., Aix, 1833.

Factum, Chansons, relatifs, &c. MSS. in the Toulon Library.

Eugène Salverte, *Sciences Occultes,* with Introduction by Littré.

A. Maury, *Les Fées,* 1843: *Magie,* 1860.

Soldan, *Histoire des Procès de Sorcellerie,* 1843.

Thos. Wright, *Narratives of Sorcery*, &c., 1851.

L. Figuier, *Histoire du Merveilleux,* 4 vols.

Ferdinand Denis, *Sciences Occultes: Monde Enchanté.*

Histoire des Sciences au Moyen Age, by Sprenger, Pouchet, Cuvier, &c.

www.ingramcontent.com/pod-product-compliance
Lightning Source LLC
Chambersburg PA
CBHW051726040426
42447CB00008B/996